the
BEST SEVEN YEARS
of my life

THE STORY OF AN
UNLIKELY CAREGIVER

GEORGE SHANNON
CHAD PATRICK SHANNON

First Printing: 2018

ISBN: 978-1-7326455-4-7

To Ma Mère and Pops,
for not only living with true grit and great spirit,
but for their courage in sharing their lives for this book.

CONTENTS

CONTENTS

foreword

Steve Thomas
Sewickley, Pa

"… for better, for worse, for richer, for poorer, in sickness and in health, 'til death do us part" is a traditional Christian marriage vow derived from the Book of Common Prayer in 17th Century England (when the average lifespan was about thirty-five years). Given today's longevity, a lifetime commitment whatever life brings can truly be a heavy one. The Best Seven Years of My Life is a love story that describes how George Shannon honors those vows as tragedy strikes when his wife Carol suffers strokes, and when it first becomes clear that she is going to need someone to care for her every hour of every day.

Most people's reaction to these circumstances would be to tumble into depression. Life has dealt you a bad hand. You're boxed in. It would have been so much easier for George to find someone else to take care of her than to do it himself. Bring strangers into the house to offer round-the-clock care. Put Carol in a home. Take the easy way out. But that isn't George. Self-pity wasn't an option for him. If he ever felt sorry for himself, he never showed it. He was all in.

When the relationship faced its drastic change, George totally accepted his fate and grew from it. He recognized anew that he was, as he puts it, "terribly in love with this woman." He found joy in a seemingly never-ending task that would buckle most of us at the knees. He moved into a state of "agape love," a Greco-Christian term describing the highest form of love known to humanity—a transcendent, unconditional, selfless love that commits one passionately to the wellbeing of others and persists regardless of circumstance. It is love with no expectation of reciprocity.

1

George talks about his relationship with Carol in delightfully amusing ways. After the strokes, her personality changed. She lost the filter that kept her from blurting out personal thoughts that might be considered inappropriate for public consumption. This resulted in Carol developing a sudden, unexpected, and riotously funny sense of humor. It changed their relationship in ways that brought George great joy, even as so much about his daily life also had to change.

George's depth of caring for Carol is truly spiritually uplifting, but the greatest surprise of all is how his expression of selfless love changed him. I relate this from the position of an insider, a close friend of George and his family for thirty years. Like many male friendships, ours was initially based upon similar interests—golf trips, poker, and jovial camaraderie over too many cocktails. Our competitive natures drew us to each other, fueled by testosterone, ego, and a mutual enjoyment of challenging one another, both verbally and in games of skill. George was a man's man, a pot-stirrer, someone you would undoubtedly enjoy having a drink with. However, a dramatic shift in his temperament was in store. As George devoted himself to Carol's wellbeing, he became a humbler, more compassionate and spiritual human being. He opened himself to vulnerability, noting that "self-defense is really not important anymore."

The Best Seven Years of My Life provides a template for others facing similar circumstances as they seek comfort and inspiration to rise above their travails. I only hope they have the good fortune to read this book and take from it the knowledge that love (and love alone) can carry us through times that can truly seem too much to bear. There is nothing wrong—and in fact, there is a lot right—with accepting and showing the softer side of your soul. When you do this, you don't have to decide how you will deal with a caregiver situation; you will find ways to accept it, embrace it, and figure out how to make your life not just as good as it ever was, but better.

CHAPTER ONE
the moment of change

We can love completely without complete understanding.
– Norman Maclean
A River Runs Through It and Other Stories

January 2017

My eyes opened to the digital numbers projected on the bedroom ceiling: 4:02 A.M., large and red. The recent years had shaped in me a powerful fixation on time. How many minutes had passed since the last time Carol woke me? Would it be better to administer her insulin five minutes or twenty minutes before breakfast? When exactly were the doctor appointments today, and what time was her physical therapy session at the rehab facility?

How long would Carol live? How long would I live?

By the time I'd shaken off enough sleep to sit up, my wife had already managed to get her little legs out of the bed. She didn't have the strength to climb down on her own, and even in the heavy darkness, I could see her big, white, fuzzy socks dangling high above the floor. There was no telling how many times she'd gotten herself stuck in this position while trying to wake me. My hearing had been going, and even before the stroke, Carol's voice was often hushed.

"I see you've got those Tweety legs ready to go," I said, my voice groggy as I delivered the same joke I'd been telling for more than forty-seven years of marriage.

"They are what they are," Carol deadpanned.

Photo: Carol with her favorite teddy bear.

I forced my fatigued body to shuffle over to her side of the bed. Her walker awaited me, but since it would only slow us down anyway, I decided to help her to the bathroom without it. I sat her straight up and wrapped my arms around her. She was a tiny thing. For as long as I'd known her, she'd claimed to be over five feet tall, but a trip to the doctor's office just yesterday had finally confirmed the sheer egregiousness of that fib. The truth was much closer to four feet, ten inches.

Balance was often a fickle friend to Carol, so I made sure to secure her arms tightly before bringing her to her feet. "I have to go really bad," she reported, drawing out the urgency of the really.

"Gotcha, honey," I replied.

We held tight to each other as we waddled to the bathroom. Since the strokes, Carol's gait had been much more of a short-stepped shuffle than a walk. Just like her physical therapists, I would often encourage her to take larger steps. Halfway through the journey, I grabbed her hand and took a step too fast for her.

"You have the wrong arm," she said.

She'd broken her right shoulder a few years back, and it still pained her to put weight on it. I slowed up to release the pressure. It probably came from a place of cranky exhaustion, but I remember thinking that it would've been nice if she'd included a "please."

When we arrived at our destination, Carol reached for the silver grab-bar we'd had installed, then let gravity do the rest as she plopped down on the seat.

"Another safe landing," she announced.

I chuckled as I lumbered out of the room to give her some modicum of privacy. The poor woman probably couldn't remember the last time she'd been left totally alone. I couldn't have been more than a step past the white-framed doorway before she called out to me.

"I think I'm done."

"Let's maybe wait another minute before we go back to bed," I suggested, my tone a mixed bag of hope and directive.

She quickly agreed, so I returned to the edge of the bed and did some plopping down of my own.

Getting up frequently wasn't anything new, but this night had been particularly rough. We'd had to wake seven times since we first went to bed during the eleven o'clock news. On the sixth time, just an hour before this latest occasion, Carol had failed to wake before trouble struck. Early in this phase of our relationship, an accident in the bed might have frustrated me, but by now, I'd performed the routine so many times I'd lost count. It had become almost mechanical. Immediately, I would go into the preprogrammed twenty-five-minute cleanup mode: Get Carol out of bed, change her clothes, help her wash herself, strip the sheets, start a load of laundry, make the bed again, and get her back to sleep.

From opposite sides of the room, we sat in silence for a moment before I heard Carol's signature rustling. For years, whenever she found herself near anything made of disposable paper—usually napkins, tissues, or toilet paper—she would fidget with it. She would fold it up and rub it on her lips, back and forth, producing that slight rustling sound. A few doctors had told me that this was likely a symptom of Vascular Parkinsonism, but we couldn't be sure.

The sound from the bathroom stopped for a second, drawing my attention. Carol had honored my request for an additional minute almost to the second, but now she was ready for help. So I began the slow, lumbering process of returning her to bed.

I sat her back into bed the same way I'd helped her up. Before she lay down, I reached over and adjusted her necklace, a silver caged heart I'd purchased in a bumbled romantic gesture on Valentine's Day many years ago. Carol wore this necklace every day, but through the night, the pendant and the chain's clasp would get bunched up on the back of her neck, so whenever I could, I would bring the pendant back to the front.

"Thank you," she said in the kindest of voices, as she always did.

As I tucked her in, I couldn't wait to lie down and maybe get the most of the next forty-five minutes—when, like clockwork, I could expect to be roused from sleep again. I hit the lights, crumbled back into bed, and covered myself. Fifteen seconds passed before the covers started to rustle again, and I knew what was coming next.

"I don't think I finished," Carol said, a tinge of apology in her voice.

I should have known better than to get comfortable. Powered by a deep sigh, I found the energy to chuck the covers aside and start the routine once more. I delivered her to the bathroom, then returned to my usual waiting spot on the bed, where I stared straight into the darkness and wondered how many times we had gotten up in the middle of the night to do this. It had been almost seven years since the event that changed our lives. Eighty months. *Multiply the months by thirty*, I thought, doing the math. *So, roughly 2,400 nights, at an average of five times per night.*

"Twelve thousand times," I whispered.

———————

It was late April of 2010, right around my birthday. My sister Barbara had earned a free trip to Cabo for her fine sales work at Howard Hannah Real Estate the previous year. Carol and I would be meeting her, along with my brothers Jimmy and Tommy and everyone's spouses, for a few days of rest and relaxation. It had been a busy spring at my job as the vice president of sales for the northern district of a water tank maintenance company, so a free trip that promised beaches, family, cocktails, and nothing to do but relax sounded like just about all I could ever ask for.

Our plane began its descent. A long way down the peninsula, on the Pacific side of Mexico, awaited Cabo San Lucas. The plane skirted the water line as we neared the little airport. Beneath us stretched a ribbon of idyllic beach, and even from 5,000 feet up, I could practically feel the fine, light-brown sand between my toes. The sky was a shade of blue whose match I'd never seen before, even in my forty years in the paint business.

As we exited the airport, we were met by a perfect breeze and comfortable evening weather. The fading sun felt warm on my skin.

Carol and I passed our twenty-minute taxi ride from the airport in the same way we'd passed the flight, and frankly, the same way we'd passed most of our time of late: in total silence, like we were leading two separate lives. I would work with my salesmen all day while Carol ran her daily errands like clockwork. At the end of the day, I would go to the driving range to work on my golf swing while Carol would plow through one book after another. We would meet up around dinner time, the meal or restaurant often left to my choice. On the weekends, I would golf with my friends while she talked on the phone with hers and read her books. She rarely tried to initiate much in our lives. Everything we did was on me to plan and schedule, including any social activity.

The more I pondered, the more I realized that Carol and I had slipped into an extended stale phase. We had been married for forty-one years, and our three kids were all grown now. In their youth, they had led active sporting lives, their athletic endeavors keeping our social calendars full, but those days had become faded memories. Our oldest son, Sean, worked in the financial world in New York City. Our youngest, Matthew, made his home and work in Montana. Chad, the middle son, lived in Pittsburgh but was often busy with his legal career and social life. Carol and I had expected to be grandparents by then, but none of the kids were married.

In this way, ours had become a boring existence. This didn't mean we didn't love each other, just that we'd grown weary. And tension was a little high between us at this moment, because somewhere over Arizona, I'd made the mistake of finally asking her if we could get rid of some of the *Vanity Fair, People,* and other assorted magazines piling up in our house. In her defense, my tone could've been politer, but at the same time, I'd just never understood why she couldn't bring herself to throw those old issues away. More than anything, though, I'd just wanted her to take a strong position on the matter, one way or another. But as was Carol's tendency, she'd shrugged off my request and retreated into silence. I had always read this as an unwillingnesson her part to be a full partner in our marriage. This made me feel alone.

Instead of asking about the magazines, I turned my frustration inward. *Why are you getting hung up on this small stuff?* I thought. I figured maybe I should try cheering myself up by reading the little black notebook I'd filled with positive or insightful quotes to remember. I'd been leaning on that book more often than usual lately, as the effort to build a new sales territory from scratch was often stressful, and reading those sayings always soothed my anxiety. Whenever I needed a breath, I would find one of my dad's quotes like "Make it a great day today," or if I had gotten too uptight about work, I would look for that truism, "Nobody on his deathbed ever said I wished I'd spent more time in the office."

At the resort, Barbara, her wide grin a fond reminder of our father, greeted us at the door of a spacious four-bedroom unit held together by a large communal area. Her infectious joy at having the whole family together managed to chase away what remained of my annoyance about the silence and the magazines, but even through the next few days of fun, laughter, and goofy jokes, I just couldn't seem to relax.

Whenever Carol and I had a few free moments together, we didn't talk much, and the chilly indifference hanging between us only heightened my sense of restlessness.

On our last full day of the trip, it finally occurred to me that the best way to make amends would be to try to squeeze out some time for Carol and me to spend alone. Eventually, I worked up the nerve to ask the question that had been churning in my mind all morning. "Why don't we do our own thing for lunch today?"

She reacted as if she hadn't heard me.

I approached and stood by her side. "Did you hear me?" I asked, immediately regretting the frustration I heard in my own voice.

"I think I'd rather just do lunch as a group today," Carol said with the level of calm that meant she was trying to avoid conflict.

Even though I knew I shouldn't allow myself to storm out of the bedroom, that's exactly what I did. Frankly, I wanted her to tell me that I was a jerk, or explain why she was upset with me. I never had any idea what she was thinking, and that lack of connection was painful. But instead of turning around and addressing those thoughts with her, I went for a walk. When I came back twenty minutes later, she'd gone with the others to the village of Cabo.

And every day since, I've pondered the question at least once: What would I be willing to trade if it meant that I could go back and change that moment? The answer, with confidence, is *anything*. I would give anything to be able to warn my sulking sack of a younger self about how drastically our lives were about to change. I didn't know it during that sun-soaked morning, but this would be the last solo conversation I would ever have with the Carol I used to know.

After a relaxing day and an early dinner, the group returned to the suite with the intention of grabbing a nightcap. I enjoyed an orange vodka as I settled into the charade of trying to read with a distracted mind.

"Hey, Georgie," Jimmy said from across the room. He

was shuffling a deck of cards. "I've got a seat at the poker table for you over here. Fifty cents a hand. I know you like a high-stakes game."

"Come on, George, sit next to your big sister," Barbara chimed in.

"I'm getting into this book," I lied. "Maybe in a little while."

"Suit yourself, buddy," Jimmy said, totally oblivious to the tremendous effort I was putting in to make a show of pouting. "I plan on making a killing over here."

This started Barbara on one of her stories, "Oh God, Jim, do you remember that one time we were at the track with Mom?"

"Before you get into that story about horses," Tommy said, "you'd better pony up the ante."

Tommy's puns always had a way of causing Barbara to go into hysterics. "You'd better rein it in before this party gets crazy," she said once she'd caught her breath.

Carol was smiling that cute little smile everyone loved. It was that same smile that had so often coaxed my dad to share his stories, Carol's nieces to divulge their latest boyfriend updates at the kitchen table, or one of our sons to disclose his challenges at school or work. The smile convinced me, like it had so many times in the past, that the time had finally come to quit pouting. All I needed was an opening to work my way into the game.

"I'm getting a beer," Jimmy announced, right on cue. "Play this one without me."

This was my chance. But before I could get up, my brother was already at my side.

"Take a good look at Carol," Jimmy said in a voice just above a whisper. "She's playing one-handed."

I stood back and watched for a while, and sure enough, Carol would pick up her cards with her right hand, then set them down and use the same hand to flip them whenever her turn came. My wife had always been rather unorthodox in the fine-motor department, so I figured maybe it was just a fluke. But then, over the next couple hands, it became clear that she was going out of her way to avoid using her left. Lately, Carol had been subject to occasional bouts with mini-strokes, episodes that left her dazed or otherwise acting a bit strange. Frightening as they were, there was really nothing we could do about them except visit the doctor as soon as possible. As I watched her playing with only her right hand, I knew it would be better to ask the resort to send in a local doctor rather than waiting until tomorrow's return to the States.

An hour later, the doctor arrived, and Carol told him about her type II diabetes and the mini-strokes. He looked her over, checked her vitals, and since her hand seemed to have improved, advised that she was likely either dehydrated or suffering from low blood sugar. She drank some orange juice and perked up quickly.

Once the excitement had died down, I finally worked my way into the card game. I listened to Tommy's jokes, watched Barbara bask in the glory of her family, tried not to let Jim win all the money, and indulged in my relief that my wife seemed okay.

Around four o'clock in the morning, I woke from an unstill sleep to find that Carol wasn't in bed. I figured she'd just gotten up to use the bathroom, but after a few minutes passed, worry crept into my mind, and I rose to go look for her.

In the bathroom, the image of Carol that greeted me was one I'll never be able to chase from my memory. She was sitting on the floor with her legs folded, Indian-style, as she stared at the ceiling. Not a day goes by that I don't wonder what was happening in her mind.

"Carol!" I cried out as I rushed to her. "What's going on?"

She just looked at me and smiled.

"Honey, what happened?"

My wife of over forty years didn't seem to recognize me. She gazed right through me for a moment, and then, trapped in some mental space I couldn't reach, she returned her attention to the ceiling, the grin frozen on her face. A moment of tremendous terror seized me from head to toe before I snapped back to reality. I could fret myself sick later, but for now, Carol needed medical attention.

My first instinct was to take her to the local hospital, but I knew nothing about the quality of the Mexican healthcare system, so I quickly started running through scenarios that would get Carol back to the States as soon as possible. I'd flown enough in my life to know that no airline would board a passenger in this condition. Fortunately, one of my oldest friends in the world was Rich Ryan, a pilot who had spent his career running various private jet companies. The expense would be overwhelming, but I dialed Rich's number and asked him for an enormous favor.

Rich was just working out the details on how he could dispatch a plane from California to Cabo when Carol started to vomit. Each time she got sick, my heart raced a little faster, and I questioned a little harder whether I should abandon the flight idea and just find the nearest emergency room. I was right on the verge of changing course when it started to seem like the worst had passed. She still had that vacant look in her eyes, but it had been a long time since she'd vomited, and a bit of color had returned to her face. So we drove to the airport and boarded Rich's eight-seater plane.

The seats were set up to face each other, four to a side. I sat across from Carol so I could keep an eye on her. At the moment of takeoff, I realized that I'd never been so terrified. We were set to fly over an incredibly barren stretch of land, and it seemed to me that if Carol's condition deteriorated, her chances of survival ranged from slim to none. Each moment that passed carried a simultaneous charge of relief that she was still fighting, and dread that the next instant might short-circuit her brain forever. If that happened, then I would have to live with the knowledge that our last solo conversation had been more like a fight.

For the next four hours, I stared into my wife's eyes, looking for changes and searching for clues to her wellbeing. Each time I asked her whether she was okay, she would reply with a wide-eyed, perpetual grin like I'd just told her the best joke of all time. My desperation to know what was happening in her mind was almost more than I could bear. I'd always been a fixer of things, but this time, my toolbox lay empty. I'd never felt so helpless.

The longer I took in Carol's expression, the more I recognized something in those eyes that I had too long taken for granted. It was trust. She had always trusted in me no matter what decision I'd made: where we lived, my career path, how many children to have. She'd put her wholesale faith in me in a way that made me realize how much she counted on me.

Then, sometime after changing planes in San Diego, and somewhere over the southwestern United States, with Carol's eyes still locked on mine, I came to a truth that forever altered the direction of my life. I told myself that if Carol survived this, then I would devote my life to making hers better. I would do whatever it took to make her healthy again. With that vow, an all-consuming feeling transcended the anxiety which had racked my world all day long:

I'm terribly in love with this woman.

For one glorious moment, that emotion filled my whole body. As the plane landed in Pittsburgh and we taxied toward the gate, I could see my son Chad's silver Hyundai Sonata awaiting us on the tarmac. Together, we carried Carol off the plane and into Chad's car. When we arrived, the doctors and nurses took Carol straight back.

The waiting room at Allegheny General's ER—a room with which I would become all too familiar—was a large, white-walled, brightly lit area lined with perpetually glowing televisions. There was as much stale coffee as your heart desired. And the tables here and there were piled high with magazines that I never got around to reading. Carol would've loved that.

We'd been up since four in the morning, had traveled thirteen hours on planes, and had been focused the whole time on getting home. With Carol in able hands, my mind could finally start organizing the questions. Our uncertain future weighed the heaviest.

"What am I going to do?" I asked Chad several times.

Neither of us had an answer.

This led me to a deluge of further questions: how long before Carol would recover and be her old self again? In the meantime, how would I manage her care? And was I even capable of doing it on my own? Then, the darker questions: what if she didn't recover? What if this was how it would always be? And then, the darkest questions: what if I would never be able to apologize to her for our last conversation? What if I would never get another chance to tell her how much I loved her? What if my wife died?

All night, I battled with these unanswerable questions. People came and went, shifts changed, and as the sun rose the next morning, Carol was finally admitted to the Stroke Unit on the ninth floor. This brought some small measure of relief, as I'd admired the staff from that unit ever since Carol was a patient there for her mini-strokes in February of 2009.

Her room was right next to the nurses' station, which added to my growing sense of comfort. Soon, I spotted the familiar face of Dr. Ashis Tayal in the hallway as he conversed with his team. Up to that point, I had never met a doctor who balanced bedside manner with the ability to be frank with such perfection. We were in good hands. I just knew that if anyone could make Carol better, it was Dr. Tayal.

The official diagnosis was as good as Greek to me: a right

anterior cerebral infarct. Ultimately, the stroke had affected the area of Carol's brain responsible for the movement of her legs, her left arm, and the initiation of speech. Her decision-making would also be impacted. The diagnosis of expressive aphasia meant that there could be some speaking and writing issues as well, but the doctor was confident that this condition could be improved. Overall, the news was as good as could be expected.

Carol was released only six days later and sent to a local rehabilitation facility for physical, occupational, and speech therapy. As a lifelong devotee of planning—and as the kind of person who writes lists for everything from shopping to the next day's chores, and even books I wanted to someday read—I reveled in the thoroughness of the plan the doctors had set up for us. We now had a clear path to Carol's return to full health, and I knew that as long as we followed that path step by step, all would be well.

Of course, it all depended on how Carol would take to rehab. Much to my surprise, she seemed more determined than ever, eating everything they put in front of her, completing every exercise they prescribed her, and even asking to be walked down the hall for additional exercise. Carol had hated exercise for as long as I could remember. Often, when I drove home from work, I would find her car parked in our friend Maris Moriarty's driveway precisely one block away from our house, and I would shake my head every time. She couldn't walk one block to visit her friend?

But now here she was, digging into her rehab, and all that hard work soon paid off. On May 22, 2010, exactly one month since I had found her in a daze on the floor of a bathroom in Cabo San Lucas, my wife was discharged home.

Hand in hand, we stepped through the front door of our two-story house in the little borough of Edgeworth, Pennsylvania, and those questions that had hounded me in the emergency room seemed so far away. Carol hadn't completely recovered from the stroke, but full recovery was in sight. All we had to do was take her regularly to outpatient therapy, so she could improve on her mobility and vocal expression.

The moment we got through our front door, a clock on the wall reminded me that Carol needed to take her medicine. So I sat her down and searched our bags and the car. I could only find prescriptions. She'd been on an extensive list of medications at the facility, but the staff had failed to send me home with any for immediate use or advise me to pick up new ones. I had no idea what to do or how to get Carol's pills, and I knew that the clock was ticking.

Thankfully, a local nurse, Sandy Travato, had heard Carol was being discharged and came to check in on us. A savior of sorts, Sandy arrived out of nowhere, took one look at Carol, and sent us to the local emergency room. They discovered that her blood sugar had spiked to 400 and gave her an insulin shot.

Meanwhile, Sandy had dropped off and picked up a full set of prescriptions from our local pharmacy, and we had everything back in order by nightfall.

After dinner, we finished our hectic day by sitting together on the couch for the first time in a month. All three of our sons called in to congratulate their mother on making it home, a fact that made me smile, because there was a time when my wife worried that her children would never love her like they did me. I still think about that anxiety often. It all came to a head one late summer day. I'd been tossing the baseball with Chad and Matthew when Sean came running through the kitchen and out the back door to tell me about his football practice and how they were going to make him a running back. It was a happy moment, but when I returned into the house, I found Carol crying at the kitchen table.

"What's wrong?" I asked, rushing to her.

It took her a moment to collect herself enough to speak. "I just don't understand why the boys never want to spend time with me," she said, gazing up at me with those dewy eyes of hers that made her look like she was always on the edge of laughter, even when sad.

"What do you mean?"

"I'll never be able to connect with them with sports like you do."

"You connect with them in other ways."

She dismissed the thought with a turn of her head. "Sean was so excited to tell you about football. But he didn't bother telling me."

My heart skipped a beat. I didn't know what to say, so instead of offering immediate hope, I looked to the future. "When our boys become men," I said, "everything will be different. You'll see."

Now here we sat in our living room, having just finished the last of the three calls from our sons, and I could see that I had been right all those years ago. The boys adored their mother and had every intention of becoming a more consistent presence in our lives.

Carol passed the next hour watching one of her favorite talent show contests on TV, and I, as I'm prone to do, fell into a deep state of thinking about the drastic changes since that moment in Mexico. Even before our vacation, and perhaps fueled by having recently elected to receive my first social security retirement check, I'd been pondering the reason for my life. On paper I'd accomplished so much, but beyond raising my three sons, I felt like I was missing true fulfillment.

My wife's stroke had presented the worthy purpose of nursing her back to health. In the first month, I'd been there every step of the way, and those efforts made me feel good. Yet the minor fiasco with the pills and insulin had shown that I could do better. I could learn more about her condition, seek out healthier meals to make for us, and research new therapies. Most importantly, I needed to be a more complete husband.

The moment I devoted myself to Carol on the plane had

been tender, but it also opened my eyes. It made me realize that I had somehow allowed inflexibility to take hold in our daily lives. A sneaky thing that way, the power of stubbornness had deposited its energy into cleanliness, routine, and order: my yard had to be landscaped a certain way, my house had to be clean, my personal things organized to my liking, and even my meals had to contain certain foods. Over time, I had hoarded the focus of our marriage and didn't even recognize how selfish I had become.

Whenever my expectations weren't met, I would succumb to prolonged periods of dwelling, and of festering to the point of general gloominess, which led me to, as my mother used to say, being "testy." The cranky person on the vacation in Cabo San Lucas came from this place. My crabbiness over the magazines ran much deeper than a cluttered home.

In this way, I also realized that Carol would need more than just my commitment. I would have to dig deep to recapture a facet of myself that I had let decay for much too long: a sense of humility. Some twenty years before, I had come to an understanding of the beauty of humility and the proper tools to maintain it, but those insights had faded with time. Over those years, my mind had been filled with the gunk of pride.

Though I'd turned my full attention to Carol over the past month, irritable George intruded on my dedication to her and invaded my mind with self-centered questions about whether I'd end up resenting my wife if she didn't get better, or got worse someday. To triumph, I'd need to confront my demons and rediscover the path to humility. In our uncertain future, would that darker side of my personality come through, or would I would find a better part of me?

A vague sense of unease crept in as I wondered whether I would succeed in achieving that purpose of returning Carol to health. More harrowing was the notion that I had no idea how much longer we would have together—she might live another ten years, even another twenty, or another stroke could take her away from us in the next moment.

I reached out for her hand under the blanket and gave it a good squeeze. She turned to me and let a little smile form on her face. In that smile, all the answers became clear: deep down, even though I had always struggled to love myself, I loved Carol with all my heart. For however long we had together, I would try my best to make sure she always knew it.

———————————

The bedroom was still dark. I peeked at the trusty red numbers on the ceiling: 4:13 A.M. Outside, the birds had already begun their predawn chirping.

"Can you come get me?" Carol asked from her perch in the bathroom.

I found her standing and holding onto the grab-bar. She blinked and smiled at me, anxious for my return. Any agitation I might have felt about the early hour or the lack of sleep or the damn birds stood no chance against this love.

Together, we started our slow amble to the mirror. No matter what the time was, Carol had to fix her hair before leaving any bathroom. After a few quick passes at her bangs, she set the brush down. Then, her hand holding mine tight, she nuzzled into my shoulder.

"Thank you for all you do for me," she said.

Back in bed, I pulled the covers over her. Then, I handed her the little brown teddy bear our youngest son Matthew had given her after her first major stroke seven years ago. She held it close. She never went to bed without it.

As I slid closer to her, I found her free hand, held it up to her cheek, squeezed tight, and did the last thing I always did before we returned to sleep.

"I love my Carol," I sang to her, terribly off-key.

"I love my Pogey," she replied with a giggle.

Within minutes, I heard her little snore. I stared at those big digital numbers on that cold January night: 4:18 A.M. In a few minutes, I would doze off, and about thirty minutes later, she would likely get me up again. In those moments before my little bouts of sleep, I thanked God for the little human embodiment of perseverance and positivity sleeping next to me. She was a wee-sized woman who defined a toughness and grit I had never known existed, someone who never let her relentless health problems get her down. What I couldn't have known back then, and what I never would have been able to face, was that my Carol would be gone less than three months later.

As I look back now, I know one thing for sure: Despite the day to day challenge between those two Aprils in 2010 and 2017, those were the best seven years of my life. This is my recollection of my time taking care of Carol. It's a tale of an unlikely caregiver, a journey toward rediscovering humility, and the story of a man blessed with the amazing chance to fall in love all over again.

I cannot control what happens to me.
I can, however, control how I react to it.

– Epictetus

CHAPTER TWO
dedication

June 1, 2010

From day one after Carol's discharge from the rehab center, I had begun making good on my promise to help her get back to her original self. We weren't going to merely accept the changes in our life; we were going to attack them. We followed an aggressive strategy for her care and therapy and kept to a regimented schedule. Until I could get the house ready for her to live in with some semblance of independence, she would spend her days in a safe place with people facing similar situations. It pained me to have to leave her in a local adult daycare center, but I knew that the process of repurposing our home to accommodate her care would require a great deal of my time and focus. So during the day, at least, it felt like it made more sense to set her up in a place where she could receive the extra attention she needed.

The first task in the effort to rebuild our lives would be the simplest: dispose of our poor eating habits. After dropping Carol off for her first day at the center, I drove to a nearby organic market to buy healthy food to replace all the junk I had cleaned out of the cupboards the night before. For two hours, I walked the aisles and studied the unfamiliar labels of a wide variety of health foods like Ezekiel bread and wild-caught salmon filets. The effort filled me with a joyful sense that we were both going to change our lives for the better, would meet the many challenges ahead of us, and we would keep to this new routine until normalcy returned.

Photo: George's favorite picture of Carol, at the house on Thorn Street.

Around lunchtime, I returned to the daycare facility to check on Carol. I found her throwing up, sick as a dog. I didn't bother waiting for an ambulance. By the time we hit the highway, I noticed that her eyes had assumed a distant, almost lost sort of glaze—a look that said she could go at any moment. We'd been told that a second stroke could happen, but neither of us could have imagined that it would crash down on her quite so soon. A consuming dread gripped my chest as I sped down the four-lane highway. I felt helpless, like we were plodding through wet cement toward a brighter future that would never come.

Full speed ahead, I flew toward Pittsburgh in whatever lane of the highway was clearest. I would tear past traffic on both the left and the right, passing other cars like they were standing still. When I exited the highway, I raced through the side streets that led to the hospital. I barely stopped the car as I whipped into the emergency room circle. The medical staff rushed out and wheeled Carol through the doors in no time flat. Inside, the intensity written on the faces of all the doctors told me that this trip would be different.

As I watched them tend to her, a sudden, reminiscent sorrow overwhelmed me. It had been many years since I'd felt this particular brand of helplessness, but I remembered it well. As I closed my eyes, my mind drifted back through several decades to when I'd first encountered the feeling.

Dad typically spent his days on sales calls, so when I saw that he'd come home I knew this had to be something serious. My body ached to the point where I couldn't get out of bed. Since I was an active, athletic eleven-year-old, my immobility had been cause enough to ask Dr. Jackson, the family doctor, to make a house call that day.

On that day back in 1956, Dr. Jackson examined me closely as my parents stood by. After he finished, he took my mom and dad into the other room. Their hushed tones confirmed what I'd been fearing: something big was happening. My parents looked crestfallen when they followed the doctor back into my bedroom.

"I'm afraid you have rheumatic fever," the doctor told me. "It most likely developed from an untreated strep throat infection."

My parents explained that they needed to help me get dressed because they were about to call an ambulance.

"The hospital?" I asked. "For how long?"

"We'll see, son," Dr. Jackson said. "At least six weeks. Maybe more."

I furrowed my brow as protest flashed through my mind. "No, sir," I said. "I'm not going to no hospital for any six weeks."

"Look, George," the doctor said with a stern gaze. "Rheumatic fever is nothing to be trifled with. If you overexert yourself, your heart could be in serious trouble. You could even..."

Die. That was what Dr. Jackson clearly wanted to say, but he stopped short—I guess to avoid terrifying a headstrong eleven-year-old kid. Back then, medicine in the US hadn't yet advanced to the point where rheumatic fever could be contained without prolonged bed rest and penicillin. If I failed to follow the doctor's orders, I would find myself at serious risk of heart inflammation, which could result in permanent damage to my heart valves, or even total heart failure.

But my mother knew me well. She had witnessed on countless occasions how stubborn I could be. And I could see from her expression that she intended to side with me.

"If he doesn't want to go, then he isn't going," she declared, cutting off the doctor before he could finish warning me about the dire consequences. Mom stood next to me and squeezed my hand as she flashed a warm smile at the confused physician. "We can take care of it here at home. You just tell me exactly what has to be done."

Dr. Jackson looked at my mother and me, then over to my father, who shrugged in confirmation that he would be of no help in the matter.

"It's important that George avoid any exertion, or it could ruin his heart," the doctor said gravely. "When he needs to get up, you have to help him. And I don't mean that you should help him climb out of bed—I mean that you must carry him wherever he needs to go. I can't stress this enough: He can't exert himself. At all."

Mom was undeterred. "Fine. How long will he need to remain in bed?"

"A minimum of six weeks."

My parents looked like the doctor had just punched them in the gut.

"That's not too bad," I cut in, hoping that the confidence in my tone would perk up my parents. "I can do six weeks in a cinch."

"Well, that's not all," Dr. Jackson added, letting the steam out of my engine. "You have to take his temperature three times a day and record it. He must go two straight weeks without an elevated temperature reading before he even thinks about getting out of bed on his own. This is critically important. If he misses a single temperature reading—even if it's abnormal just once—he has to start all over and begin another two-week testing period."

"Done," my mother replied immediately, and even if she'd felt it, she never showed one second of doubt.

The doctor wrote out the instructions and went on his way.

My mom and dad procured a double bed, which they set up in the living room. We never had any money, so I don't know how they managed it or where it came from, but it dominated the leisure space of our little second-floor apartment in Brentwood, Pennsylvania, a neighborhood at the edge of Pittsburgh's city limits. They rearranged what furniture they had and set me up to face our black and white television with nothing more than the three networks the rabbit ears could muster. My dad would make sure that I always had the daily sports page from the newspaper and the latest Sport Illustrated—my favorite magazine as a kid by a long shot.

For the first couple weeks, every day was the same. Mom would get up in the morning and turn on the television while I waited for breakfast. I would eat my breakfast slowly and drink tons of water. I would watch the tube until lunch came, and then I would repeat the process. The same would happen for dinner. Every time I had to go to the bathroom, or got tired of my position on the bed, I would call my mother to help me. My siblings, Barbara, Jimmy, and Tommy, would drop in to say hello after school, but otherwise, I was all alone as the rest of my family went about their lives.

At some point in those initial two weeks, I came across an article about a paralyzed college football player. His family needed help paying the medical bills, so they set up a foundation to accept donations. Right there and then, I knew I had to help. I couldn't move, but I could sure have my mother teach me how to knit a potholder, and that process consumed quite a bit of my time. At first, it was slow going, but within a month's time, I could knit a tight potholder in no time flat. Once I had completed enough of them, Mom helped me sell them to the family and neighbors, and then donate the money to the football player I'd read about.

Apart from that, it was all routine. For the first few days of my time in bed, Mom took the temperatures and marked them down, but eventually, I told her that I could do it. I'm not sure why she decided it would be okay to trust the word of an eleven-year-old, but she agreed. I made a chart of perfect little boxes drawn with a ruler and pencil. Heading the vertical column, I wrote the days of the week, and in the horizontal rows, I listed the times of day when I would take my temperature. Morning, noon, and night, I would record the readings in those meticulous little squares. Over the first few weeks, the temperatures landed all over the place, but then they started to stabilize. Like clockwork, three normal readings would come back to me every day, until I found myself celebrating a full week of perfect results. This continued for the eighth day, then the ninth, and so on.

On day fourteen—the day that would be my last in that bed after weeks of intense boredom—my morning reading turned out to be normal, as well. I only had two more to go. Right before lunch, with great excitement, I put the thermometer under my tongue, closed my eyes, and waited. After a couple minutes, I pulled it out and took the reading. Up one degree. Heartbroken, I double-checked. Then, I repeated the process, hoping that it had been an error. But no. Even after the third try, my temperature was still over by one lousy degree.

This was when, as an eleven-year-old kid, I faced my first real crisis of conscience. I knew I could fudge the number. It wasn't like anyone checked my work. I could just write down a normal reading and then get back to my regular life. Most eleven-year-old kids would do exactly that. And besides, what was one little temperature reading out of the dozens I'd done over the past eleven weeks? Hadn't I suffered enough? Couldn't I be forgiven for moving the goalposts just this once?

Of course I knew the answer. I had no choice. I was an honest kid. Out came the ruler and pencil. I made a new two-week chart and resolved to start the process anew the next morning. My parents were beside themselves about the whole thing. They couldn't believe that I would be willing to subject myself to another long stretch in that bed when I'd come so close to completing the course.

At the end of the thirteenth week, I called my mom into the living room, and she checked the chart. It looked to me like she'd waited up all night in anticipation of the final result. She clearly couldn't wait to call the doctor and get me cleared.

"Well, George did it!" my mother proudly announced into

the phone. "Fourteen straight days of perfect readings."

A long pause followed, Mom's expression slowly fading from excited to confused as she turned away from the phone and looked to my dad. "He said that George should get his sneakers on and jog up to the doctor's office," she said, sounding perplexed.

"That can't be right," Dad said. "Ask him again."

So she did. "You want the same kid that's been in bed for over three months to run a mile and half uphill?"

My mother nodded as she listened to the doctor's explanation. When it was done, she shrugged and said she would tell me to get my shoes. Dad seemed less sold by the idea. He watched patiently as I laced up. Then, he trailed me outside and got into his car.

"I'll follow you," he explained. "Just to make sure you're okay."

At the time, we lived in what was then called the Hollows—a section of town below the village of Brentwood. The doctor's office was in the same area that now houses Brentwood Town Square, a steep climb from our home both then and now.

"How ya' feeling, son?" Dad would holler out the window every hundred yards or so.

"Good, Dad, good," I would confirm quickly, motivated as I was to avoid having to return to that bed.

I ran the whole way up the hill, into the building, and straight into the doctor's office. At no point did I feel even remotely exhausted. It was just so exhilarating to be outside again, to use my legs, to draw fresh air into my lungs.

After a thorough checkup, the doctor cleared me to return to my normal activities. I got to be a kid again.

Having been laid up in that bed for over three months, I learned some things about myself. First, I learned that I liked being organized and reaching goals. Also, I learned the power of dedication, that if you committed yourself to something, gave it everything you had, and stayed the course, great things could happen. And even though I was just eleven at the time, I learned what it was like to be bedridden, to need help doing simple things like getting out of bed, and the vulnerabilities such a situation creates. Little did I know then how important those lessons would become decades later, when I would be tasked with helping my dear wife through her own health crisis.

––––––––––––––

Though Carol had been admitted to the familiar confines of the Stroke Unit at AGH, and though she was under the exceptional care of Dr. Tayal, things had definitely taken a turn for the worse. Dr. Tayal explained that the stroke had reached the basal ganglia area of Carol's brain, which would suppress her communication skills, profoundly impact her balance and movement, and strip away her ability to think before taking an action. On top of that, to avoid further strokes, she would require a blood-thinner for the rest of her life. This would make it more difficult for her blood to clot, and it would send the risks associated with future falls and surgeries soaring.

The damage to her brain threatened to cripple the life that Carol had carved out for herself. Each affected area seemed like a direct attack on the best aspects of her character. Communication skills? Sure, we had our struggles interacting, but she was a great listener. Many nights, when the boys were still young, I would walk in the door from work and find her counseling one of our sons' friends. Plus, talking on the phone was her main connection to her family in Ohio. Balance and movement? She had a whole daily routine that required her to buzz around town in her Jeep Cherokee: stopping by to visit friends, swinging by the grocery store and other errands, and working at the local Penguin bookstore several days a week. Also, it was almost impossible to imagine my wife not being cautious.

On several occasions during the first couple days after her admittance, with this latest damage to her brain causing disorientation and confusion, Carol tried to pull out her various tubes and IVs. After the most recent attempt, the nursing staff outfitted her with a pair of protective gloves to prevent her from continuing the behavior. The gloves made her look like a felled boxer flailing limply at the air. The feeding tube plunging into her throat reminded me that she might never be able to eat on her own again, and that she hadn't said much in the several days since her second stroke.

In a couple of days, she would be undergoing something called a barium swallow test, a critical examination that would determine whether she would ever be able to eat solid foods again or would have to remain on a feeding tube for the rest of her life. I'd seen firsthand from friends and family how quickly life tended to degrade once a feeding tube became permanent, so I left the hospital with a foreboding sense that our future hung in the balance.

I lay awake the rest of the night, pondering how to solve Carol's many new medical issues. She would need so much help, so much care. I vowed to do for her just as my parents had done for me during my bout with rheumatic fever: prepare her food, take her to the bathroom, carry her from place to place, and help her make the best of it. The morning, the day of the swallow test, and the answers to our future couldn't come fast enough. So when the birds started chirping, I sprang out of bed and headed back to the hospital.

Though I knew Dr. Tayal wasn't rounding that day, I figured there had to be at least one doctor there who could answer my long list of questions about the barium swallow test scheduled for the following day. So I headed up to the ninth floor with a warm cup of coffee in my hand and a charge in my step. When I stepped into my wife's room, I met a familiar face. The doctor checking Carol's chart was a neurologist I had known socially for a long time. In the interest of anonymity, I'll call him Dr. Short. Seeing someone I knew helped calm my frayed nerves.

He nodded for me to join him in a conversation outside the room.

"The truth is that Carol's very sick," he told me once we were in the hall. "And she won't live very long."

The blunt force of the statement rendered me unable to speak.

"Sorry, George," the doctor said. Then, he patted my shoulder stiffly and headed down the hall.

A shock of anger rushed through me. *How can you drop a bombshell like that without letting me ask a single question?* But then, the anger was shoved aside by a gut-twisting fear. *How long is not very long?* With a shake of the head, I cleared my mind to avoid the answer to that question, and told myself that this guy had to be wrong. That sense of defiance only lasted for a moment, chased away as it was by the sight of my wife lying in that hospital bed, the reality of all those tubes and wires snaking around and into her.

I found one of the visitors' lounges down the hall. The little alcove was poorly lit. With my face buried in my hands, a memory of our fortieth wedding anniversary came to mind—Carol standing in the crowd of a hundred people and, despite her fear of public speaking, giving a heartfelt and well-delivered speech in honor of the friends and family who'd come. She'd looked healthy and happy that night, chatting with all the guests and laughing at every joke. At the time, I believed that we would breeze past our fiftieth anniversary, and if all the cards fell right, we might even make it to the sixtieth. But the year that had passed since that party felt like a lifetime. And now we faced a new reality, one where Carol's days were severely numbered.

In that small waiting room, I negotiated with anyone or anything that might be listening—an unplanned prayer of sorts—for any extra time I could get. The idea that I might be able to enjoy two more years with her seemed more than reasonable, but also rather abstract. For now, I just wanted her to stay alive for the next hour. Then, a whole day. And after we'd strung together a few days, we could start thinking about weeks.

I sat alone in my kitchen later that night, sipping on an orange vodka and mulling the importance of the swallow test. Just a month ago, Carol had been walking on the beach, and now I couldn't help but fret that she might not live another day without a feeding tube. The looming prospect of another devastating stroke felt like a ticking, unreadable clock hanging over our heads. How much longer would we have together? A year? A month? A day? And how would we spend that time?

Failing the test would be disastrous for anyone's quality of life. But for Carol, it would also mean no more white wine on ice or fountain-poured Diet Cokes, two of her greatest loves. Almost every day over the three decades we'd lived in Sewickley, Carol would drive to the local gas station or bagel shop to get a Diet Coke in a cup filled to the brim with ice. And her bar order of a glass of chardonnay on the rocks had become so predictable that most of the local bartenders would start scooping the ice into the glass the moment they saw us walking through the door. One of my longtime friends had taken to greeting Carol as "Lady Chardonnay."

The pleasure she took in those two simple things was especially unusual for a woman who never much cared about the quality of the food she ate and never spent an overabundance of time on shopping for clothes or jewelry. If she could enjoy a Diet Coke in the afternoon and a glass of wine at night, then she could go to bed entirely content with life. Even though I'd just cleared out all the Diet Coke from our fridge and had vowed to reduce our alcohol intake, I found myself desperately hoping that she would get to enjoy those two great loves again someday. But it all hinged on that barium swallow test—the outcome of which I had no control over.

The next morning, before heading up to Carol's room, I stopped for a quick prayer in the hospital's chapel. Prior to the downturn in Carol's health, it had been a while since I had made a meaningful trip to any house of faith. But I had come up in the old-school way of thinking about these matters, the one that said if you were going to ask God for something, then your butt had better be in a pew. That was why, since the time of Carol's second stroke, just about every Saturday night, right after Communion, you could find me in deal-making mode. The deal was always the same: I'll do whatever it takes to earn more time with Carol. I made this same prayer in the chapel that morning, then headed off to join my wife for one of the biggest moments of her life—and mine, for that matter.

Family members were permitted to watch the procedure through a large glass window. I cringed as Carol refused the test liquid. At first, the technician refused to let me go back into the lab to support her, but I persisted, and he finally relented. I pushed through the heavy lab door and hurried over to my wife. When I got closer, her eyes showed fear, and a depth of vulnerability that cut to my core. The nurses had removed her boxing gloves in advance of the procedure, so I grabbed her hand, which was ice-cold, and held it until it warmed. I told her how important it was to take the test, and asked if she would try. She nodded. Two minutes later, it was done.

As Carol got situated back in her room on the ninth floor, it was clear that the test and the emotions of the day had exhausted her. She was so fatigued that she didn't bother fighting the boxing gloves. Once the nurse had finished securing her and we were alone, I closed the door, slipped off one of the mitts, and held her hand. Carol's grip was so weak, it broke my heart.

Just then, there was a knock on the door. Dr. Tayal and his team had arrived. He assumed his typically kind expression as he addressed us from the end of the bed, and I braced myself to soften the blow of bad news.

"We're going to need to put Carol onto a thickened liquid diet," he said with a sigh.

Since I'd readied myself for the worst news, I had to replay his words in my head just to make sure I hadn't mistaken him. "She doesn't need a full-time feeding tube?" I said, feeling oddly excited about the medically-termed diet I knew nothing about.

"Not for now," he answered in stride. "But any food she consumes must be pureed, and all liquids must be thickened with cornstarch."

I fought the urge to give Dr. Tayal a high-five or a hug.

"Can we thicken wine and Diet Coke?" I asked hopefully, badly needing a win for Carol.

Dr. Tayal measured his response. "We should minimize such things, but yes."

Carol's gaze searched the room in a confused, lost way—and maybe I'd imagined it, but I could have sworn I saw a momentary flicker in her eyes at the thought of returning to her liquid luxuries. When I felt her little hand grab for mine, I scooted my chair in closer to the bed and began combing her hair with my free hand. My wife wouldn't be leaving me that day, the next day, or even the next week. A month or longer still seemed too far ahead to consider, but at least we weren't going hour by hour anymore. Now I could return to my focus of giving her every chance to get stronger and prove Dr. Short wrong about her longevity. We would start by helping her improve her swallowing, day by day. I would make sure that she received the latest and greatest in speech therapy. And once we overcame that, we would move on to the next challenge of relearning how to walk.

Though the irrefutable facts of her brain damage posed potential limits to how high up the hill of health we could climb and what quality of life she could maintain, I was certain I would dedicate my life to maintaining whatever stage she achieved. No matter what condition Carol was in, we would make it work. If we needed to move into a new home to accommodate her disability, we would do it. If I needed to pull away from my job, or retire, I would. And for as long as Carol could stand on two feet, we would continue our life much as we had before. We would still go out to dinner, still find new ways to take vacations, and still create new activities to enjoy together.

Soon after Dr. Tayal left, a nurse arrived with a pureed tomato soup and a cornstarch-thickened cup of water. I found the buttons to move the bed and bring Carol to a seated position. She pointed at the water, so I scooped a spoonful of the grainy gel and fed it to her. Her reaction was to twist her expression and turn away like a toddler who doesn't want her carrots.

Curious, I tried it too. Carol had the right of it. It was an awful, mealy, salty mess. She tried the soup next, which didn't seem to rate quite as bad. I could tell because she looked at the bowl, then at me, and then back at the bowl. I made a note to myself to explore other soup-like meals at the grocery store.

I wanted to encourage her, so I made a big promise. "Someday, you can have as many cold and un-thickened Diet Cokes as you want."

Though she was weak and hushed, and though it was her first full sentence since the second stroke, my wife managed to bowl me over with, "That sounds *so* good."

CHAPTER THREE
unrelenting

Don't give up. Don't ever give up.
– Jimmy Valvano
speaking about his battle with cancer

March 2011

Light poured through the bedroom window. Had I slept in? I whipped around, already knowing that I would see nothing but crumpled sheets in the place where my wife always slept.

"Carol?" I called out.

No response. I rushed into the bathroom and found it empty.

Damn it, Carol. We talked about this. You have to wake me up.

I ran into the long hallway of our new home, relieved that I had installed a baby gate in the entryway heading down to our finished basement. It wasn't possible for her to have tumbled down the steep stairwell.

Finally, I made it to the kitchen, out of breath, and found my wife sitting at the table with a bowl of cereal, a full glass of juice, and one of her ubiquitous magazines. The little countertop television flickered behind her. Having heard me enter, she turned to look back at me.

Instead of following my instinct to sternly remind her that she wasn't supposed to be up and around on her own, I grumbled, "Why didn't you get me up?"

"What's going on?" she deadpanned before turning back

Photo: Carol's favorite look, "You have a problem with this?"

41

to her cereal.

I wanted to laugh, but I knew if I did, it would only encourage her to continue this dangerous behavior. "Jesus, I almost had a heart attack."

She shrugged and went back to her reading. This was a scene I'd encountered thousands of times in my life. It wasn't difficult to drum up the image of her sitting Indian-style at our many kitchen tables over the years, smirking, book in her lap, chin down, engrossed in the words, turning the page with one hand and twirling her hair with the other. In those moments, I had often wondered whether Carol preferred her books over me, but this time, as scared as I had been to wake up and find her missing, the sight of her reading gave me great joy.

As I retrieved a coffee cup and a single-serve pod from the cupboard, my heart finally slowed. Carol had come a long way in the nine months since her second stroke. She had progressed to the point where she could make short trips around the house without my help, but it was still imperative that I get up with her in the mornings. The problem was that her balance hadn't fully recovered, and she would trip over her own feet, tumbling to the floor. The fact that she hadn't fallen during the breakfast trapeze performance amazed me.

Much had changed about our lives since Carol's most recent stroke. Shortly after her discharge from the rehab facility, I'd traded our two-story and handicap-unfriendly home for a reverse-ranch-style home in the hills, which allowed us to live on a single floor. Additionally, Carol's mother, Char Perry, passed away. Her father, Stew Perry, had moved in with us. And, I'd finally found some in-home help. Angie, a registered nurse, arrived every morning to check Carol's vitals and blood sugar, work with her on any therapy exercises, and get her ready for the day. As an added benefit, Carol's mornings with Angie gave me a chance to get ahead in my work.

Much had changed about our lives since her most recent stroke. Though she would probably always need caregiving,

Carol had made significant advancements. After three challenging months of soupy meals and thickened liquids, she finally passed her barium swallow test. Her hit-or-miss communication persisted, but she had at least started trying to express herself more often, and when she delivered a cogent line, it was often uncharacteristically comedic.

Once, on the way to PNC Park to see a Pittsburgh Pirates game, Carol and I found ourselves in one-lane, bumper-to-bumper traffic because an ambulance had parked in the middle of the right lane. From my perspective, the paramedics appeared to be off duty. Carol wasn't speaking much—she never spoke much during our car rides—so I filled the time grousing as we crawled along. The closer we got, the more I griped about the terrible choice to park an ambulance in a way that choked off a full lane of traffic.

When we finally pulled up next to the ambulance, I caught the driver's gaze. And just then, Carol rolled down the window, turned to me, and calmly asked, "You got anything to say now?"

Frozen with surprise, I said nothing. After the silence hung for a second, Carol rolled the window right back up while staring straight ahead. "That was kind of cute," she said, "if I don't mind saying so myself."

I don't think I stopped laughing until the third inning. Her irreverence and comedic timing at that moment had floored me, and it would continue to do so for the next several years.

Though I had come to realize that there would be some permanent disabilities, I felt content in knowing that we were working toward steady improvement. Carol attended physical, occupational, and speech therapy throughout the week, and every month or so we would see some incremental advancement in the speed and length of her steps, and an increasing confidence to speak with authority. Eventually I started to harbor hope that she might at least get close to an independent life.

Her father was a beacon of punctuality and positivity. That morning, Stew came around the corner into the kitchen right at 9 A.M., wearing a wide smile, just like always. As soon as Carol saw him, just as she did every morning, she returned the smile. The two of them had been close for as long as I could remember, a fact I always attributed to how difficult and insulting Carol's mother, Char, had been.

This thought had first occurred to me many years prior. We had just moved to Kent, Ohio, and once our little Ryan-built home was ready, we invited Carol's parents to visit. The minute Char came through the door, she started criticizing everything: the fact that we'd moved to Kent, the placement and choices of the photographs and art on the walls, the dish Carol was using to cook the casserole she'd spent all afternoon preparing, the temperature she'd set the oven, and on and on. It didn't stop for fifteen minutes. Though my wife didn't show it, I could see that the judgments hurt her deeply.

Stew politely waited for the barrage to end, then tried to lift his daughter's spirits with a cheery attitude and gracious words. It was his tactful handling of moments like this that had caused his relationship with his daughter to flourish over the years.

I greatly appreciated his presence in our new situation. He served as a kind of buddy for Carol while also providing me peace of mind that if anything terrible happened while I was in the other room, he would be there to alert me.

Now that Stew had joined his daughter for breakfast, I could get started on my workday. I grabbed my coffee and headed toward the hall. On my way out, I told my father-in-law that he might want to have a talk with his daughter. "She was a bad one this morning," I quipped. "Did you get up without ringing the bell again?" I heard Stew ask her as I hurried downstairs to my office. "What are we going to do with you?"

We had placed diner-style kitchen bells throughout the

house, including on the table next to Carol's side of the bed, so she could ring for us if she needed help. She never used them, despite her many promises that she would, until early the following morning when she rang one of the bells for the first time. My anxiety still high after the previous morning's scare, I woke in a hurry and fought through the fatigue to help her with whatever it was she needed.

"Can you get me up?" she asked.

I peeked over at the clock, which read just shy of 4 A.M. We had slept for several hours straight—a small miracle on its own, but what thrilled me most was that finally Carol had remembered to ask for help. Pleased that she'd warned me, I went around the bed and assumed my usual position. I noticed that her Valentine's necklace was in disarray as usual, but since time was of the essence, I figured it could wait until I returned her to bed.

"Okay," I said, anticipating the shift of her weight onto my arm. "One, two, three."

She didn't budge. This was not unexpected, as sometimes she would be fighting her own sleepiness and would take a little longer to respond.

I pressed a little closer to the bed. "Here we go," I said, but she remained a dead weight. "Maybe a little help here?" I quipped.

"I can't get up," she said, sounding like she was somewhere between laughter and tears. "I'm trying."

I bent so low and wrapped my arms around her so tight that we were basically hugging. Without aid, I lifted her. She weighed in at only a little over a hundred pounds, but she was limp as a child in a tantrum, so it took my full strength to pull her to her feet.

"Don't worry," I said. "I'll hold you tight."

I took a step, but she didn't move. She stared at her feet as if to will them to operate, but lost her balance and fell back on the bed.

Oh, dear Lord, I thought grimly. *Please, not another stroke.*

Our son Chad had been coming to stay with us from time to time, and he happened to be there that night. I rushed to his room and roused him from sleep. He and I carried Carol to the bathroom. When she was finished, we got her dressed and headed down to Allegheny General Hospital for a CT scan, but not before grabbing my trusty brown bag. I'd learned to be prepared with all the pertinent medical records, the full list of Carol's prescriptions, and a day's worth of pills.

Many hours later, we learned the good news: the scan showed no signs of a stroke. But Carol still struggled to move. I called Dr. Tayal to make an appointment, and he fit us in for later that day.

After calling Carol in from the waiting room, Dr. Tayal watched her intently as she made her way into the examination suite. "How are you?" he asked.

"I'm fine," she replied with a shrug. That was Carol. Always fine. The reply had become something of a mantra, one of her most shining attributes during her waning years.

The doctor glanced at me, and I shook my head.

"I understand you've been having trouble using your legs," the doctor probed.

"Well, I'm fine," she shot back, straight-faced. "That's all I'm saying."

Dr. Tayal's physician's assistant Judy started snickering, which caused me to chuckle as well.

The doctor explained that Carol had a condition known as Vascular Parkinsonism, which occurs with some frequency in a basal ganglia stroke. We learned that the difference between Vascular Parkinsonism and the more commonly known Parkinson's Disease was that while both conditions came with symptoms like slow movement, tremors, difficulty walking, and trouble with balance, Carol's condition would be free of the nerve cell loss typical of Parkinson's. The crushing news was that there was no treatment, and the progressive nature of the disease couldn't be overcome with physical therapy.

"I'm afraid she's going to need a walker or wheelchair to get around," the doctor said. He didn't put it bluntly, but it was clear that, at least in terms of her motor skills development, Carol's progress had ended. Not only would she never get any better with her walking; she would get worse as time wore on.

I felt terrible for Carol, who just couldn't seem to catch a break. I also sensed a creeping resentment about the seemingly endless attacks on my own life. Then I immediately felt guilty as hell for even thinking about myself in such a situation. I forced a smile so Carol wouldn't see the bleak feeling coursing through my body.

"Well, honey," I said with a chuckle, "it looks like you're just going to have to deal with a hunk like me holding your hand wherever we go."

"Whatever," Carol quipped as she rolled her eyes in Judy's direction.

As we worked our way out of the parking garage, I found myself thinking about Hilton Head. In the early 1990s, we had purchased a two-bedroom condo on the island, which back then was still little more than a sleepy golfing destination. But since I was fond of golf and Carol enjoyed the beach, we fell in love with the island immediately. One of Carol's favorite activities in life was to make the trek from our little house in Shipyard to the beach, where she would comb for shells for an hour or two before heading home.

After our youngest son graduated high school, we lived there every winter. Those months down in the low country were some of the best of our marriage. We had the beach, a great group of friends, and an evening ritual that made us quite content. At around happy hour every night, we would take two chairs, a bottle of wine, and our books down to the beach to take in the sunset. Inevitably, we would ignore the books in favor of conversation about our sons or a dreamy retirement. When our sons came to visit, we included them in our five o'clock beach tradition, which always made the evenings even more pleasant than usual.

For obvious reasons, we had missed the season the year after the strokes. Undeterred, Chad and I had taken Carol down for a few days to see how she would manage. Even with our assistance, she struggled mightily to get from the parking lot to the beach. The boardwalk made it easier, but the sand proved impossible to traverse. We wound up having to carry her to the beach chairs. The best shells always lie at the tide's edge, making for something of an uneven minefield for a person with walking issues. So we passed on the idea of searching for shells.

Despite the difficulties, for a time I'd remained confident that Carol would rehabilitate enough to make it possible for us to return to wintering in our favorite place. But this latest turn with her health essentially washed those hopes out to sea.

Before Carol's strokes, my greatest personal pleasures were working and golfing, mostly because of the routine and social life that both provided. Maintaining my success in my sales region for my current company meant long and focused phone calls or quick trips to visit my salesmen's territories. The time for that had already gotten significantly limited after Carol's strokes, but now with the care related to her Parkinsonism, it was clear that I would have even less time to manage my job, and less contact with the outside world.

Losing the golf would represent a particular challenge, as the hobby had always functioned as my primary form of stress relief and my only source of exercise in recent times. Before the strokes, from April through September, I would work throughout the day, head to the golf course for a few holes of practice, catch up with my friends, enjoy a post-match drink, and then join Carol for dinner. That custom had become my touchstone of happiness.

As we drove from the appointment to complete a list of

errands for the day, I tried to give myself a pep talk to drum up some much-needed resolve. Eventually, the perfect source of inspiration came to me. Whether it was as a bed-bound child trying to get two weeks' worth of good temperature readings or as a young man playing to the whistle in every game I ever suited up for, I'd never given up.

Back in 1963, when I was a freshman at Edinboro State College (now Edinboro University of Pennsylvania), all I wanted to do was earn a spot on the basketball team. Even though I was only 5'8" and 135 pounds with shoes on, I knew my fundamentals and hustled more than anyone. In those days, college teams had both freshman and varsity teams, but Edinboro was a Division II basketball program, and so their two teams only had space for scholarship players. I went to tryouts anyhow, but due to my size was never given a chance. So I joined the intramural team.

By midseason, the freshman team had lost two of its players. The head coach had been scouting our league, and he picked a dozen of us to try out. I made the team, and even got into the second half of the first game. That turned into a starting spot just a few games later. By the end of the season, I lettered and was asked to come back on the team the next fall on partial scholarship.

When freshman classes ended, I hurried home to join a semi-pro baseball summer team. Just as our team got going, Edinboro University notified me that I'd failed two classes and needed to go to summer school. Though I hated giving up baseball, I knew I had no other choice if I wanted to get back on the hardwood and continue my education.

I'd flunked English Literature and another course I can no longer recall. Before the summer makeup classes got started, I had to meet with the dean. He informed me that I'd have to get two Bs to be let back in school. I figured the English class would be full of strugglers like me, so I was halfway back to getting that basketball in my hand. Instead, they placed me with eleven eager English majors who were taking their required course before the fall semester. Five minutes into the class, the professor announced that he would be grading on a curve, so to get a B in the course, this meant that I had to beat at least eight other students at Shakespeare. I'd never worked so hard to make a grade. Six weeks later, my expulsion loomed. I requested a meeting with the dean. I had to give it one last shot. My mother had arrived to pick me up and take me home, so she came along.

"Son," he said sternly, "we made a deal and you didn't honor it."

I'd never in my life had to tell my mother I'd failed. I stared at the floor. When it became clear that I couldn't find the words, the dean excused us. Dejected, I followed my mom to the door, but just as I reached the hall, I turned and took a deep breath.

"Can I tell you a story?" I asked.

The dean nodded.

"Sir," I said before I cleared my throat. "You're right. I did make a promise to you."

His gaze followed me as I worked my way closer to his desk.

"But when I made that promise, I couldn't have known that I would be graded on a curve in a class full of English majors. Given another chance, I know I'd pass."

I stood there, tall and proud of my honest and direct pitch. He smiled and stuck out his hand for my papers. I avoided eye contact with my mother, who had to have been confused.

"All right, Shannon," the dean replied. "You're back in, but on academic probation."

"Thanks," I said as I handed him the papers. It was then that I learned a lesson that carried me fifty years in the sales business: know when the deal has closed. Instead of walking out the door, I spoke. "I really appreciate the extra chance, since I really did the best I could."

He looked at me for a long, uncomfortable moment before tearing up my papers. "If that's the absolute best you can do," he said, "then there's no reason to come back." He stood and offered me his hand. "Best of luck to you."

I gave him a strong shake and stood there in shock for a good half-minute.

In the end, my overzealousness with the dean was what got me the boot from Edinboro. Otherwise, I worked as hard as I could to make the team and stay on it, and that mentality had stuck with me for the decades since. Though Carol's medical issues had come hurtling at us at an unrelenting pace, she didn't plan on quitting, and neither did I.

Life for us had already drastically changed, and the difficulty level would soon rise. For years, people I knew had told me I was crazy for trying to take care of my wife in my own home, that a wise man would find the best possible assisted living facility or nursing home and let the professionals handle it. Sure, it would have been easy to give in to the temptation offered in those whispers from friends, and it didn't even seem like it would be a particular indictment of my tenacity. And yet, I never really gave that idea a second thought.

Next, we stopped at Costco for my wife's medicines and some groceries. As usual, Carol was quiet. A sense of loneliness and isolation hung over me. I kept my eye on her as she pushed the shopping cart through the massive discount store. Dr. Tayal had said that as long as her legs would allow, she should continue to use them, and her legs appeared to be doing well. The sight of Carol trucking down those long aisles raised my spirits some. Then it occurred to me that she hadn't seemed depressed even for a moment about the latest medical news. To the contrary, she'd essentially shrugged it off. Tenacious and unwilling to quit, Carol may or may not have grasped the full weight of Dr. Tayal's prognosis, but for today, she moved toward the tall stacks of bottled Diet Coke while she tried to sneak sweets into the cart. She wasn't going to let yet another blow to her health affect her quality of life, and I admired her for this.

It was while standing in the frozen foods section of Costco that I decided I would never willingly place Carol in a home. Perhaps I'd heard echoes of my parents' teachings in my ears, and certainly a good part of me just didn't want to quit. But most of all, I'd made a commitment to this woman, a commitment to be there *in sickness* and in health, and I intended to honor my promise.

The exercise in the store had worn her out, so it took me a while to get Carol back to the car. As we drove the back roads home, I gripped the steering wheel and tried to summon up as much strength as I could and fight off my growing sense of crankiness. I had spent a lifetime teaching my boys not to harbor the woe-is-me attitude, under the belief that it prevented a person from reaching success or true happiness. Yet there I was, feeling sorry for myself over my loss of freedom.

When I got into a mood like this, I knew to be on the alert. A life of self-analysis had taught me it was only a matter of time before someone would do something that I perceived to be wrong, and I would unconsciously drift into that agitated state. In this case, it was that circumstance had robbed me of my carefully planned life of retirement with my wife.

Worry about that later, I told myself, shoving that brewing negativity to the back of my skull.

Just as we pulled into the garage back home, I realized that I had forgotten to cross off an important item on my list. Normally I might have considered leaving Carol with Stew and heading back out on my own, but Chad had taken Stew out for an early dinner. "I forgot something in the village," I said as I reopened the garage door and shifted into reverse. Carol had already swung the door open, released the seatbelt, and was turning to get out. "I have to get my purse," she said.

Seriously? I thought, feeling the crabbiness starting to win. Sure, we'd forgotten her purse that morning because we'd left in such a hurry, but the thing was little more than an oversized lipstick-carrier anyway, so what would it matter if she went another twenty minutes without it?

I threw the car back into park and hurried to her side of the car, but Carol seemed like she was trying to do everything possible to make the process of getting her back into the house as difficult as possible. When finally we reached the coat closet, and I helped put the big bag around her shoulder, I apparently did it wrong.

"I hate when you do it like that," she snapped. "I hate it, I hate it."

For a moment, I saw the darkness in my mind perching in the shadows, ready to pounce. I headed for the door, red-faced. Too little, too late. "For Christ's sake!" The words hurled from my mouth before I could tell myself to calm down and swallow my bitter thoughts. But then, one look back at her washed them away in a heartbeat.

"I'm so sorry you have to do all this," she said demurely.

"Do what?" I asked, hating myself for lashing out.

"All this shit," she said, a modern-day Carol-ism if there ever was one. "Taking care of me and having to do everything."

In the instant she spoke the words, all those pesky, lingering, and poisonous thoughts evaporated. I loved her so much at that moment.

"I wouldn't have it any other way," I replied, patting her on the hand.

I led her to her favorite seat in the house, then sat beside her and stroked her hand. The cold truth was that my unwillingness to ever quit, though a good quality, had also put a lot of pressure on me, her, and the whole situation. For too long, I'd been telling myself if/then. If Carol just had some more speech therapy, then she would talk more. If we focused more intently on her therapy exercise, then her legs and balance might come back. And so on. By telling myself these things, I was setting myself up for growing frustration about our lives, her happiness, and my independence. The only "if" I was sure of at this point was that if I kept going at this rate, then I would burn out and likely bring everyone around me down in those flames.

I wanted nothing more than to be a good man to Carol, and to entirely dedicate my life to her. This meant I would have to do something more than just make a promise to be humble. I would have to go beyond not quitting on her. I would need to just be with my wife, embrace the situation, and let life unfold. If I was going to be any good to her, then I would need to find ways to overcome my tendency toward crankiness when things didn't go as I planned.

I went to my office and pulled out the small, black moleskin journal I'd been keeping for years. I popped it open and found a nugget of borrowed wisdom that my past self had left for my future self:

The way out is through it.
– Robert Frost

CHAPTER FOUR
a search for inner peace

If I do not forgive myself for my imperfections
I cannot love myself enough to fully love others.
– Robert Furey, PhD
So I'm Not Perfect: A Psychology of Humility

That near blow-up over Carol's purse deeply concerned me. Instances like it had been becoming more common, but that was the closest I'd felt to losing my cool in a long time. My near loss of control had nothing to do with the small interruption of time it would have taken for me to help Carol fetch her bag. Frankly, it probably would've been wise, since we could've made a pit stop to the restroom. What happened that day was a symptom of something I'd been dealing with my whole life. Though I'd made good on my promise to devote time and energy to taking care of my wife, those old personal demons still lingered.

It's true what they say, that one must take the good with the bad. And that goes for genetics, too. I'd been lucky in so many respects. I had my father's dream-big nature, along with my mother's ability to socialize with anyone. With all that good luck, I suppose I shouldn't have been too surprised that I got saddled with the streak of sensitivity and agitation that ran in my mother's family as well.

My parents both had big families full of people who rarely moved away. At least once a week, my mother's family would swarm to the house that had the most beer. My siblings

---

Photo: 40th wedding Anniversary in 2009.

and I loved going to these gatherings when we were kids because so many of our family's funniest characters would be in attendance. We didn't understand it then, but with those gatherings came a complex web of family dynamics: great stories and big laughter, but also explosive sensitivity and long-held grudges.

Almost every party took a wrong turn along the way, with one family member getting in another's face over some usually inconsequential issue. Something as simple as one person paying a compliment to one family member could cause another to feel aggrieved. The insults would start flying into an argument, quickly marking the end of another gathering.

Each time, as my parents hurried us kids out to the car, I stood in awe of how intense the arguments would become. I can still see how quickly the smiling faces of my aunts and uncles would turn into nasty scowls, how the soft voices would become high pitched, and how they would be sitting one minute but standing and pointing a finger the next. Every time our car pulled away, I would worry that we would never see the family again. That concern would last right up until the following Sunday, when word would invariably get out that someone else was holding a case of beer.

While I'm certain that alcohol played a factor in some of those moments, even as a young kid, I knew there was something deeper. No matter what the issue was, and even though mere time to cool off would have healed all the hurts, it always came down to one of the involved participants needing to set the record straight. Though there was always a high premium on being right, the details of why this was important would usually get lost in the fray.

As I grew into an adult, I began to recognize my own feisty nature, especially when someone disagreed with an idea of mine. I would feel my heart beat a little faster, and a tightness in my chest would wipe away my calm demeanor.

My jaw muscles would clench into a grimace, and I would start talking a little faster. Each time, I would hear that little voice in my mind point out how damn wrong the offending party had been, and my lips would part to deliver whatever incredibly astute observation leapt to my mind. But just then, I would muster up the strength to keep my mouth shut. Here's why: I had seen how my family acted with one another, and it scared me to my core. I never wanted to be that way.

Though I learned to put a clamp on it, the heat-up in my mind was inevitable. The one big drawback to this tendency was that the people who offended me never knew how or why they had done so. Instead of seeking confrontation, I would internalize it. My philosophy became, "Keep a lid on it, and it will go away."

Sometimes it worked. I would battle those moments, and the frustration would fade fast. More often, something would happen, and the agitation would fester. During those stretches, my mind would feel like something of a prison. As I went through college and my first handful of jobs, my ability to contain the feistiness weakened.

These episodes only became more frequent after I moved our family back to Pittsburgh and started my own business as an independent sales representative in the architectural coatings industry. One February a few years into that business, it all came to a head. I'd enjoyed some successes, but our overall financial situation was tenuous. I needed every account I could get. So I decided that I would make a trip up to Erie, a small, blue-collar city in the northwestern part of Pennsylvania, to see if I could close some deals. In winter, cloud formations crossing Lake Erie dump blankets of snow on the city, along with frigid snaps of wind. Spending any time outside is a terrible idea. But there's also no better time to visit potential customers who are preparing for major coatings jobs in the spring and early summer.

On that trip in February, despite the success in lining up

some meetings, I found myself out of sorts throughout the day. It was nothing specific—just mild agitation—but at the same time, I should have known by then how to read the signs of a feisty streak brewing. With each new interaction with a colleague, I became increasingly annoyed by their attitudes and the tones of their voices.

When I got home that night, nobody in my family seemed to notice. The boys kept to their rooms. Carol was reading. On the stovetop simmered a pot of chili, the third batch in a week. I grumbled my dissatisfaction with the menu choice, but Carol barely looked up from the depths of whatever book she was reading.

"Boys!" I hollered up the stairs. "Come down for dinner." The tone of my voice was what alerted me to my mood. I didn't need a mirror to see that my expression reinforced my irritation. Memories of the bickering at the family parties flooded my mind. So I took a deep breath, grabbed an Irish whiskey, and retreated to the living room.

The sight of my favorite painting, a John Stobart landscape depicting one of the rivers in Pittsburgh in the 1800s, put me in a somber mood. I alternated between stewing and feeling sorry for myself as I slowly finished off the whiskey. Then, with a sigh, I rose from my chair and returned to the kitchen. As I set my empty cocktail glass in the sink, I reminded myself that my mood had nothing to do with my wife, my kids, or even my colleagues. This was just the same internal battle I'd been battling for years.

I awoke the next day and drove to Erie for a series of new appointments. Some of them broke my way, and some of them didn't. At the end of the day, I stopped by one of my most reliable customers in the hopes of capping the day on a positive note, but he hit me with some upsetting news: another coatings rep was poaching a high-end customer I had been targeting in the eastern Ohio portion of my territory.

The frustration rose to my face, but I buried it quickly

in front of my customer. We went on to have a productive meeting, even though I felt the whole time like I couldn't get it over with soon enough. I had to confront this other rep as soon as possible.

The snow was coming down hard and darkness had already set in by the time I hit the road at 4:30. Interstate 79 starts in Erie and runs straight south through a mostly rural landscape until you reach Pittsburgh. The first fifty miles out of Erie have always been quite barren, and I wasn't in the mood for the radio. Instead, I started chewing over the possible interloper in my territory. For that next half-hour, I grinded through his lack of professional courtesy and business ethics.

Who in the hell does this guy think he is? Who does he think I am?

My brooding was so deep that I failed to notice the exit signs for Edinboro University, which had never failed to prompt memories of basketball games and lessons learned. A firm grip on the wheel, I started looking for the next rest stop. It was time to call my mentor, Harold Righter, to object to the interference and set the record straight. Harold had run his own coatings agency for twenty years in New England, so I figured he could help.

As I pumped quarters into the payphone, I felt my neck and chest tighten. A roaring headache had started by the time I finished dialing his number.

I didn't even let him say hello before I started in about how this SOB was sneaking into my territory.

"George!" Harold tried to chime in, but I blew past him.

For the next three minutes, I explained how unfair the situation was, how I planned to contact our coatings supplier to raise hell, and how I would demand a meeting with the guy, then get in the car the next morning and drive all the way to Cleveland, where I would catch this turkey in all his lies. When I finally slowed down, a long, quiet moment ensued.

"I can hear you shaking through the phone, George," Harold said in his thick Boston accent.

The words snapped me back to reality. I hung up the phone without saying goodbye. Then I returned to my car and leaned back onto the hood. The last bit of light was fading over the trees to my right. The wind had picked up. Images of my temperamental family flashed through my mind. I closed my eyes and thought of my wife and three boys. From the ash tray in my car, I grabbed a couple more quarters, then returned to the payphone. I had to do something about this. I couldn't wage this battle alone anymore.

A familiar and loving voice answered on the other end of the line.

"Dad," I said with a sigh. "What was the name of the retreat you used to go to in the city?"

St. Paul's Catholic Church and Monastery sat high on a bluff overlooking Pittsburgh's historic Southside neighborhood. As I came upon the iron gate at the outer edge of the notable church, I felt equal parts excited and anxious. A few members of my family, like my dad, had long encouraged me to attend as they saw the troubles in me well before I did. So there I was, like my father and uncle before me, waiting for the bell to ring to begin the weekend.

Having arrived a few minutes early, I decided to pass the time with a stroll through the grounds. I reached the garden and breathed in the beautiful view of Pittsburgh.

I began to feel silly. When was the last time I'd been to church and meant it? How would I plan to find peace here? And why was I being so hard on myself? I had led a successful life. I was married to an adorable and easygoing wife, and I had three good sons. I owned my own house and ran my business from an office less than a mile from where I lived. I was forty-five years old, and everything was going my way.

Sure, just beneath the surface, I'd battled with that agitated self, but apart from my occasional crankiness, I rarely acted out. I figured I'd find a way to ignore the inner turmoil and headed for the gate and back to my car.

When I was halfway back to the gate, the St. Paul's church bell rang, freezing me in my path. I'm not sure if it was Catholic guilt, a sense of obligation, or the fact that the sound also meant dinner was ready, but I turned around to join the group heading for the cafeteria. A short Mass followed, after which we learned that we would be on our own for the rest of the night. There was no whiskey or wine, or any other libations. No TV or radio, either, and I hadn't brought anything to read. I was totally out of my element.

Right then, as if by cosmic reminder, I was paged to the reception area, where I picked up the phone sitting on the desk. My good friend Joe Curtin was on the other end of the line.

"George Shannon at a church retreat," he said. "This is sacrilegious."

"I'm trying to do something good in my life," I replied.

He laughed. "When Carol told me you were there, I had to call and confirm it for myself. I'll be at Froggy's tonight if you change your mind." I shouldn't have been surprised. I was always one of the guys. Always having a good time. And I certainly understood why none of my friends could believe that I'd cloister myself in a seminary over a weekend, trying to make myself a better person.

After hanging up with Joe, my instinct was to find someone to chat up, but I fought that urge and wandered into the seminary library and sat down. The quiet of the room made me uncomfortable. Though back then I'd never have understood why, it has become very clear that the total lack of distraction forced me to face the uncomfortable: true self-reflection. I'd convinced myself up to this point that taking control of my life and striving for perfection had been the tools I needed to achieve happiness, but instead I'd been feeling worse. In those painfully quiet moments, I resolved to change, but I had no idea how. As I waited for an answer, it occurred to me that I was sitting among hundreds of books—spiritual ones no less.

I knew my reading tendencies, so I figured I would need to find a smaller book. I paced up and down the aisle until a thinner, black-bound title jumped out at me: *So I'm Not Perfect: A Psychology of Humility,* by Robert J. Furey, PhD. I read the first few paragraphs and was immediately gripped. For the next hour, I sat on the leather chair in the library, soaking up one nugget of insight after another. It was as if this book had been written directly to me. Each passage seemed to reveal something new that would absolutely floor me.

When I glanced at the library clock, I discovered how late it had become, and realized I had to get to my assigned bunk for the night. Though I'd seen the sign that asked visitors to leave the books in the library I wanted neither to stop reading nor risk having another self-reflective soul getting their hands on these one hundred fifty pages of wisdom. I scanned to make sure nobody was around and palmed the book to my side like I was sneaking out top secrets. Since I planned on returning the book at the end of the weekend, I figured no sins had been committed.

The minute I returned to my room, I pulled out a little black notebook in which I'd been keeping some personal observations as well as any inspirational quotes I'd heard or come across. I found a page in the Dr. Furey book I'd earmarked and transcribed the passage word for word into my notebook:

"Without humility, pride becomes conceit and arrogance."

And then I read that wonderful sentence again and again. Those eight words shot through my mind, shining a bright light on my behavior of late and beyond. I didn't have a full grasp of the concept of humility then, but I knew one thing, that I had to stop always wanting things to be my way or needing things to be perfect. So what if Carol had made three batches of chili in one week? Was she loyal? Yes. Was she taking care of the house like we'd agreed upon? Check. Had she done her part to raise our kids as independent young men as we planned? Yep.

The truth was, I owed it to her. She always bore the brunt of my self-important streak. Just as I had convinced myself that in striving for perfection, I was only trying to be successful in business, that faulty belief had served as something of a trap for my marriage in my many attempts to "help" her. It wasn't a failure to get my way that always triggered me. That was just a symptom of my problem. To overcome, I would have to start seeing things for how they were, rather than for how I thought they should be or imposing my own version of what ought to be.

I should have known better; I'd seen my family bicker over a hundred little injustices that were likely created out of their own minds. What would I accomplish if I drove to eastern Ohio and gave that coatings rep a piece of my mind? Nothing, and frankly it would've been an act of selfishness. It all made so much sense. Immediately, I realized that I needed to be more tolerant. It was, after all, that same desire for tolerance that had caused me to enroll in this retreat in the first place. Perhaps I could sit down with the guy and figure out ways to make both of our agencies better. If not, at least I tried.

To me, humility meant thinking of others more than I had been, and that's what I intended to do. I spent the rest of the weekend sneaking back to my room and jotting down every last one of my favorite passages of wisdom.

I left that wonderful retreat full of energy and hope for the future. When I got home, I went to the local bookstore and ordered a handful of copies of *So I'm Not Perfect*. I made my peace with the encroacher from eastern Ohio. I became more tolerant of others in my workplace. I found ways of introducing new meal ideas to Carol and tried to enjoy my kids' busy lives as best I could. I couldn't have been happier that first month. Right around that point, I ran into an old friend and shared my awesome experience with him. He smiled and bluntly, though politely, told me it wouldn't last. I blew it off and ignored his comments. It turned out he was right; six months later, I'd fallen back into my normal patterns: delving deep into work, building and maintaining impeccable landscaping at my home, and losing my tolerance and humility.

The truth was that the more I asserted myself in life, the better I felt. To see order and neatness in my world felt comforting. In those times, the confrontational thoughts would stay mostly in the background, a quiet but constant murmur. When life got messy, literally or figuratively, those tenaciously righteous thoughts would demand to be heard, and I would battle them with all my might before eventually winning the day. I figured that the idea of inner peace was something like a mirage, just something pleasing to ponder but never all that attainable. I assumed someone like me would never find true happiness and come to terms with that truth. There are few moments I can remember in life where I am more grateful to have been wrong.

[A humble man] will not be thinking about humility:
he will not be thinking about himself at all.

– C.S. Lewis
Mere Christianity

CHAPTER FIVE
the healing power of humility

By December of 2012, I'd been taking care of my wife for a little over two years. I had approached her new health situation like I had everything else since I was a child: head-on. I learned everything I could about her condition, discovered ways to improve her health, and provided those opportunities, all while keeping things organized and on track. My unwillingness to quit was something I could finally put to good use. Trying to make Carol's situation the best I could had created an unexpected happiness and sense of fulfillment. I began to think that my purpose in life had become clear.

Unfortunately, over the years, my inner dialogue had evolved cleverer and cleverer ways to undermine any happiness I ever managed to find. Even now, it was exhibiting its craftiness on my newly discovered sense of peace. I soon became frustrated by the lack of options to improve Carol's health, and it seemed to me that suddenly even the aspects I had mastered—like keeping her diabetes under control—became quite unpredictable. A bad sugar reading would feel like a failure on my part, and this would send my thoughts down a road toward crankiness and negativity.

No matter how hard I tried, I couldn't make Carol better. If my very purpose for living was to take care of my wife, then the chatter in my mind always had the means to twist the knife. I feared that eventually my demons would win.

That was my somewhat brittle mental state at the time I received the call.

Photo: With friends Robert E. McCarthy Jr., Janet McCarthy, Linda Hoehl, and Greg Hoehl.

"I'm sorry, George," came the news, "but the treatments weren't effective. You still have cancer."

I had been diagnosed with prostate cancer at a time when the dust had barely settled on my sixtieth birthday. Carol was still healthy then. My oncologist recommended that we forgo any radiation treatment and instead go straight to surgery to remove my prostate. Follow-up tests showed that the surgery had failed to deliver me a perfectly clean bill of health. A small amount of detectable cancer matter remained in my prostate bed. At the doctor's recommendation, we made the decision to wait on radiation treatment, based on my relatively young age and the likely side effects. I submitted to regular checkups and blood tests, and we started radiation at what the doctor felt was the appropriate juncture.

But now I sat there dumbfounded with the phone in my hand, having learned the hard way that we'd missed the appropriate juncture. That's a difficult enough thing to hear on its own, but the worst part was that I didn't even hear it from my doctor. The call had come from his secretary. The inner boil spilled over in an instant.

What kind of doctor has his secretary do his dirty work? This is cancer, for Christ's sake.

As soon as I managed to collect myself, I called the doctor directly. "Tell me what these results mean," I said, trying to keep a level tone.

"It means you'll never be cancer-free," he said flatly.

When I heard those words, it took every stitch of what I had to fight against my anger. Many years of taming down that predisposed agitation of mine went to tatters in an instant. Though I wanted to take him to task for not calling in the first place, I got off the phone without incident.

I won the immediate battle in my mind with that doctor, but the rest of my day was full of sour thoughts as I ruminated on how I had just learned that, like my wife, I would spend the rest of my life battling a terminal condition.

A couple weeks went by, and the bitterness in my mind only grew as I sat alone with my pain. Within a month, I reached a breaking point. One night, my son Chad stopped by unexpectedly and found me sitting gloomily in the dark. He tried to cheer me up by staying with me for a couple hours and discussing the situation, but it was no use.

The somewhat embarrassing experience left me with the feeling that I needed to do something about my dark mood. The next morning, I went to my office to see if I still had any copies left of that wonderful little book about humility I'd read twenty years prior. Once I opened the book, it was as if I'd never left the quiet confines of the church library.

I reread the passage about how arrogance grows in the absence of humility. In my younger days, I must have missed the basic meaning behind that critical observation: unless you can remove yourself from the center of your universe, you will suffer from being at the center of your universe. To be humble is to break down the energy-sucking ego that can never be satisfied. I had spent a large part of my life battling with my own tendencies to seek out the imperfections, whether that meant obsessing over the details in my business environment or being hard on Carol because she hadn't done things the way I preferred.

All my life, I had convinced myself that taking charge was a virtue, and it certainly served its purpose of helping me building my business and therefore providing for my family. That tactic required that I put me first. Yes, it gave me the strength to see anything through, including the goal of caring for my ailing wife, but it also originally stemmed from a desire to serve my world, my needs, and my ego. I still hadn't let go of my goal of getting her healthy again, and had been banking my hopes on the idea that she was going to get better. My goals and expectations weren't being met, which had given rise to the kind of gloominess that made me forget my place.

If I was going to last in the face of cancer and a

progressively ailing wife, I needed to find a new path. The question then arose as to which route to take. I kept reading, and when I came across the words, I remembered them as clear as the day I'd jotted them in my notebook many years prior.

"Our very first problem is to accept our present circumstances as they are, ourselves as we are, and the people about us as they are."

There were no more fixes, but acceptance does not equal quitting. Like a fog lifting, it became wildly clear to me. My never-quit mentality had fed the chatter in my mind and thus prevented me from possessing true clarity regarding my situation. I sat down in my office chair and sighed, a long breath of both relief and sadness. It felt good to shed the burden of trying to fix everything and keep my life in perfect order. And the grief that overcame me arose from the realization that my wife and I were sick. I scanned my office walls with all the pictures of my family and awards in business. Time was moving fast, and our lives on this earth were limited.

My mind became still, perhaps for the first time in my life, but certainly for the first time in the last two decades. *Accept the cancer. Accept me. Accept Carol. Accept the world around me.* The next few moments were as exhilarating as I'd ever experienced. Ever since Carol's strokes, I'd been saying that I wanted to make her feel the love, but for the first time, that phrase made sense. It was about more than being a reliable husband or stepping up to the initial challenge of her disability. I wanted to make my life about her, all about her, for the rest of her life—or mine, if that was the case. To be a vessel for her happiness, fulfillment, and enjoyment of her life.

Cancer was a difficult prospect, but I couldn't change it. In some ways, it made my desire to be fully selfless more intense. If I was destined to die before Carol, then I wanted to make sure I went down having given her everything I had.

The thought that I would get to spend the sunset phase of my life with my one-of-a-kind wife made me feel almost giddy in that moment.

Before closing the book that day, I found one more critical lesson: "If I do not allow for my own imperfection, I will never really know myself."

It wouldn't be easy. Life would throw me curveballs and some days would be quite difficult. If I lost sight of this truth, I would slip back into the same patterns and allow my old self to rule the day. Remembering my own imperfection would be the compass to guide the rest of my journey. From this moment on, these became the words I called on whenever I needed to identify my true north.

A few months later, I would face a major test. One of my oldest friends put me on to a cancer doctor named Dave Parda. When I first met with Dr. Parda, he explained we could make one last-ditch effort, a radiation laser-focused blast at the tumor site, and with this strategy came a glimmer of hope. Dr. Parda's team spent many sessions with me, fine-tuning their blast location based on my anatomical measurements and the assistance of high-end computing. I found myself thinking that maybe we'd beat this thing after all.

The following week, the radiation went off without a hitch. But the subsequent meeting with Dr. Parda didn't deliver the best news. Despite the perfect precision, the zap of radiation had stunned the tumor into submission, but hadn't destroyed it. The short of it was that my cancer would never be cured, and our next step would be to find ways to manage the slow-growing disease. We'd start hormone therapy soon and eventually move on to chemotherapy.

Now, considering I'd gotten my hopes up, I'll be the first to admit that I expected a wave of anger to destroy me in that moment, but it never came. As I left the cancer center and got in my car, I waited for the swirling thoughts of injustice to clutter my mind, but they failed to appear. Instead, I found myself thinking about the practical implications of taking care of Carol during chemo treatments. Driving down the highway, I took the quiet time to check for lurking demons of old, but my search turned up empty.

My relationship with Carol had flourished as of late. Though we had normal marital challenges, life had been so much more interesting. We'd been having such fun and so many laughs, and had spent more time together in that period than we had in the whole of the decade prior. I didn't want news of a terminal illness to ruin all that, so I decided I'd downplay it with her. When I entered our front door, I found my wife in her usual spot in her chair, her tiny legs propped up on the ottoman, a magazine in her lap as she brushed her lips with a business reply card in the way that always soothed her.

Her eyes met mine. "Oh, there he is," she said, as she often did when eager to see me.

I marched straight to her and gave her a long hug, and the mantra crossed my mind as naturally as the blood flowed from my heart: *Accept me, accept her, and all your circumstances.*

I really should have expected the blunt question that followed.

"Are you going to die or something?"

Some younger version of myself would have jumped all over that remark as being less than tactful. Instead, I focused on how much I enjoyed her offbeat and frank manner.

"I'll be with you for all your days," I whispered in her ear. "All your days. Do you understand?"

A year or so later, I elected to undergo a new chemotherapy treatment, which rendered me physically useless and bound to the couch.

After a chemo treatment, I felt the absolute worst, like a toothache and the worst flu had simultaneously invaded every fiber of my body. As I sat on the living room couch, wishing nothing more than to be able to curl up and go to sleep for the next three days, I glanced over at Carol. She must have sensed my attention on her, as she looked away from Doctor Oz on TV.

"Why don't you try to sleep?" she asked.

Restlessly, she wiggled about in her chair while glancing at me every few seconds. I had learned that this jumpiness meant Carol was feeling like a burden, but it went beyond that. She wanted to be an active part of our lives together. She wanted to do something for us, take care of things for a while, and just be her own person. She wanted to water and prune her orchids, swing by her favorite store to buy some thoughtful cards for family and friends, or even just make her own peanut butter toast for breakfast. These were the times I felt the worst for Carol.

"I'm okay," I said, stretching the truth beyond recognition. "Just need to rest my feet a little while."

She gave me one of her patented headshakes with a little shoulder shrug, a move that translated directly as "I know you're bullshitting me, but what else can I do?" She kept her eyes locked on me as I battled that coveted sleep. I must have dozed for a moment, because the next thing I knew, Carol had worked her way up on the walker and moved a few feet away from the chair. Instead of making her customary left down the hall in the direction of the bathroom, she went straight into the kitchen toward the refrigerator.

"Whatcha' doing, honey?"

"Making you lunch," she replied loudly. "You got a problem with that?" She turned around to stare me down.

For a split second, I considered telling her not to worry. Instead, I just chuckled at the stern delivery. I also remembered how important it had been for her to take care of me when I was first diagnosed with this disease a decade ago. So I forced my weary body up from the couch and stood near her in case she lost her balance. Other than having me grab the plates from an unreachable shelf, she did the rest. In about ten minutes, we both had American cheese sandwiches with mustard, and we split a Diet Coke.

When we finished, Carol scooted herself back to her chair while I trudged through the full list of tasks and household chores that needed to be done. An hour or so later, and running on empty, I flopped down on the couch. Though I wanted to, out of my own fear for my wife's wellbeing, I couldn't let myself fall asleep. I had noticed that Carol was fidgeting with the newspaper, and I knew what she wanted.

"Anything good in there?"

"I want to see all of them," she replied. "Do you want to pick?"

I rolled off the couch, grabbed the movie section of the paper, and picked one for later in the afternoon. Sure, the pain would be unbearable, but making every day of Carol's life the best day of her life had become the thing that gave me the most happiness, the thing that made me feel at peace with myself. Not even the misery caused by chemo could take the value of that away from me. After all, I didn't know how many more days I would get.

Was our life perfect from then on? Certainly not. The big difference after that day I first picked up *So I'm Not Perfect* during my retreat in the 90s was that I had accepted my own faults and could finally love myself enough to make my love available to my wife in a way we had never reached before. This gave me the chance to know her—and us—in a whole new light.

That was how I learned to smile instead of being angry, be kind over confrontational, and humble over self-righteous. My old inner self still knocked on the door a dozen times a day, but my understanding of what humility required gave me the edge to refuse entry. When I made mistakes, I apologized. If I felt like I was losing the battle, I picked up my notes and reviewed them. I reminded myself that life, even at its best, would never be perfect, but the key was to accept it on its own terms.

CHAPTER SIX
better days

We are not the same persons this year as last; nor
are those we love. It is a happy chance if we,
changing, continue to love a changed person.
– W. Somerset Maugham
The Summing Up

Even though I'd been a fan of the University of
Pittsburgh's football team as a kid, I'd always thought of
Notre Dame as a nearly mystical place. Maybe I'd fallen for
the Knute Rockne story. Whatever the case, it was 1967, and
Joe Curtin, a good friend from high school, had made Pitt's
team as a defensive back. When I heard he'd moved up to the
starting job, it made the annual matchup with Notre Dame
seem even more exciting. I circled the day on the calendar:
Saturday, November 11th, and made sure I got the time off
from my job in Youngstown, where I was working my way
through college at the time.

I arrived home that Friday night in enough time to catch a
drink with another high school buddy, Tommy Ryan, at a local
pizza parlor called Pinchero's. The moment we opened the
door to the restaurant, I spotted that easy smile of the woman
I would come to love. On either side of my future wife sat a
pair of her friends, Linda and Janet. This trio would remain
the best of friends for decades after.

But in the meantime, I only had eyes for the girl in the
center. Carol Perry didn't seem like she had a care in the

Photo: Wedding Day, March 15, 1969

79

world. This attitude permeated everything she did, from the way she held her cigarette to the way she laughed so easily. Tommy introduced us, and we talked about everything from my fascination with Bobby Kennedy to our dreams in life, and even to my uncertainty about what I would do after graduating from college. Mostly we laughed for the next few hours. In her quiet but attentive way, she made me feel like the most important person in the room, or in all of Pittsburgh, for that matter. As we got up to leave, she stood as well. That was when I first noticed that Carol couldn't have been a centimeter taller than five feet. She was the most adorable thing I'd ever seen. Just as I was about to go, I felt a tug on my sleeve. Carol had written her phone number on a slip of paper, and was reaching out to hand it to me. With a grin, I took it and left.

"Watch out," Tommy said once we'd gotten out to the parking lot. "That Perry girl is looking for the hoop."

My friend's assessment was on the money, but neither of us could have figured that I would soon be willing to oblige.

Carol and I dated for just under a year. The rare times I made it back to Brentwood, I would take her for a bite to eat, and we would invariably end up at one of our families' houses. When we went to her house, we would quietly watch television with her parents. But Carol preferred to spend time at my family's parties, where drinking, teasing, and dancing were always the order of the night.

One weekend, I was home from Youngstown to visit her. Between finishing up my senior year and my full-time job at the bank, these visits were painfully few and far between. Just a couple months earlier, I'd made our relationship a lot more official by giving her a lavalier, a necklace bearing my fraternity's name. She'd been so excited that she flashed that beautiful smile of hers everywhere we went.

On this occasion, the last night home before heading back to school, I picked Carol up in my black Chevy Camaro—I was so proud of that car—and took her on a date. We were heading to South Hills Village, a new mall, when we pulled up to a stoplight at one of the main intersections in town. I was bobbing my head to the radio and keeping an eye on the red light when she turned to me and blinked her big blue eyes. I braced myself, because she'd never really looked at me quite so theatrically.

"So," she said, "are we going to get married or what?"

The truth was that I was enamored with Carol, but hadn't been thinking about marriage just yet because distance had prevented us from spending much time together in the eleven months since we'd first met. Given that I was someone who'd led an almost entirely practical life up to that point, my reply surprised even me.

"Yes," I said. "Let's get married."

When the light turned green, we drove off and spent the rest of the night celebrating.

We wasted no time setting the date: March 15, 1969. In those days, weddings were relatively simple affairs. The one stipulation I asked for was to get married at the Catholic church I'd grown up in, St. Sylvester's in Brentwood. We had our reception in the banquet hall of a little mom and pop hotel nearby. My extended family was enormous, so it felt almost more like a Shannon/Kramer reunion than a wedding.

At some point later into the night, I finally had the chance to dance with my new wife. She looked so beautiful in her dress. I remember thinking how crazy it was that I'd married this woman just eighteen months after meeting her. But the longer we danced, the more that feeling gave way to a sense that Carol was the one for me, and that someday soon we would start a family.

When it was time for us to leave the reception, my brother Jim brought the car around for us. My Uncle Charlie, truly one of the silliest people to have ever lived, waited for Carol to climb into the car before he jumped into the driver's seat and sped away without me. The crowd went wild. Fifteen minutes later, he returned my car and new wife to me. I can only imagine how he must have teased her during that ride.

As he was handing me the keys, he grabbed me and said loud enough for everyone to hear, "Hey, kid. She's a real keeper, so don't mess it up."

Everyone got a good laugh at that one. When I hopped in the car, I was met by the same smile that caught my attention in the pizza parlor. I told her I would keep my promise, and she kissed me.

As we made our way to the Pennsylvania Turnpike, my new wife tallied up the wedding envelope proceeds, so we could figure out how many honeymoon days we could afford. The location had been my choice. Long in love with American history and intrigued by government, I wanted to see everything Washington DC had to offer, and Carol went right along with me. For three straight days, I took her to one historical site after another. Though the constant movement clearly exhausted her, Carol kept on trudging at my side.

Toward the end of the trip, she indulged me one last time. I couldn't leave the city without seeing Ford's Theatre. I've always been fascinated by the Civil War. Imagine my heartbreak when we found that while the museum was open, the theater itself was closed. The entrance had been covered by a makeshift door marked with a sign reading "under renovation." Undeterred, I pulled back the plywood barrier just enough for Carol and me to slide in before letting it clap shut behind us.

Alone in that theater, I grabbed my wife's hand and led the way to the spot where John Wilkes Boothe had spied on Lincoln. The whole way up, she voiced her concerns about getting caught. But when we looked through the peephole that Boothe had made, she seemed to become just as enthralled as I was. Hand in hand, we ventured into the viewing booth where Lincoln had watched the play, and we finished by sitting in the very same seat where the president had passed his last moments.

Our time in Ford's Theatre was like a microcosm of our life together. I had always been willing to race after what I wanted, and Carol had always chosen to come along, open and accepting of whatever our newest adventure might bring. Now, some forty-plus years later, it was my wife's needs that dictated the day's journey, and I'd become the willing participant.

September 2016

The living room clock read 7:00 A.M. The last time I'd peeked in on Carol, right after my quick read of the morning paper, she'd been snoring away. So I settled into my desk chair, second cup of coffee in hand. The next sixty minutes would be the only stretch in the day that belonged to me alone. I clicked my desk lamp on low and tucked into the beautiful silence. Every extra minute that Carol slept in the morning would make her day better. The correlation was remarkable. If she slept well, we almost always would have an incident-free day. But if she woke early, something troublesome would happen. Perhaps she would be more fatigued than usual and take a tumble on the way to the car, or something in her metabolism would be off, sending her into a low blood sugar state. Whatever the case, more sleep meant fewer problems.

As Carol slept, I checked my calendar for appointments, grabbed a pen and notepad, and started a list. Fifteen minutes later, I had assembled a game plan for the day. Predictably, the dishwasher beeped. I emptied it with an almost comic dedication to quiet, then moved on to Carol's morning setup. I set out a glass of water, a *USA Today* reassembled with the Life section on top, an array of her pills, a placemat, a spoon, and a bowl of dry cereal. I would wait until she reached the counter to add her almond milk—a necessity because of her lactose intolerance. Next to her breakfast, I placed her glucometer, which we would use to test her morning blood sugar levels. Finally came the tissue we would use to wipe off the drop of blood that would follow pricking her finger with the glucometer's needle.

I drifted back to my computer to glance at the video monitor that allowed me to keep an eye on Carol while tending the morning tasks. The only change since last I checked the monitor was that she had flipped from facing the window to facing the bathroom side of the bed. I knew I would have about fifteen minutes until she tried her daily morning escape to the bathroom without telling me.

I gazed through the monitor at my wife, tucked cozily into a ball of comforter and sheets in the dark bedroom. Since the second stroke, I had thought of Carol like a little injured bird I was keeping safe in the palm of my hand. I hadn't always held such a tender view of our relationship. In fact, there had been a series of losing battles in our marriage when I had tried to change Carol, or to make her think differently about things, or maybe to just convince her to hold stronger opinions or take more charge of the life we shared.

Before we got married, I tried my hand at teaching middle school kids. While I had a few memorable moments—like when my class wrote me personal notes after Bobby Kennedy was killed—education was a profession for which I found myself ill suited. Then, a few months after Carol and I tied the knot came one of the shortest military service stints in the history of the Marines. I'd been excited about the chance to serve my country, but two weeks into basic training, they discovered my heart murmur and issued me an honorable discharge. Uncertain of what to do next, I applied for a series of sales jobs and landed one with Koppers Inc. The only trouble with this new job was that we would have to transfer to Minnesota in the dead of winter. Despite the fact that Carol worked at TWA, a job she loved to death, and that we would have to move away from our families, Carol proved totally fine with the move.

It didn't take long for us to become unhappy in the Great White North. I was new to sales, and I had zero direction at work, hated the cold, and missed my family. Carol struggled to adjust to life away from Pittsburgh as well. But when I asked her what she wanted to do next, she claimed that it didn't matter. This irritated me, as I wanted her to participate in the decision-making process, or at least share some insight. But instead, I got nothing. We moved five times in the next seven years, and each time, I felt like the decision rested solely on my shoulders, as Carol claimed that she would be fine anywhere. Perhaps my feeling that we had merely been spouses and not partners in our marriage went way back to the beginning.

The way I'd seen it back then, this was just one of the many signs of Carol's lack of initiative. Whether the matter was as trivial as choosing a vacation destination or as serious as finally following through on confronting her overbearing mother, she never showed much interest in sharing her opinion. I had always figured I could change that. I was wrong, but she did have a quiet way of doing things on her terms, even as she went with the flow. I just failed to see this wonderful attribute, or better yet *accept* this until much later in our marriage.

The gentle tone signifying the end of the dryer cycle called me to our laundry room to begin the process of gathering and folding a load of warm towels.

Just as I finished folding the towels and setting them on my desk in the living area, the ring of the landline phone carved through the blissful silence. The loud intrusion into Carol's best moments of sleep forced a cringe. Caller ID announced that it was the local pharmacy calling to notify that the next batch of medicine was ready for pickup. Another item to add to the day's list.

I placed the phone back into the cradle and, out of instinct, turned to the monitor. Carol had those Tweety legs pointed straight up in the air, and the slowest escape in the history of mankind was underway. I pulled the door open, the soft living room light casting into the room.

"Oh, shit," Carol muttered, caught in the act yet again.

"Where were you going, buster?"

"Were you spying on me again? I hate when you do that."

Truth be told, I hated the necessity of it, too, but what could I do? Carol's condition had regressed to the point where she was far less capable of guarding against poor choices. The minute I would look away, she would be off trying to walk on her own, and she just wasn't capable of that anymore. Even so, I couldn't blame her for the desire. Imagine what it must feel like to be under constant supervision.

Before the strokes, Carol had enjoyed a life all her own. She had once co-owned with her good friend Mareena a customized gift store called Perfect Presents. Carol had loved that little business and wished it had lasted longer. She often mentioned fond memories of how our boys would visit her at the store's location in the village. At least once a week, Chad, who has always had a sweet tooth, would hit her up for one of the fancy chocolate bars she used for gifts.

As our kids grew older, Carol clerked at the local Penguin bookstore and worked part-time for a florist, helping with the arrangements. She would also spend one Monday a month at the women's shelter in downtown Pittsburgh. In the last few years before her life took that drastic change, she volunteered a few days a week at the hospital just up the street from the center of town.

For someone like Carol, that sense that she was always being watched and that she had lost any real measure of independence must have been frustrating.

I went to the bed and helped her to her feet. "Maybe I just couldn't wait to see my honey."

"That's a good one," she replied. "Is she here yet?"

I chuckled. "You've got me today."

"Oh, Christ."

One thing that always struck me about Carol was that she could deliver more emotion in those two words than most inspirational speeches I'd ever heard. In this case, she was conveying her preference to be bathed by Jennifer, whose bathing technique far surpassed her husband's "hosing down" approach. Several mornings a week, Jennifer, who was a certified nursing assistant, would come over and help with Carol's morning care. As part of the routine, she would apply lotion that would leave Carol smelling like some kind of exotic flower. Of course my wife cared little about the lotion's scent. What she was after was the massage-like experience of the application. This luxurious routine was one of the many reasons that Jennifer would become one of Carol's closest friends in the last few years of her life.

After helping Carol to the bathroom, I had just enough time to make the bed and fetch the folded towels I had left on my desk. Like clockwork, I found her standing in the doorway of the bathroom right when I returned. Just like every day, we lumbered slowly and steadily off to the kitchen. As we passed the stack of towels, Carol reached out and patted them, almost as if to thank me for doing the laundry.

"Look at that," she said, delighted at the sight of the array I had prepared for her on the counter. "It's all ready for me. Thank you." Carol made this same observation every day as if she had never seen the spread before.

I helped her to her seat, then applied the glucometer to the finger she held up reflexively. With her free hand, she'd already started leafing through the Life section of the paper. The glucometer returned "121," a good number. With a healthy blood sugar reading and a sound few hours of sleep, this felt like it would be a good day.

The pills went down without a hitch, which was also a good sign, because Carol's stiff esophagus typically made for a struggle with the bigger ones. I poured the almond milk. The oven clock read 8:15. This left us half an hour—along with sufficient contingency time for the inevitable surprise or hurdle that each day presented—before I would need to help Carol brush her teeth and then get her in the bath. If all went well, we would make it to her first doctor's appointment at 10 o'clock with plenty of time to spare.

She would need every bit of that thirty minutes to eat her bowl of Puffins Peanut Butter cereal, the eventual winner after a year-long search for a low-sugar and fiber-rich brand she actually enjoyed. Each spoonful would bring to her lips only one to two Puffins at most, the rest of them slipping back into the bowl during their shaky ascent. While she slogged through breakfast, I passed the time replying to any emails or texts that had landed in my inbox since yesterday morning.

Right on schedule, we had Carol in the bath. Many F-bombs later, we were finished. Next, just like always, she sat on the bed in a bathrobe while I stood in her closet and failed at several attempts to find a shirt she wanted to wear. Eventually she agreed to a blue sweater with a rolled neck, always one of her favorites.

As I helped her dress, I noticed that she was bleeding just above the knee. If, prior to her strokes, someone had told me what an obstacle a simple bloody knee could be, I never would have believed it. I'd seen it often enough by then to know that this would complicate the day pretty drastically. Various vascular issues left Carol prone to bruising. Simple bumps against a chair or a table or the edge of the bath could sometimes lead to an impossibly slow-healing wound. Some grew serious enough to require an emergency room visit. This wound, though, looked manageable. We started applying pressure, and after a half-hour, the bleeding slowed enough to where we could finish dressing and make it to the appointment on time.

I helped her into the wheelchair and guided her down the

hallway to the elevator. In our building's parking garage, I lifted her into the car and folded the chair into the trunk. Then I drove us to the doctor's office, parked in the handicapped spot, lifted her back out of the car, and then wheeled her into the appointment. Like always, the process took over twenty minutes. Even so, we arrived two minutes early for our 10 A.M. session and were told that the nurse would come for us shortly.

The more time Carol and I spent together, pushed along by my growing acceptance of myself, Carol, and my circumstances, the more I reflected on how much of a strain my personality had put on our marriage in the years past. I sincerely believed that by trying to help her, I was fixing her, but she was never the one who needed fixing.

When we were younger, I feared that if Carol didn't get a little exercise once in a while, she would end up like her mother, who was in rough physical shape for most of her adult life. In my tendency to try to fix things before they were even broken, I urged my wife to join the YMCA, or some other fitness club. Sometimes she humored me and attended a yoga session or an aerobics class, but those efforts always faded.

Then, one day, she seemingly took my advice to heart. Our three sons had moved out, so we downsized to a smaller home and soon started to feel a little cooped up.

"Maybe it would be good to get out and take walks every day," I suggested.

Carol agreed, and went for a walk into Sewickley Village, a mile from where we lived at the time. The next day, she went out again. This became a full week of walking every day. My second-floor office looked out over the driveway, and I would see her depart every day around 10 A.M. Two hours later, I would see those little legs chugging back toward the house. Even at her typically pokey walking pace, I figured she'd walked a good six miles. I praised her on a regular basis for taking the bull by the horns. She would smile and go about her business.

This continued for several years. I probably patted myself on the back a time or two, taking some small amount of credit for the change.

Until one day when I went for a jog into town about twenty minutes after Carol had left for her morning walk. When I came to the edge of the village, I spotted her, a giant soft drink in her hand, as she made a turn up the street toward her best friend Linda's house and went inside.

Confused and frustrated, I finished my run, took a shower, and waited for my wife to return. An hour later, she came up the driveway.

"So," I said knowingly. "How was your walk?"

"Oh, fine," she said. "Same as always."

I smirked and presented my evidence. Whether I had expected her to twist about getting caught in a lie, I can't be sure. But she just shrugged it off. For years, I had thought that I'd changed her somehow, but every day, Carol had been walking to the local bagel shop and grabbing a Diet Coke before heading straight to Linda's to gab for an hour or so. As I write this now, I kick myself for being such a pain-in-the-ass husband. That walk to Linda's and back was still a two-mile jaunt, and I should have just been happy with it instead of needing to be right.

The nurse took us back to an exam room, patched up Carol's knee, and took an INR reading to check her Coumadin levels. Anytime she dealt with one of those long-lasting bleeds, I worried that the dosage had gotten out of control. If her blood became too thin, it could be deadly.

After a little tape and gauze and a good INR reading, we headed home for a quick lunch and the noon pills. We had about forty-five minutes to enjoy lunch before we would need to leave for the podiatrist appointment at one o'clock. I had hoped to have enough time to get Carol a little rest, and maybe even run out to Sam's Club to pick up the prescriptions, but both would have to wait. As we drove home, we went past our church, St. James, which reminded me to make sure we attended Mass again soon. It had been a few weeks since our last visit, and both of us always felt better when we made it there on the regular.

I threw together some sandwiches for us—tuna for me and cheese with French's yellow mustard for her. I ate mine standing up and checking my emails while she picked through hers. Even though she didn't eat the crusts of her sandwiches, it still took my wife a solid fifteen minutes to get through an average-sized sandwich and wash down her pills.

As I put the lunch items away in our fridge full of food, I recalled how we'd always butted heads about the way Carol grocery shopped. In our little town, there used to be three grocery markets: a chain, a medium-sized independent, and a small corner store. Carol shopped at the smallest of them. And when she went, she would always pick up only the essentials: enough eggs for a few mornings, the fixings for a couple sandwiches, and a six-pack of Diet Coke. When that store closed, she promptly gave her business to the remaining independent store, never changing her habits.

This was fine, except that the bare shelves at home always bothered me, so I would nag her about at least getting some dinner supplies from time to time. When Carol was in charge of the shopping, the contents of our fridge always made it seem like we were moving out. Whenever the shopping fell to me, I would do exactly the opposite, as I loved buying in bulk. My backups always had backups.

I often let her know that I thought there was a better way to shop, and in doing so was imposing my own need for order and the way things ought to be. I'd convinced myself that Carol needed to be explained how things worked. In reality, all I'd been doing was trying to satisfy my own ego's needs. She would always acknowledge me with a polite nod before casually going about her day. This frustrated me, as it reinforced my mistaken belief that I was in this marriage alone.

After I started taking care of all the shopping post strokes, I learned that her shopping style had nothing to do with the purchase of food. When she went to the stores, she would listen to the cashiers' stories or problems, and they would always love her for it. That was also part of why she always shopped so small—she liked going more frequently because it gave her a chance to be out with her friends in the community. That was the Carol I'd come to eventually know, quietly going about life in her own way and without fanfare. After ten minutes of post-lunch chair rest in front of the TV, we had to leave, but not before a trip to the bathroom and an ill-timed tinkering with the many orchids and other potted flowers she kept all around the house. As always, on the way out the door, I grabbed my brown bag of meds and records. I threw her dinner pills in as well, in case we decided to eat out. We nearly made it all the way to the elevator before she asked for her purse. I hustled back for it, and we were on our way.

We arrived at the podiatrist precisely on time, which put us in good shape schedule-wise, because they could always get us out of there in twenty minutes. This was a good thing in part because I hated being late, but also because this was Monday, and Monday was movie day, Carol's favorite. As long as we remained on schedule, we would be done with our daily routine in time for a 4:30 screening.

Nothing compared to Carol's love for movies. Between Jennifer and me, she would see every new release, often twice. Of course, part of that was because every time she went to the theater, she enjoyed the biggest Diet Coke and largest box of popcorn she could get her hands on. My side of the bargain was that, from the moment we left the house until the moment we exited the theater, I would get to enjoy the perpetual little smile of excitement on Carol's face.

She needed those trips, and I needed them too.

We were called back to see the doctor almost immediately. As always, I held her hand while they clipped her nails, since she feared the sharp instrument the podiatrist used. By 1:40, we were hitting the road for the rehab facility and her two o'clock therapy appointment. I knew this trip would perk her up. She would be over the moon to see Wendy, Keirnan, and Debbie, to give everyone a virtual standup act, and to do exactly half of her exercises—no more, no less.

This trip didn't disappoint. It started with a few physical activities, then shifted to some mental exercises to stimulate her brain.

"Okay, Peanut," Debbie said, using the nickname she'd given Carol. "I'll ask you a question and you give me a list."

"Gotcha," Carol replied.

"Try not to overthink it. Just tell me the first things that come to mind."

Carol nodded, and Debbie looked down at the sheet on the clipboard she held.

"What are five things that you use only once?"

Before I could come up with an answer in my own mind, Carol had her first response ready.

"A rubber?"

I laughed so hard I fell into a fit of coughing.

After Debbie gathered herself, she pushed the list away. Carol had shut the test down in two words. But that was Carol—always clever. It's just that before the strokes, she had never really shared these kinds of thoughts with the world. Or maybe she'd just never shared them with me. To this day, her friends tell me that Carol was one of the funniest people around when they were younger. It's a mystery to me how I didn't know that. Perhaps it was me who'd had to open his eyes.

Although she hadn't gone to college, Carol was always one of smartest people I knew. Before her strokes, she was a voracious reader. I can't remember a time when she didn't have a book in her hand. She must have read three books a week. Sometimes she would go for the lighter reads, like James Patterson, but most times, she would be holding something in the John Irving category. She also loved television shows about medicine, whether a drama series or something more educational.

When we were younger, I often mentioned to Carol that she should go back to school for nursing, since she liked to learn about these things and could manage the heavy reading load. She always politely passed on the notion. But that was never enough for me, so in the leadup to every new fall semester at the local colleges, I would ask again. Every time, she would oppose the idea with trademark silence. It was these instances where I'd start feeling underappreciated for my well-intended efforts. In retrospect, that was just my hungry ego finding a clever way to make an issue out of nothing and otherwise convince me that I was doing right by Carol. That's the Catch-22 about self-involvement, you are too involved with yourself to see the problem.

From the rehab facility, we had just enough time to make the movie. I knew I would need every minute of it, since the balancing act of buying the tickets and the concessions, and then getting situated in our seats always proved to be tricky. To complicate the matter, we were catching a movie at the theater she frequented with Jennifer, and I wasn't as used to it.

The refreshment stand sat in the center of the lobby, with the cashiers right next to the ticket taker. Usually, I took Carol to our seats and came back to get the food, but this was a movie I had been eager to see, so I didn't want to miss the start. With Carol locked in my arm, I began the tightrope walk of collecting two drinks and a popcorn while watching out for her safety. We stepped up to the self-serve soda station, and I grabbed a couple of smaller cups. "I want a bigger one," Carol said politely at a volume I could barely hear.

She had been such a trooper all day, so I grabbed the

medium—which of course is an extra-large anywhere other than in a movie theater—and filled it with ice to minimize the fluids. Next, we stepped up to the popcorn counter, where I pointed to the second smallest size, plenty for an afternoon snack.

"We'll take the small bag there," I told the clerk.

"I want that one," Carol muttered, pointing.

I looked over at the popcorn receptacle lineup to note that the container she wanted was almost as large as her torso, let alone her stomach. This made me figure that the matter was negotiable.

"How about the middle one there?" I said.

"I want the big box," Carol announced, loud and clear.

The popcorn clerk leaned in and smiled. "You know, she always *does* get the big box."

I gave him a sidelong look. He wasn't helping.

"We still have dinner—"

"I want the fucking box," Carol hollered. It was the loudest I'd ever heard her speak in a year, and it caught the attention of everyone standing within thirty feet of us.

The clerk looked like he was stifling a laugh.

"You heard the lady," I said with a shrug. "Give her the fucking box."

"I guess she told you," the clerk replied as he started filling the fucking box.

I joined him in a belly laugh.

"It was kind of cute, huh?" Carol quipped.

The clerk held his smile for as long as it took him to fill the practically oil-drum-sized container. Somehow I managed to balance that gigantic tub, the two drinks, and my wife while grabbing my wallet as we worked our way over to the cashier.

We settled into our seats, and out came the afternoon pills.

About halfway through the movie, I noticed that Carol had somehow managed to dispose of half the giant box of popcorn. So I waited for her attention to be drawn and covertly slid the box under my seat. Later, with maybe fifteen minutes left in the film, she announced that she had to use the restroom. This was no surprise, as I'd gotten rather used to missing the climax of every movie. As we exited our seats, I was not surprised to hear my feet crunch through the massive pile of popcorn that had missed Carol's mouth. This had become such a common occurrence that the cleaning crew would always start with our mess first.

After we'd finished the long walk to the family restroom and completed her comb and lipstick routine at the sink, there didn't seem much point in returning just in time to see the credits roll. So we headed to the car.

We stopped at a favorite chain restaurant on the way home, a place where we always loved sitting at the bar. Once we had our seats, I pulled out her evening pills, and she shot me a dirty look. She hated having to take her pills in public.

"I'll have a Diet Coke please," she said to the smiling bartender.

I put my hand up. "Cancel that."

Carol furrowed her brow, looking ready to repeat her popcorn-tub performance, but I chased the expression away with a soft gaze. Due to Carol's blood-thinner, we had to limit her alcohol intake, so the routine had been to avoid any alcohol until 8 P.M., and even then, she could only have one or maybe two glasses of wine. But it had been a great day, so I figured it would be good to celebrate with an earlier drink.

"How about one of your big glasses of Chardonnay instead?" I asked. "With ice on the side, of course."

The bartender looked for confirmation from Carol, who had straightened up in approval.

"I'd love that." She beamed, and that smile hung on her face as we placed our standard order: a chicken Romano salad for the both of us.

We pulled back into the garage a few minutes before 8 P.M. I got Carol up to the condo and settled her into her chair with a rerun of *Frasier*. Then, I went to prepare a nightcap for the both of us. An Irish whiskey for me and a diluted Chardonnay for her. She barely even noticed me making us drinks. It never took more than a minute of that wonderful show to get her chuckling.

Though they were miles and miles away, I could easily picture our three boys sitting at her feet on the rug watching TV with us as we'd done so many times before. When they were young, we would gather around during Christmastime with mugs of hot chocolate and watch all their favorites: *Rudolph the Red Nosed Reindeer*, *Frosty the Snowman*, *Emmet Otter's Jug Band Christmas*, and *Charlie Brown*. As they got older, we traded the mugs for glasses of wine and the cartoons for *National Lampoon's Christmas Vacation*, but Carol and I would always look forward to the holiday season.

I caught her attention long enough to hand her that coveted white wine, and she blinked at me with breathtaking tenderness before looking back to the television. In those few blinks of the eye, an incredible shift in my thinking occurred. I'd let my relative inflexibility infiltrate our relationship too deeply for too long.

All those years, I had thought that by trying to fix Carol, I was loving her—that, in my tinkering with her life, I had been looking out for her best interests and otherwise taking care of her. Being a fixer, a neat freak, and expecting her to live my way must have made me tough to be with at times, but she had put up with me every day. During that time, I had failed to consider how that would have felt for Carol. She likely felt suffocated by my personality. For decades, I'd been squeezing my precious little bird too tight.

But all these things Carol did, she did out of deference, or affability, or maybe just to accommodate my more hardline views about how we should live. Did I have legitimate marital gripes along the way? Of course. We all do. But underlying my behavior for a lot of those years was a fundamental failure to appreciate my loyal and caring wife.

My thinking suddenly became clear: Carol was my little bird with a broken wing, and the only way to bring her back to health was to cradle her gently, always show kindness, and let her breathe and experience the world as she healed. The time for trying to change my wife had ended. I had squandered too many years on failing to show her the compassion she deserved, and to just let Carol be Carol. In this new phase of our relationship, I would do everything in my power to right that wrong.

Her contagious laughter punctuated the thought, and suddenly I felt lighter than I had in years. In my relaxed state, I noticed that my own laughter sounded heartier than usual. We watched a couple more episodes before my eyes grew heavy.

"Are you awake?" Carol asked me.

When I startled, I had a sudden sense that this was about the tenth time she'd had to ask me before I finally broke from my slumber. Falling asleep in my chair while watching TV at night had become something of a habit, and Carol woke me up the same way every time.

"I am now," I replied groggily.

"I'm ready for bed."

She had turned the TV off. I shook off the sleepiness and helped her to the bedroom, where we changed her into her pajamas and tucked her in. I gave her the teddy bear Matthew had gifted her at the hospital, hit the lights, and slid in next to her. Like every night, I found her free hand and squeezed tight.

"I love my Carol," I whispered.

"I love my Pogey," she whispered back.

Sleep wouldn't come. Carol was breathing heavily and would soon start to snore. My gaze found the big, red, digital numbers on the ceiling: 11:11 P.M. There would be just a moment of complete stillness in my mind before the anxiety about tomorrow would begin to pour in. On this night, I took immense pleasure in the rare lack of mental chatter.

Inspiration move me brightly,
light the song with sense and color.

– Robert Hunter
Terrapin Station

CHAPTER SEVEN
whether tragedy or turkey

It had been four years since Carol's strokes. One thing Dr. Tayal never told me was how quick-witted, comically irreverent, and observant my wife would become. Though her humor had been stunning since then, she'd also shown a tenacity beyond anything I could have ever imagined. At first, I attributed her changed personality to some sort of neurological loss of a mental filter, which would have explained her nearly immediate transition from a mild-mannered mother of three into a sparkplug of a woman with the vernacular and doggedness of a drunken sailor.

But then, after I'd had a little more time to observe how she handled her disability, I began to wonder if maybe I was in fact seeing the original Carol, the one who had always wanted to express herself this way. A particularly comic moment in our past came to mind, which supported that theory.

One winter in our home in Hilton Head, I was traveling to Kansas City for work almost weekly. I would pack my clothes every Sunday morning before leaving for the airport. Then, one Sunday, I discovered that one of the legs on a pair of pants I needed was badly wrinkled. Of course, this irked my meticulous nature.

"Is it really that hard to find the time to iron our clothes?" I groused.

As usual, she didn't reply.

"I don't ask much," I calmly argued, "but could you please make sure my travel clothes are ironed each week?"

Photo: Singing Take Me Out to the Ball Game with her father Steward Perry.

She said she would, but then the same thing happened as I was preparing for my weekly trip the next Sunday. And then again the next. Every Thursday night, I would return home from Kansas City for a few nice days with my wife, but then every Sunday morning, I would find one pair of half-pressed pants as I packed for my Sunday evening flight.

Finally, I'd gotten myself worked into a bit of a mood about it, and trudged down the stairs to find Carol casually reading the newspaper in the dining room.

"I'm at a total loss," I said, with a smidge of scold in my voice. "Can you explain to me how this keeps happening?"

She snapped a dirty look at me, got up, and stalked off to the kitchen. I was so surprised by her uncharacteristically curt departure that I didn't follow her. But through the doorway, I could see her rummaging around in her purse. Finally, she found what she wanted and stormed back into the room.

"Listen, asshole," she said, "if you have a problem with these pants, go see the source!" With that, she slapped a piece of paper onto the counter.

My eyes wide, I leaned in to examine the paper. It was a dry-cleaning ticket. All that time, my clever wife had been hauling my clothes to the cleaners while I was away, and then taking credit for the ironing when I returned. She would just wheel them over to the cleaners on Monday morning, then pick them up on Thursday, remove the tags and any other evidence, and hang them in the closet. So that was the last time I complained about the pants, but we did find a better dry-cleaner.

My wife's infectious positivity permeated every facet of her life, but perhaps it shined brightest at the rehab facility. She had become a minor celebrity in that place, having been a patient there for five years. Everyone knew that when she walked in the door, they would be both entertained and moved. Their amusement would come from her inevitable cheating on her exercises, where Carol would routinely skip from her fourth rep to her fifteenth in any set of twenty. Or how she would drop a dozen F-bombs as she performed a therapy drill she didn't like. Though she hated the work, Carol never wanted to miss a visit. She never explicitly said it, but it was clear that she counted all those wonderful folks among her friends.

And they were moved by the same thing we all were: her one-of-a-kind, inspiring fortitude. One of the last times we visited that place was a few months before Carol's final hospitalization. She had been getting weaker for no apparent reason. We didn't know it at the time, but her heart was rapidly failing. As we entered the lobby area in the physical therapy room, the faces of the staff lit up, as they usually did upon her arrival. Carol saved her biggest smile for Wendy, one of her two main therapists. We hadn't been in for a session in almost two years, so Wendy was eager to give Carol a big hug.

"What's happened in the last two years?" she asked.

"Nothing much," Carol replied, blasé as ever.

Wendy glanced at me, and I rolled my eyes.

"How are you feeling?" Wendy asked, playing it straight.

All the gazes in the room found their way to Carol as we awaited her response.

"I'm fine."

The giggles kicked up all around us.

"Well," Wendy said as she took Carol's hand, "when I spoke to George earlier, he told me that since the last time we saw you, you broke a hip and got three pins, broke your shoulder, and had a heart attack, along with triple bypass surgery."

Carol gave a shoulder shrug, her message clear: *Nothing has gotten me down yet, so what's the big deal?*

Baffled as I'd always been about my wife's ability to let these various medical setbacks just roll right past her, I found that it was making perfect sense to me. She had always responded this way—to anything and everything—so why,

103

when she'd come so close to death, should it be any different now?

––––––––––––

2009. Early in November. Carol and I had just settled into our routine in Hilton Head, having arrived a week or so earlier. I'll never forget the call. We had returned with takeout from our favorite little Greek restaurant. I was arranging the plates as she took the boxes out of the bag. Whenever the phone rang, Carol would usually leap to pick it up, hopeful as she was that one of the boys would be calling. But this time, I was closer, so I picked it up.

"Hey, Dad," came the familiar voice. It was Chad. "I'm with the McCarthys, and it's not good."

My son sounded near tears. Carol must have seen the change in my expression, as she went for the other landline.

"Okay, you have both of us," she said.

"I'm at AGH," Chad explained. "Janet's not going to make it. She has some rare disease called Creutzfeldt-Jacobs. She might only live a month or so, at best."

It sounded to me like neither Chad nor his mother wanted to stay on the line a second longer, so I suggested that we hang up for now. By the time we got back in the same room, and I had taken her into my arms, Carol had lost her composure. I could picture Chad doing the same, some 700 miles away.

We had heard that Janet was seeing doctors, but the working theory had been that she was suffering from a vitamin deficiency, not a universally fatal brain disorder, so the news came as an overwhelming shock. For over fifty years, Janet and Carol, along with their friend Linda, had been the dearest of friends. We'd raised our kids together, attended their sporting events together, and enjoyed many dinners at each other's homes over the years. And just two months prior, at our fortieth wedding anniversary celebration, Janet had been the life of the party.

She and Carol were so close that the former would call the latter every morning at the same time, just to talk. Most of the time, the phone would hardly even be off the hook before Carol would start giggling. That was Janet, always able to make my wife laugh at will. And if I'd had anything I needed to say to Carol after that call came in every morning, I might as well have forgotten it, because nothing short of a three-alarm fire could ever hope to interrupt them. It was a perfect relationship; Janet got to be her silly and hysterically funny self, while Carol enjoyed a beautiful friendship, laughing the whole way through.

I suppose I should have sensed that something was amiss, since Janet hadn't called for the past few days.

As Carol's sobbing subsided, I promised her that we would immediately book flights back to Pittsburgh to say goodbye and make our peace. It was a good thing we did, as Janet would be gone less than two weeks later, at the age of sixty-two.

Carol had endured a ridiculously unfair, lifelong run of tragic deaths among her closest friends and family. It started with the untimely demise of two friends when Carol was still in high school. Then, from the late 1980s through the mid-1990s, the sheer number of dear friends and family members that my wife lost would have wrecked most people.

Carol lost her dear friend Polly Phillips, in 1993, from breast cancer at the age of forty-three. Despite her early death, Polly's memory remained strong in our lives.

"Do you remember that weekend with Polly and John?" I could ask Carol, and she would burst into laughter despite the pain of loss that accompanied the memory.

Polly Phillips may have brought Carol and me one of our favorite weekends ever. Sometime in the early 1980s, we had fallen in love with Cape Cod, particularly the small island of Martha's Vineyard. We had vacationed there for several summers with our boys, and had tried to get away there for long weekends as often as we could.

One September, Polly and her husband John joined us for a quick trip. Like Janet, Polly Phillips never took life too seriously and had an infectious laugh that would bowl you over.

We arrived at the rented cottage just as the sun had started to set. The four of us had barely brought in the first load of luggage and groceries from the rental car when John went on a mad search for towels and blankets. Not but a minute later, he reappeared and whispered in Polly's ear. She dropped her bag and grabbed his hand.

"I hate to do this," he said. "But my wife and I must take our leave."

"What the hell are you talking about?" I asked.

They looked at each other, and Carol knowingly giggled.

"If you must know," John announced coyly. "I've never done it on the beach before."

I chuckled through my disbelief. "Well don't let me stop you!"

Quickly they took their leave, scurrying over the deck and out into the fading light. It wasn't long before they returned through the sliding door, because Carol and I were still putting the last of the items into the fridge.

"That was fast," my wife quipped.

"I couldn't do it," John said.

A moment of awkward silence followed.

"Not that," he protested. "The minute we laid down, I couldn't stop hearing that damn Jaws song. *Dun-dunh...dun-dunh...dun-dunh.*"

We almost lost our balance from the laughter. John tore open a bottle of wine, and into the night, stories were told.

Carol's own smile and laugh were like a big candle in the room. I had watched so many people over the years set a spark to it and then soak in its joyous and extraordinary light. For the next four days and three nights, Polly and John had kept that flame lit. Every day and on into the night, we laughed until it hurt. We would lose Polly soon after, but those memories never faded.

About a year later, Mareena, her close friend and partner in the Perfect Presents business lost her life to domestic violence. Carol had a knack for befriending good-hearted, caring, and giving people, and Mareena was one of those folks. My wife had jumped at the opportunity to spend large swaths of time with one of her closest friends, and the one occasion when I stopped by their office unannounced showed me the sort of time they were having.

They had been putting together a retirement gift for a post office worker, and Carol had pulled it all together in an incredibly creative way: a bronze mailbox to hold the gifts which doubled as a useful container, a box of chocolates that looked like stamps, and a small American flag, among many other clever goodies. She was so proud of it and her shop. Mareena had a way of highlighting some of my wife's best attributes—creativity, thoughtfulness, and making people happy.

Next, she would lose her favorite aunt, and Stew's sister, Carolyn. Between that trio, I'm not sure you could put together a warmer set of people. When Carolyn visited from Columbus, the three of them would get together and gab and grin about life until the moment she left. I remember one long-weekend visit, they'd decided to go on a walk, so I went about my elaborate day of yard work. Every time I saw them come around the block, they'd be laughing, and Carol would give me a cute wave and a smile. Carol just wanted to enjoy life, and her aunt always brought that spark to make to it happen. In 1995, while visiting Carol's sister, Lyn Anzalone, in San Diego, Carolyn suffered a massive brain aneurysm while sitting next to Carol.

At that time, we'd been living in the same house for over a decade, and Carol had developed a very close relationship with one of our neighbors, Kathy Gratton. Early in the summer of 1996, I joined Kathy and Carol at our recently purchased home in Hilton Head and got to see first-hand their wonderful connection, which was based on listening to each other, sharing their love of family, and laughing until their faces hurt. A few weeks later, while in the Charlotte (North Carolina) Airport, we received news that Kathy had suddenly passed. Carol, after four years of heartbreak, broke down into terrible tears that made my own heart break.

It always amazed me how Carol could find her way back after losing one great friend after another. She would cry her eyes out with each loss, and I would often find her looking through old pictures of the departed. But she would never succumb to self-pity or dwell on the unfairness of it all. Though I never asked her the question directly, my sense was that Carol had learned to live life in the moment, even long before that ethos became a cultural phenomenon. More than anyone I've ever known, she could cherish the memories in a way that kept those people alive in her heart.

I never really understood the true depth of my wife's personality—and perhaps the source of her sense of humor—until I had the occasion to live with Stew. Carol's father was like a Jimmy Stewart character: kind, gentle, compassionate, and principled—and after five years of living with him, it became clear how completely he had passed those qualities on to his daughter.

After Carol's strokes, when we moved to the new single story home, I had the place remodeled so the living room would be right in the middle of everything, making it easier for Carol and Stew to get to the spots where they could be the most comfortable. I installed a big television and new, plush sofas, the biggest sofa facing the front door and the gated stairwell at the opposite end of the open floor plan. From there, one could see just about everything and everyone in the main living space. Plus, this layout would allow me to pass Carol's favorite spot at least twenty-five times a day. This made it easier to ensure that she always had everything she needed.

Every morning, after we'd gotten her ready for the day, Carol would sit on that couch. Stew would join her a few minutes later, after he'd read the morning paper, and would sit at the opposite end. Some days, the schedule would be empty, leaving the two of them to sit side-by-side all day long. On the days with more activities, I would always make sure to return Carol to her favorite spot beside her father. Eventually, Stew would move out to San Diego to live with Lyn, but the few wonderful years he and Carol had together were spent smiling at each other from one end of the couch to the other.

Around five o'clock, I would make my way to the kitchen to start dinner for the three of us, but would first stop at the big entryway to the living room to check in on dinner plans.

"What are you in the mood for tonight?"

"Doesn't matter to me," Carol always replied.

"Whatever the chef wants," Stew would say.

"Neither of you have a preference?"

Two simultaneous shoulder shrugs.

For nearly five years, if we stayed in for dinner, this was the way it would go down. Then, one night, I pressed the issue, figuring that giving them some more specific options might help them contribute a decision.

"We have chicken breasts," I said. "And I think we have a few premade crab-cakes, plus some of that chili I froze last week."

"They all sound tasty to me," Stew answered, turning to his daughter. "What sounds good to you?"

"Doesn't matter to me," Carol said.

I threw my arms up in the air, grabbed some ground turkey breast and an orange vodka, and went out to the grill. From the patio, as I performed my usual overcooking of the turkey,

I watched them sitting on the couch. They could sit there all day without saying a word to each other. Whenever a decision came up, they would always defer to the other. If I changed plans, no problem. If I changed them back, still no problem.

It wasn't until that moment on the patio that it truly struck me. Suddenly, Carol's behind-the-scenes and acquiescent disposition all made sense. It had been inescapable—like father, like daughter. Whether by genetics or learned behavior, they had become the two most easygoing people in the world.

They also shared an unparalleled level of humility. Nothing in their life was ever about them. Though Stew boasted of nothing, we all knew that his proudest accomplishment was the work he'd done to open the Brentwood Community Food Bank in the basement of his church. But that was Stew. His joy revolved around selflessly giving. This made him deferential to others in every decision, and gracious about everything good that ever happened to him.

But as I emptied that orange vodka, and as the turkey burgers continued their race past well done, something deeper occurred to me: Carol had also inherited her father's unyielding optimism. The old saying goes, "There's a silver lining in every cloud." I suspect that most people are like me, in that those clouds can quickly get thick enough to where they lose sight of any sign of silver streaks. Carol, though, could find them in a tornado.

That thought carried me back into the house with a smile on my face and three extra-crispy turkey burgers on the serving dish. Stew had worked his way over to Carol on his walker and was helping her get to her feet so she could stand at her own walker. Ever the gentleman, he let her lead the way into the kitchen. As they took their seats, I examined those charred discs of turkey and decided that I'd eliminated any chance they would still bear flavor.

Even so, I couldn't help but ask. "So, what's the verdict?"

"So tasty," Stew eagerly replied. "Thank you, George, for

your fine work."

"Very good," Carol echoed.

I didn't learn this until much later, but Stew would wait until I exited the room to start delivering one-liners, along with the occasional eye-roll, about my subpar grilling skills. Apparently, he would get Carol, and sometimes my son Chad, into a good chuckle.

Whether tragedy or turkey, Carol always kept an even keel. The tragedy side required toughness beyond anything I could ever hope to display in my own life, and the patience it must have taken to endure my burned turkey called for a level of understanding that I've never been able to absorb, no matter how I try. Carol put it best one night before one of her many late-in-life surgeries. I asked her how she always found the will to overcome her health issues.

"Nothing gets me down," she said, offering that signature shrug.

Though I didn't realize it happening at first, I did manage to learn some measure of that resilience. Before Carol's strokes, I wouldn't have been the kind of man who could get up at odd hours of the night without complaint. Even those times when I did get grouchy, Carol's effect on me squashed those feelings in a hurry. Her spirit for life kept my chin up when things didn't go our way. How could I possibly be negative about such small matters in the face of this beaming light of positivity I called my wife? Even when I learned that my cancer had reached the point of incurability, and I was facing my own mortality for the first time, I knew exactly how to react. The answer was sitting right next to me.

That was the unfiltered Carol in a nutshell. Perhaps some strand of brain cells had been altered during those strokes, and the effect was to encourage a higher level of assertiveness. Or maybe she'd realized that there was nothing left to lose from being herself. Either way, she'd stepped out from her demure and unassuming persona and wandered into the limelight. Even more impressively, she carried on with the same carefree nature that had always endeared the world to her. She was now dependent on many other people to keep her healthy, and yet she was living life on her terms and making everyone laugh and feel inspired along the way.

CHAPTER EIGHT
feel the love

Courage is not having the strength to go on; it is
going on when you don't have the strength.
– President Theodore Roosevelt

One night in June of 2015, a social engagement put us
on the road past the regular dinner hour. Since Carol's blood
sugar numbers had been particularly wild of late, I decided to
swing by a drive-through for a quick meal that might help us
hedge against returning home to a low-blood-sugar situation.
But when I handed Carol a chicken wrap and a fresh Diet
Coke, she did something she had never done since her first
stroke: she ignored them.

"What's wrong?" I said.

She gave a wide-eyed glance. "I can't breathe."

The day before, on Dr. Tayal's recommendation, we'd
had our first scheduled appointment with a cardiologist named
Dr. Suad Ismail. During this appointment, we learned that the
warning signs for a heart attack are typically quite different
for women than for men.

"Women don't experience chest or shoulder pains," Dr.
Ismail said. "For us, heart attacks present as something more
like a change in how we typically feel. If you see something
out of the ordinary, head for the hospital."

Now, as we idled in that fast food parking lot, the terrifying
picture started to fall into place. Ever since the strokes, we
could always count on Carol eating anything you put in front

Photo: With son Chad at PNC Park

of her. She never passed up a Diet Coke. Coupled with the difficulty breathing, this suddenly looked like an emergency situation. I roared for the highway that would bear us into Pittsburgh.

The nurses at AGH immediately ushered Carol into an exam room, where they performed a few tests that confirmed that she had in fact suffered a heart attack. Whenever I think back on this moment, I'm struck by how different things would have been if we hadn't met Dr. Ismail when we did. If we hadn't stopped for chicken, we wouldn't have had the warning sign, and Carol might have died in her sleep that night.

My wife looked frightened and tired as they admitted her for the night, but otherwise, she acted like herself. I called all the people I normally called in these situations: my kids, her father and sister in San Diego, Jennifer, her cousin Jodi Jaynes in Ohio, and Linda Hoehl. When I spoke with the boys, I assured them that their mother wasn't in any present danger. Chad insisted on coming back from Nashville to visit anyway, since he hadn't been home in a while. He and his then-fiancée Catherine had moved there to embark on new careers. Though it could have been under better circumstances, I knew that Carol would be thrilled to see him.

Next, I left a message for Dr. George Magovern, Jr., the only heart surgeon I knew, and also one of the top cardio-thoracic surgeons in the country. I knew that heart attacks sometimes repeated themselves, so I figured if I could get Dr. Magovern involved, Carol would be in good hands.

The next morning, I picked Chad up at the airport.

"How's Mom?" he asked the moment he slid into the car.

"You know the answer to that."

"She's fine."

We had a good laugh.

"Are we worried?" Chad asked.

"Just tests right now. No further heart attacks, so that's

good."

The moment we came through the door to Carol's room at AGH, the proud mother's eyes grew wide. I'd kept the visit a surprise, so the reunion was a bubbly one. Linda visited later that morning, as did another good friend, Mary Jane Platt. Jennifer stopped in around lunch, as well. They all brought laughter and stories, while Carol told everyone she was doing just fine.

That afternoon, after the nurses wheeled Carol off for further testing, Chad and I retreated to the cafeteria. We caught up on life, Nashville, and his thoughts about where he and Catherine might live after the wedding. I missed them terribly and prayed every day that they would return to Pittsburgh.

Back from the cafeteria, we found Carol's room empty. A nurse stopped in and told us she would escort us to the interventional cardiologist's office. He had loaded the films from the scans of Carol's heart onto his computer, and he had some thoughts on how we might proceed. The doctor had turned the large monitor on his desk so it faced the two chairs set up for guests. The image on the screen looked like black and white abstract art. Our host demonstrated an excellent demeanor as he explained all the preliminaries in a way I could understand. The gist was that they had run the tests so they could assess the level of Carol's blood flow near her heart.

"So, how does it look?" I asked.

"May I be frank?"

I nodded, as a tight knot formed in my stomach.

"I don't know how she's alive right now," he said, his eyes kind but intense. He pointed to a spot on the image. "This little aortic area is known as the widow-maker. It's more than ninety-five percent blocked. What that means is that Carol is hanging from the edge of a cliff by her fingers. And that's not even considering the mitral valve issue."

The knot leapt from my throat to my eyes, where it

presented in the form of tears.

"She's on her way to the cardiac ICU right now," the doctor added gently. "I don't want to take any chances."

"Surely, something can be done," I said.

"There's three ways you deal with this. First, a stent. But if I tried that, it would likely cause her whole arterial system to explode. So that's out."

A tear spilled over my cheek.

"Second, there's medication. But unfortunately, her disease is too far advanced for that option."

He took a long pause. "Ordinarily, surgery would be an option, but the cardiology report says that her left ventricle isn't pumping strong enough to withstand it."

The harsh reality robbed me of my ability to speak. And I knew I couldn't look over at Chad, or I would lose what remained of my composure.

"I don't have anything to tell you that you can put your hopes into," the doctor said. "If surgery isn't an option, then I'm afraid Carol's time will be very short."

The dam burst. I fell into a shoulder-lurching sob, the kind of cry that I didn't even know I had in me. I grabbed a couple tissues from the well-placed box on the desk and rejoined the conversation that my son had continued with the doctor.

"What do we do next?" Chad was asking.

"I'm not a surgeon," the doctor said, "so it's not my place to make that decision." He sighed and looked steadily at me. "But I'd get your affairs in order."

Chad and I left his office with all the grace of a couple of zombies. We stood in one of the hospital's many bright corridors, the bold light and the ad-barren walls making me feel anxious. The hospital wasn't allowing visitors to the cardiac ICU, so we returned to the cozier confines of the cafeteria. On the way down, since I couldn't bear repeating the situation to my other two sons, I asked Chad to call his brothers and get them to town.

By the evenings at AGH, the cafeteria always seemed to echo the day's activity. It was never as busy, and those in the room typically appeared either tired or reflective. In this quiet atmosphere, I attempted to process the news we'd just heard. I finished my first cup of coffee quickly, and was just getting back up for more when I ran into another cardiologist managing Carol's case. He told me that he had seen the films and agreed that not much could be done.

Dazed, I returned to my seat across from Chad. "Everybody seems to be counting her out," I said.

After a long and quiet second cup of coffee, we went to the fifth floor and found our way to the Cardiothoracic Specialty Care Unit. I saw Carol sleeping through the sliding glass door to her room. She had more leads coming from her body than I had ever seen before, and at least three large monitors set up around her beeped and whirred and blinked numbers in different colors. I choked back a fresh round of tears, pulled the door open, and rushed to the chair next to the bed. For the next several minutes, I watched those numbers blink. The whole room felt as critical as my wife's condition.

Soon after, her nurse Taylor entered for a checkup, and proceeded to explain every monitor and the meaning of every number they displayed. In a nutshell, it all boiled down to a constant calibration of Carol's blood pressure with a wide variety of medicines. I had always been a numbers person, so I asked for the normal ranges, and he related them to me.

About an hour later, Dr. Ismail stepped up to the sliding glass door with a concerned smile. She waved me to join her in the hall. I complied. Gracefully and honestly, she broke down the situation: it was a cardiac Catch-22. First, she confirmed that, without surgery, death was likely imminent. But for surgery to be possible, we would have to wean her off the blood thinner. Meanwhile, thicker blood presented a danger because of the widow-maker blockage. To make matters worse, the mitral valve was causing wild blood pressure fluctuations, which meant that Carol could quickly drop into heart failure or have another attack. Dr. Ismail wrapped up with a polite dodge of my questions about whether Carol could survive surgery, but assured me that they would do their best to keep her alive until then.

The knot jumped from my stomach and radiated across my chest.

I squeezed Carol's hand and fixated on the flashing numbers. It felt like I had to wait an eternity for every new update, even though the truth was that they happened precisely every minute. In those tense seconds waiting for them to refresh, the discussions about death repeated in my head. I wasn't ready to let Carol go. I wasn't ready to be alone. The thought of losing her made me think about what my life, her life, our lives had meant. Though I would end up asking myself the question a thousand times, that was the first moment it had formed in my brain: had I done enough for her?

For our whole life together, Carol had deferred to my preferences, and in so doing, had allowed me to reach higher with my career. But at some point, I had lost my way and started casting onto her the burdens of what I expected of marriage. And what did she do? She shouldered them. She soldiered on, always trying to please me and make things right. It wasn't that we had ever fallen out of love; it was that I had found ways to dodge humility or convince myself that the things I'd been doing were satisfying my half of the bargain.

In my mind, providing a steady income, a home, a faithful man, and a father to three sons had been enough. And if you were grading my obligations as a husband in the traditional sense, I'd have passed. But marriage didn't equate to love unless you gave it love. This was what I first truly discovered in those moments after the first stroke, and understood even more so after the second. With that knowledge, and for the five years since, my goal had been to do what I could to let her feel the love.

In pursuit of that objective, I'd traveled unwittingly along a journey of romance, experiencing it in a whole new manner, getting to know her in this wonderful new way. Carol, with her emboldened individualism, and me with my newfound openness, tolerance, and tenderness were what made it all possible. Like new lovers in their early twenties, we'd developed inside jokes, ways of being intimate, and even the normal tension that occurs as two become one. We'd travelled, laughed, sung songs to each other, and recited those three most important words more often than ever. Still, as I sat at her bedside—next to what I feared might be her deathbed—the question nagged at me. Had my efforts been enough?

Carol's quiet whisper broke me from my trance, but I couldn't quite make out what she said.

"Sorry, can you say that again?" I asked as I leaned in closer.

She tried to sit up a little straighter. "So..." she said, her lips softening into a clever smile. "How's everything going?"

Taken aback by the question, I cocked my head to one side.

After the strokes, the responsibility for starting and sustaining conversations fell almost exclusively to me. Sometimes Carol would engage, and sometimes, she wouldn't. I would always run out of things to say after a while, and we would wind up sitting in uncomfortable silence. During a long car ride earlier that year, I'd implored her to feel free to start conversations from time to time. In reply, she'd turned to me and said, "So...how's everything going?"

I'd had a good, long laugh in the car, and there I was having it again in that hospital room.

Chad returned, and we decided that the two of us would stay the night in the hospital. But as we began to situate our chairs and pillows, the nurse coming on for the night shift seemed like she was preparing to tell us to leave. Taylor talked to her for about a minute. Eventually, after quite a lot of nodding, the other nurse relented. My son and I settled in for the night.

Over the last couple hours, Carol's numbers had been trending in the wrong direction. The worry crept back into my mind. I kept picturing the image the doctor painted of my wife holding onto the edge of a cliff by her fingers. *Can she make it to surgery?* I wondered anxiously. *Can her weakened body sustain it? What will I do without my wife and best friend?*

Somewhere in the middle of my fretting, Dr. Magovern returned my call. It felt like a week since I'd left that message. After a brief exchange about how he'd be stuck out of town until Saturday night, he said something calming, if only slightly.

"I'm hearing the same thing you are," he said. "That she's not going to make it. But just remember, I haven't seen the films yet."

One of the top heart surgeons in the country had given me a sliver of hope. Now, we just needed to keep Carol alive until Dr. Magovern could get home.

The nurse stepped in and turned out the light, leaving us with the bright blue glow of the monitors. Between unwanted dozes, I would sit up and watch those flashing numbers and beeping sounds. These indicators would become something of an obsession for me for the next hundred hours. Any time the numbers fell out of range, the alarm bell sounded, and I worried that she might pass away, right there in front of me, at any moment. I would pop up from my chair in a desperate search for a nurse, even though I knew they were always quick to respond. Only after they had steadied the situation, and calm returned to the room, would I relax even a little.

Early the next morning, sunlight poured through the window, rousing me from my half-sleep. I sprang up reflexively, afraid that Carol had gotten up to go to the bathroom. To my relief, I found my wife and son snoring the morning away. I sat up in the chair and assessed Carol's numbers. So far, so good. Though I had been happy to wake to relative normalcy, the intensity of the surroundings concerned me. Even if Carol made it through, she might still have entered the downhill phase in her life. That familiar pang of pain returned to my stomach.

Chad soon stirred, and we went in search of coffee and breakfast. Around this time, Sean arrived from the airport and joined us. Carol lit up like a firework when she saw him trailing us through the door.

"Oh, there you are!" she said.

The way Carol's relationships with the boys flourished as they became adults was a joy for me to watch. Looking back now, I have to smile at how there was a time when she thought that because of sports she would never be as important to them as their father. Of course I had told her back then that they would grow closer as the boys grew older. To my great pride and delight, they proved me right and then some, particularly during the home stretch of their mother's life.

By this point, Sean was always reaching out and doting on Carol like never before. She clearly loved every second of it. Watching him greet and attend to her now reminded me of the Thanksgiving when I first noticed this tendency in him. For years, Carol had taken care of Thanksgiving dinner at our house. Her two specialties were her moist-yet-crispy stuffing, and a sweet potato casserole that was out of this world. At some point, Sean started to help her with these dishes. Then, after the strokes, when she'd become unable to prepare the food on her own, Sean reversed the roles and had Carol help him. They always laughed whenever she would drop a quarter of the ingredients on the floor. Every year, she would get so excited about Thanksgiving, and I knew that a huge part of the reason was her cooking time with Sean.

Sean stroked his mother's hair as he sat beside her hospital bed.

"I love it when you do that shit," Carol said.

Taylor had entered just in time to overhear. He erupted in laughter with the rest of us. "It's good to know she doesn't just talk like that with me," he said.

Later that day, my good friend Howard Cohen stopped by to see us. Howard practiced as a cardiologist and specialized in cardiovascular disease, so he wanted to see if he could help. Since we were still waiting for Dr. Magovern, and didn't know what his verdict would be, I figured it couldn't hurt to authorize my friend to look at Carol's records and X-rays.

We went out to the nurses' station, where Howard proceeded to draw a simplified version of what he would do if given the chance to perform such a procedure. Although I'll never fully understand the medical reasoning behind it, by Howard's own admission, his drawing represented an inventive strategy. The basic gist was that he would enter via an artery and use some sort of robot to sneak past the widow-maker blockage and create a bypass, which would then allow him the chance to work on the mitral valve.

I stepped away from the diagram for a minute and glanced in at Carol, who was one bad blood pressure swing from death. I considered Howard to be one of the most even-tempered and intelligent people I knew, and I still think that. So, if he was telling us that this would be our best solution, I was all for it. Howard promised to reach out to Dr. Magovern to discuss. For now, we would have to wait.

The next morning, as Sean, Chad, and I sat on the window side of Carol's bed, Matthew strode up to the sliding glass door. Carol followed our gazes and lit up. The trip from Montana to Pittsburgh required at least two flights that cost Matthew over a thousand dollars each time. He had started making the journey more frequently since his mother's strokes, but his presence still tended to coincide with downturns in Carol's health. This realization seemed to occur to my wife in the next moment, as she turned away from greeting Matthew and shot a glare at me.

"What's going on here?" she asked.

I remained silent.

By then, Matthew had come to the side of the bed. He had bought his mother another teddy bear.

She smiled wide as she pulled it close. Then, ever the direct one, she said, "Seriously, why are you here, Matthew?"

The way the question came out made us all laugh. The truth was that everyone involved believed that it wouldn't be good for Carol's heart to include her in the stress of every medical discussion. Since nothing concrete had been decided yet, I'd been okay with it, but I could see that the boys and I needed to figure out a way to deliver the stark truth. We exchanged some hangdog looks, none of us sure of what to say. Taylor returned to collect Carol for tests, so we were saved by the bell.

After the tests were over and Carol was back in her bed, my sons and I gathered around her bedside and explained that the doctors might need to perform a corrective surgery, but that we would wait for Dr. Magovern to give us his thoughts before proceeding with anything. Like she always did, Carol took the news in stride, and said very little. She was courageous that way, rarely ever showing her fear.

From that point forward, we camped out in that little room, breaking all the visiting hours rules related to time and number of guests. After a couple days we began to take shifts, but there was always at least one Shannon in the room in addition to Carol from 7 A.M. to 7 P.M. There were occasional bouts of laughter, and a few stories told, but mostly we concerned ourselves with being next to this woman who meant so much to all of us.

As the week wore on, I could see that something needed to be done. Carol's numbers trended further from normal, and the medical team's efforts to stabilize her took longer and longer. Every time they got her back into a safe zone, those vitals would immediately head in the other direction, causing another mini-crisis. The whole thing felt like a long volley in a tennis match, with nobody wanting to give up the point. Time had become the worthiest of adversaries.

At 9 P.M. that Saturday night, Dr. Magovern called me as he disembarked his plane from Chicago. We set a meeting for first thing the next morning. Chad and I arrived an hour early. As we sat in silence, I couldn't help but dwell on the cardiologist's opinion that Carol wasn't suited for surgery, and on Howard's plan for how to overcome a supposedly insurmountable obstacle.

Dr. Magovern broke the spell of worry when he appeared in the hall and waved us out of Carol's room. I approached him with a mouthful of questions, and a pit of swirling doubt in my mind. He beat me to the punch by a mile.

"I've scheduled Carol tomorrow for a triple bypass at six in the morning."

I didn't know how to respond. I had to replay the words I'd heard, just to make sure I had them right. Eventually, I managed a half-coherent question about the condition of Carol's arteries. "The plaque?"

He explained in clear terms that it was a genetic condition that led to Carol's arteries being full of plaque, and that, yes, the existence of this plaque posed a high risk of triggering another stroke, especially since Carol would be off her Coumadin for surgery.

But then he said, "I took a long look at those films, and I think I found a tiny place I can clamp onto."

Meanwhile, I was willing to clamp onto any little hint of hope. I knew the procedure would be risky, but Dr. Magovern's confidence brought significant relief. I may have even smiled.

"Is she ready?" I asked.

"We don't have a choice," he replied. "If we don't do something soon, she won't make it."

The answer, though terrifying, didn't come as a surprise, as I'd been hearing it all week.

"Besides," he added. "I know I'm not going to sleep tonight. And you certainly aren't going to sleep. So, let's get on with it."

With that, he strode confidently from the room.

This was how the door on Carol's chances cracked open just enough to let in a slice of light. We had a plan in place. It was still a long shot, and despite our surgeon's renowned skill, I knew that there was a very distinct possibility that the door would slam shut in just a short twenty-four hours. First, we had to get her to tomorrow morning.

Sean and Matthew joined us a while later, and we spent the whole day as a family in Carol's little room. We took turns sitting in the seat at the head of the bed, holding Carol's hand and talking with her. Like most families, we had our complexities, but I felt overwhelmed with pride at the way we supported each other. We shared the news with Carol, albeit with the breeziest possible spin we could give it. Then, with the dangerous surgery just hours away, we all had a few final words with her.

Sean led off with the pep-talk Carol needed. In the last handful of years, Sean had been much sillier with Carol, so the talk came from a place of humor. She giggled appreciatively. Then, he planted a peck on her forehead as he relinquished the chair to Chad.

"I know you'll be fine," Chad told her. "Because Catherine's going to need help picking out flowers for the wedding."

It was true. Carol would have to make it through this surgery because there was no way she would allow herself to miss that wedding. She had been thinking about that day for the whole year since we learned of the engagement. Chad kissed his mother on the forehead and gave up the chair to Matthew.

Before Matthew could sit, she reached out and grabbed his hand.

"I don't want to die," she said, loud and clear.

The boys and I all glanced at each other, acknowledging the rare expression of concern Carol had just shared. We didn't want that either.

My heart ached and warmed at the same time. I felt the fear that my wife was expressing but also experienced a wave of affection for their connection and the way Matthew responded. The two of them had spent a lot of time together back when I was traveling for work, and it gave me great joy to see them bonding again. He assured her that she would make it through, and after a few more minutes of this, he kissed her on the forehead and rose from the chair. The boys then left us to be alone.

Now it was my turn in the seat. Had I done enough to make her feel the love? With my wife's life in the balance, and with these being possibly our last moments together, the answer became a bit clearer. It was likely that I would never convince myself that I'd done enough, but I did feel like the luckiest guy in the world in that I'd had the chance to fall in love with this woman again. That wonderful revelation spurred, in all its unfettered glory, this all-consuming feeling of love. It buzzed through me, the beautiful noise of it drowning out any thought, opinion, or expectation I'd ever had.

In that moment of purest love, panic crystalized in the form of a question: *Is this really all the time I have left with her?* From Carol's bedside, just as I had so many times from the pew after Communion, I started making desperate offers. *What's it going to take? My life for hers?* No immediate answers came.

I sighed, and might even have gotten mad for a moment at the thought that we had no sooner fallen in love again than I risked losing this wonderful wife of mine. Fear came directly from love, because when you have something extraordinary, you don't want to lose a single bit of it. It didn't take me the better part of five decades to fall in love. It just took me a lifelong journey toward humility to fall all the way.

Carol tugged at my hand and repeated her fear of dying. Though I shared that same fear, I promised that we wouldn't let that happen to her. After a few minutes of encouragement, I just sat still with her, running my fingers through her hair and over her hand, trying to comfort her. At one point, I adjusted her caged-heart necklace, prompting a silent smile.

We had experienced so many bouts with silence in our later years. Sometimes, I would want nothing more than just to reach out and make a connection on something, a way for us both to feel the love. At some point along the way, I found a little bond that tied us together, and I would break these quiet moments with a tune—my take on a number I'd often heard Bing Crosby sing on the radio when I was a child.

"Over in Killarney..."

And despite the fear that this day might be her last, she responded to the call right on cue.

"...many years ago."

I squeezed her hand.

"Me mother sang a song to me..."

She squeezed back.

"...in tones, so sweet and low."

"Just a simple little ditty..."

I brushed her hair with my fingers.

"...in her good old Irish way."

She closed her eyes.

"For I'd give the world for her to sing..."

And we sang the last line together.

"...that song to me this day."

I leaned in and kissed her. Not long after, she was asleep and breathing softly. I took one last, long look at those heart numbers just before I left the room. For tonight, at least, my darling wife would be okay.

HAPPY BIRTHDAY
to my husband,
my soul mate,
my very best friend.
I love you.

Love CAROL

– Carol Shannon
*Carol's message on the birthday card she gave me in
2014, 2015, and 2016. Out of the 5,000 greeting cards
at Rite Aid, she chose the same one
three consecutive years without realizing it.*

CHAPTER NINE
it finds you

December 28, 2016

Carol's first surprise birthday party was New Year's Eve, 1987. In the eighteen years of our marriage up to that point, we'd lived in four states and moved five times. But we'd lived in that house on Thorn Street for four years, which was tied for our longest stretch yet. I had missed making a big deal over her fortieth, so I went full bore for her forty-first. At the time of that party, Sean was sixteen, Chad was thirteen, and Matthew was ten. They did a great job helping keep the sixty or so guests quiet as her friends Linda and Janet led Carol into the house.

The look on her face was one that I've never forgotten. Most of our family and all our friends at the time were there. The kids transformed the dining room's hardwood into a dance floor, and there, through a steady stream of Motown and oldies, Carol and I danced all night, a relatively new thing for us.

Much to the disappointment of my wife, I never danced until about a year before her surprise party. I'd secretly taken six weeks of Arthur Murray dance classes. When the first song came on at a big New Year's Eve party that year, I asked Carol to dance. She nearly fell over in shock, and once again when she got a gander at my new moves. We took to the dance floor and never left, letting it all hang out.

Her surprise party proved no different. For days after, Carol often mentioned that she couldn't believe how all these

Photo: Carol's seventieth surprise birthday party, her last.

people had gathered just for her. She'd always been that way: so humbled and moved by the gestures of others.

Here we were again, nearly thirty years later, an hour before Carol's seventieth birthday party, and she had no idea the surprise in store for her. I peeked in on her and asked if she was excited to check out the new restaurant in town. She nodded and went back to putting on her lipstick. She looked beautiful in the new outfit I'd bought her for Christmas, a spiffy black and white number purchased just for this occasion.

In some ways, I couldn't believe we had reached this milestone. She had started down the path of troubled health at the age of sixty-three, and back then, the odds of her making it to seventy seemed slim. The doctor had implied as much. When the second stroke hit, it seemed that these events might occur repeatedly, and each time, they would take a little piece of her life along with them. Her closest brush with death had come when she faced that nearly miraculous heart surgery. Post-bypass, her first words to Dr. Magovern were, "I'm fine."

Even though it all seemed so far away now, I couldn't help but smile at the memory of her one-year post-stroke follow-up with Dr. Tayal in May of 2011. I'd felt a sense of pride that day as my wife and I walked hand-in-hand from the parking garage down the long corridor to the hospital. She had come such a long way from boxing gloves and thickened liquids. She hadn't even needed a wheelchair or a walker to make the long trek.

When we stepped off the elevator in the medical office building, we stood face to face with Dr. Short, the same doctor who had predicted a swan song for Carol the year prior. His eyes bulged when he saw her. He shot a look at me and then back at her.

"Oh, I see you are still with us," he said.

You're still with us? I thought. *Anger boiled within me. Still unkind, still cold. Some things never change.* Then, I took a deep breath. *Humility, George.*

"We're doing just fine," I said, nicking my wife's favorite line.

As we glided down the hall, I muttered less than complimentary things about that doctor under my breath. Carol tried to tell me to be quiet, but she couldn't stop giggling.

My eldest son tapped his watch, his signal that we had to go. Sean had first suggested that we make it a big birthday bash, and I could see that he was excited about it. So was I. The surprise would go off without a hitch. We used the cover of the holiday season to explain why all three of our sons were in town.

Carol's birthday was on New Year's Eve, so we decided to pick an off night for the celebration, December 28th. Carol loved to go out to eat, and a local restauranteur, Robin Fernandez, had just opened a new place in town, Bruneaux, which provided the perfect pretense to get her out of the house none the wiser. Plus, some recently arriving visitors could help cover the story. Chad and Catherine had just returned from spending Christmas with Catherine's family in Scranton. That summer, the two of them were married in a lovely ceremony at a local nature center on a perfect blue-sky day. Carol had indeed gotten her chance to help Catherine pick out a wonderful array of flowers for the occasion, which served as a memorable backdrop for a day filled with laughter and nearly enough dancing to last a lifetime. Given how much Carol still loved chatting with her son and new daughter-in-law about the wedding, I knew they would provide compelling misdirection for the upcoming surprise.

As they settled in with Carol, Sean and I slipped out under the auspices of running to the wine store to get some special bottles for the occasion.

When we arrived at the restaurant, and I saw firsthand how many people were so incredibly fond of my wife, it felt like an electric charge was climbing up my spine. I couldn't wait to see that unforgettable look of joy on her face once more. I texted for the boys and Catherine to lead Carol down. Our friend Chris Wu started preparing his fiddle.

I chanced a look outside and spotted the wheelchair rolling toward the place—we had since moved back from the hills to a smaller condo just a block from downtown Sewickley. Carol couldn't walk very far on her own anymore, and as much as she'd always hated that wheelchair, we had managed to come to an agreement. She would allow us to push her around in it, so long as we promised to ditch the thing just before we entered any public places.

When they arrived, I stepped into the small vestibule and prepared to walk her into the building. As per our pact, Chad, Catherine, and Matthew stopped just short of the door to help Carol out of the chair.

You can see into the forward edge of the restaurant from inside the vestibule, so as Matthew and Chad helped Carol to me, she managed to catch a glimpse of the Hoehl family standing in front of the waiting crowd. It was apparently at this moment that she sniffed out the surprise, because the second I opened the door, she loudly posed a simple question:

"What the fuck is going on?"

The twenty people closest to the door went to pieces. In retrospect, I couldn't have imagined a better way for her to enter her seventieth birthday party.

When she saw the size of the crowd, she lit up in a way that made my wish come true and then some. Though I don't have video from the 1987 party, the reaction for her seventieth wins in a landslide. Linda and Greg's son Matt recorded the scene, and I have watched that video over and over in the days since. My favorite part is the way her giddy laughter turns into open-mouthed amazement the moment she sees the crowd. If dementia ever robs my memory bank, those five seconds will be among the last precious gems I'll hold onto.

As the calls of surprise subsided, Chris started up with a beautiful rendition of "Happy Birthday," and the crowd joined in. As the serenade concluded, Carol delivered her signature move, the left arm shoulder shrug punctuated by an upturned palm.

Our sons had prepared a few words, with Matthew beginning. A few seconds into his speech, Carol spotted someone special in the crowd, and cut in.

"Oh!" she exclaimed. "There's Wendy!"

Wendy replied with a cheerful wave. The crowd erupted with laughter. When it died down, Matthew concluded his speech.

"Mom," he said, "you have been my strength, and I love you."

"You better love me a lot," she fired back, sending the crowd into hysterics.

Chad noted in his remarks that when he was a child, his mother had given him the sage advice to be kind to everyone, and that the crowd that night was a perfect example of that wisdom. People from every era of Carol's life were there, from old friends to new. My sister Barb, having buried their youngest daughter just a couple months prior, had come with her entire heartbroken family. The Jaynes had made the trip from Columbus.

Sean finished up with a sentiment that had become true of the whole family. Whenever the boys came to see us, they would always give Carol a long, tight hug, to which she would always respond, "I love you, and don't you ever forget it." I'd heard her say it to each of them many times. And now here was Sean, returning the thought in kind.

"Everyone in this room loves you, and don't you ever forget it."

That was about as much standing as Carol could do in a stretch, so we sat down right in the middle of the restaurant at a table. It felt like a wedding, the way people kept coming over to see us. Every time I got up to mingle, I would glance back at the table, and there was always someone new there, talking with her, making her laugh and feel special.

My daughter-in-law Catherine had made a large poster centered by one of my all-time favorite photos of Carol, a silly yet somehow glamorous pose at a Saturday afternoon barbecue for the high school football team. In it, she has her head cocked to the side like a movie star, a slight smile, and a lit cigarette in her hand—a perfect snapshot of my wife's carefree attitude. Next to it, she left a big white space forpeople to sign. By the end of the night, warm words filled the space to capacity. There was just so much love in that room.

The next morning, I went for a long walk, taking one of Carol's favorite routes from those couple years when she'd feigned exercise while she was really visiting her friend Linda. I walked past an old swimming and tennis club. Carol took tennis lessons there one summer, and quickly proved to be one of the worst players in the history of the sport. She hated every minute of it, but had tried anyway, and in part because of my encouragement.

As I walked on, I couldn't help but be overwhelmed by the outpouring of support we had witnessed the night before. But it went beyond just a night—a whole community of assistance had been present from day one. Though I knew we had raised good kids, I never could've imagined how wonderful each of them would be with their mother. Matthew called all the time. Sean visited as often as he could. Chad would often take on my role as caregiver so I could get away for a few days.

My siblings, Jimmy and Lennie, visited frequently and made Carol feel special. Barb would come stay for a couple nights now and then, always providing us with some laughter and help. Tommy checked in on us often, his conversations with Carol always leaving her delightfully silly. Jodi and David would sneak away from their busy lives raising a family, whether the occasion for a visit was a good or a bad one.

My walk took me to one of the most beautiful spots in town, a street lined with trees that must be at least 150 years old. I thought about the generosity our friends had shown over the years, how they had opened their homes for visits, invited us to dinner, reached out to spend time with Carol, or stopped by with food, especially when we had just returned from a hospital visit. Their selflessness humbled me. The truth was that they had all played the role of caregiver in their own ways.

When I hit my turnaround point near Little Sewickley Creek, I knew there was one last place I needed to see: the location of Carol's first surprise party.

As I made the two-plus mile walk to our old house, I thought about how, a few months after Carol's second stroke, we'd started going back to church. Because of my wife's extensive morning routine, we had started going to Saturday five o'clock Mass rather than forcing the issue on Sundays. We would get Carol dressed up in her best clothes—which basically just meant dress pants instead of the usual athletic pants, and maybe a little extra jewelry. At communion, I would let a good portion of the congregants go ahead of us, because I didn't want to halt the procession with our slow pace. When we would finally reach the front, Father Dan would see us, smile, and come down the aisle to meet us.

To return to our seats, we passed the front of the altar, which meant that we also passed the additional sacrament of wine. It probably would have been better for her legs to get back to the pew quickly, but there was zero chance that Carol wouldn't stop for a sip of the good stuff. She always gave the appearance of wanting to do her duty as a good Catholic, but I knew she was sneaking an extra nip.

We would be met with warm smiles and kind faces during our slow walk back. Back at our seats, I would have just enough time to kneel and ask God for more days for Carol. Since that blunt doctor had sent me into impromptu prayer in the darkened alcove, my wife had lived six-and-a-half years beyond the strokes. In this way, it had become a daily renegotiation, and I would take any time I could get.

Our Saturday night routine became taking our good feelings from Mass to our favorite dinner destination. We kept a 7 P.M. reservation, allowing for just enough time to belly up at the bar for a pre-dinner drink. Every time we pulled into the roundabout of the restaurant, Ron, the head valet, would help me perform a perfectly choreographed routine to ensure Carol's swift passage from the car to a cozy glass of Chardonnay.

The large set of windows at the head of the restaurant afforded Lynn, the regular Saturday night bartender, the chance to see us coming. While Ron and I helped Carol from the car, Lynn would scoop a glass of ice and pour the chilled white into the proper wine glass. Then, she would come from around the bar and wait until we rounded the corner to the long hall leading to the lounge area.

"Oh, there's Lynn," Carol would remark with delight, and her steps would always get a little longer and a little faster.

Sometimes, along the way, she would start veering in the direction of the cookie tray, and I would always have to hold her a little tighter.

"After dinner, honey."

Her reply would always come in the form of a furrowed brow. Once we finally reached the lounge area, Lynn would help me get Carol situated on a stool.

"You are too good to me," Carol would say.

"My pleasure, Mrs. Shannon," Lynn invariably replied before giving me a wink. She would pour the wine onto the ice and head around the bar to find something for me. By the time I'd finished the reminiscence, my feet had taken me to 13 Thorn Street. I had walked four miles or so in total, and my body felt good and my heart warm. Though the last couple owners had made some smaller aesthetic changes, the place looked fundamentally the same as it always had. On this quiet morning, I stood in front of our old home remembering Christmases, family gatherings, parties for the football teams, graduation parties, the five of us just sitting in front of the television.

My mind then landed on that birthday night twenty-nine years ago. I saw Carol with her frosted, shoulder-length hair and her stylish fashion. I saw myself with a thick mustache, tight haircut, and a sweater vest. I watched us approach that door with Carol none the wiser. The eruption of joy from our guests, and Carol getting swept into the dining room happened as clearly now as it had back then.

On this chilly morning in the waning days of 2016, instead of taking a right to follow Carol into that large, makeshift dance room full of boozy chatter and laughter, I mentally made a left into our empty living room. I sat down, but not before catching a glimpse of myself. My hair and scruff had gone white, and I'd put on a few pounds since my running days. Like the last fifteen seconds of a song on a record, the sounds of the party faded slowly into silence. I mentally scanned the room and found our old records situated in the wall-sized bookshelf, and the Stobart painting of early Pittsburgh above the fireplace. I spied the couches and chairs, situated in their perfect little spots, and our family pictures scattered around the room. It looked exactly like it did in 1987.

In that silence, I heard something, but it wasn't audible, nor did it come from the constant babble of my mind. It came from within, perhaps even from my soul. It was truth.

I didn't know how to give unconditional love back then.

At the relatively tender age of forty-two, I favored feeding my ambition and having my expectations met, and I hadn't yet attended the retreat at St. Paul's. I was a confident man, to be sure, but I employed a strong will to deny my own imperfections. I spent so many of those years trying to make everything and everyone around me just right. The drive for perfection had created an incredible amount of stress, which often expressed itself in outward agitation. I'd missed the point that nothing was perfect, including me.

Even after St. Paul's, I didn't always embody that enlightenment I'd found, which left me feeling privately ashamed and relying on pride to get me through. Don't get me wrong, during those years between the retreat and the strokes, we celebrated graduations and career successes, enjoyed many anniversaries, and the joys of our life in Hilton Head, but they were also speckled with moments of deep personal guilt. Shame and guilt remind us of our flaws—our lack of perfection. Left untreated, they eat away at one's core. Properly acknowledging and accepting them heals and bolsters the power to love.

All my life, I have been in search of peace. In some ways, I was on the right track in valuing the idea of humility I had discovered in that church library during the retreat. But there's a problem with actively seeking humility: you don't find it; it finds you. It discovered me when I was dealing with a terminal illness and felt ready to give up control of my world, to stop focusing on my own needs and truly focus on Carol's. In so doing, humility freed my soul to accept my life's circumstances as they were, myself for who I was, and Carol for who she was. That was when the joy in my life truly arrived. I wasn't perfect, nor would I ever be. Our life wasn't perfect, but it was wonderful. Perhaps most importantly, I realized that I had a partner in love, a love that had become unconditional.

I could have been a better man back then. I could list the apologies and hugs I wished I had given, but if I was ever going to fully heal, I would need to find a way to forgive myself.

A few days after the seventieth birthday party, Chad paid us a visit. It had gotten to be later in the evening, so I had taken Carol to the master bathroom for her bedtime routine.

When it was finished, I returned to the kitchen to continue talking with my son. We were just discussing the nature of Carol's perseverance when she scooted in from around the corner, standing in her pajamas and holding onto her walker. We kept having our discussion as she approached. Then, when it looked like she was starting to announce something—very much a rarity in those days—we stopped to listen.

"I guess you thought I was going to die or something," she said proudly. "Well, I guess I showed you something. Here I am. Living proof."

She said it better than I ever could. Every time she was knocked down, she got right back up. She'd outlived everyone's expectations, probably even mine. I had begun to wonder if she might even outlive me. She did all this by being the perfect embodiment of the power of perseverance, the inspiration of humility, and the willingness to live each moment as if it was her last. Her strong will to live rekindled a love some forty-plus years beyond its original spark, and she brought her family and a whole community closer.

As Chad and I settled into the brilliance of my wife's words, she proceeded past us and took a seat in her favorite chair in the house. Each time she sat down on her own, she did it the same way. She would get her walker to the side of the chair, shuffle her feet until her body was fully square with the destination, feel for the armrest with her right hand, and then let her backside perform a dramatic freefall into the seat. At impact, her feet would kick up off the ground, and she would ride the momentum to where she could set those little legs on the ottoman in front of her chair. Somehow, she would do all this while simultaneously leaning left to pick up whatever glass happened to be sitting beside the chair. And whether it was water, soda, or wine, she never once spilled a drop.

"Another perfect landing," I said, just like I always did.

"That's all I'm saying," she replied.

The voice of the sea speaks to the soul.
– Kate Chopin

CHAPTER TEN
the mighty fight

February 12, 2017

In that half-second between asleep and awake, I sometimes experienced a moment of prescience. Maybe it came from a life lived in perpetual and generalized worry. On this dark winter morning, it told me I was alone in bed. Startled, I snapped awake and reached for Carol, but came up with a clump of empty sheets.

A loud bang followed.

I flipped the lights on and raced to the bathroom, where I found my wife splayed across the beige tiled floor. Carol had fallen more times than I cared to count, but this instance immediately felt more serious than the rest. I asked her where she felt the pain, and, breathless and wincing, she pointed at her leg and knee.

I ran into the bedroom and called 911. I'd been through this headed-for-the-hospital routine enough to know that they wouldn't let her eat all day just in case they had to do an operation. But since they would have to wean her off the blood thinner for at least a few days, I knew there was zero chance of a surgery happening today anyway. I helped her sit up and went to the kitchen for a bowl of Peanut Butter Puffins, which she dug right into and continued to eat even as the paramedics came through the bathroom door. Soon, we were in the ambulance and off to the hospital. As per usual, I snatched up my brown bag on the way out the door.

By the end of the day, we had another diagnosis to add

Photo: Carol with son Sean in New York City.

to Carol's fragile condition: a broken right hip. The news couldn't have been much worse. The way she'd broken the bone, they were going to need to perform an extensive surgery and implant more hardware than she'd ever gotten before. As predicted, they would need a day or so to get her Coumadin pulled back, but they scheduled the surgery for as soon as they could manage.

I spent every minute of the next day with my wife in her hospital room. By nightfall, she couldn't do much more than gaze at the TV with tired eyes. They had given her some strong pain meds. Just then, I noticed her Valentine's necklace was all bound up, so I pulled the pendant away from the clasp, just like I'd always done.

For the better part of our marriage, as Valentine's Day approached, Carol would ask me how we were going to celebrate the holiday. I would always shrug it off on the basis that it was a made-up holiday. In her usual way, she would accept that answer and say nothing more. Then, on the day of, I would get a little card from her. One year, maybe around 1999, she asked me the same question, and I gave the same response, but I could clearly see that my rejection had hurt her feelings. I thought about it all day, and decided that I'd been harsh about it. If she wanted to have that holiday, why should I get in the way?

We were in Hilton Head, so I went to her favorite shop, a local boutique. The owner of the store didn't wait a second to show me a silver caged heart, which I immediately loved. Apparently, Carol had been eyeing this piece for quite some time. That night, I surprised her with the gift at her favorite restaurant. She beamed all night. Now, with me being among the worst romantics in history, I asked her if she would only wear it on Valentine's Day. In my mind, that would make it extra special. She didn't flinch. Rather, she just nodded in agreement. In retrospect, that was a ridiculous notion. But that's what made Carol so wonderful: my silly rule didn't matter to her. A few years later, I sensed that my request was unreasonable and told her that she could wear it whenever she wanted, which she promptly did. Later still, it turned out that "whenever she wanted" meant "every day."

Now, with another risky surgery looming, I just wanted to see my wife make it through, so she could continue wearing that caged heart whenever she wanted.

When I entered the inpatient surgery waiting room the next morning, I found the massive area packed with patients and their families. On the long wall next to the check-in desk hung four large screens tracking every surgery happening in the hospital. I glanced up at the board. "Carol S," it read. "Pre-op."

I'd been told to expect a three-hour operation, and yet one o'clock came and went, and Carol's status on the board remained "in surgery." Time wore on, and as the crowded room began to thin out, concern settled in. Each hour, the list on the monitors grew smaller, as did the crowd in the waiting room. By 8 P.M., it was just me, an empty board, a quiet room, and my windmill of anxiety. Finally, the call came that they had found a room for Carol on the seventh floor.

To gain access to the wing, I had to press a button and announce my name into the intercom. It felt like an hour before they finallybuzzed me in. The moment I burst through her door, Carol looked up at me with those doe eyes of hers.

"What's going on?" she said.

The familiarity of the greeting set me at ease almost immediately. Carol's unabashed casualness always had a way of cutting through my stress. I dragged a reclining chair over to her bed, and for the next couple hours, we held hands and laughed at *Frasier*.

Those past couple days had been full of worry, but as I sat there watching the television, I breathed a gigantic sigh of relief. The first time she'd broken a hip, it took her a solid three months to reach a full recovery. Though I knew it would be a long road to that point again, I could clearly see visions of us heading down the highways and making the most of our seventies. Throughout the evening, I'd thumbed through various websites looking for the right vehicle to make that happen.

We'd done it once before, at the beginning of 2015. A voyage that I often referred to as the best trip of our lives. I'd traded my retirement convertible for an eight-passenger Dodge Ram ProMaster van, which I packed with enough stuff to last us an eternity, including a portable toilet that Carol could use instead of exiting the highway to address her frequent bathroom needs. For an entire month, Carol and I zig-zagged through the south visiting friends and family, before ending up in Florida in mid-March to attend an annual symphony fundraiser concert hosted by our dear friends Lori and Juergen.

This particular event happened to fall on the evening before our 46th anniversary, and our last night of that fantastic road trip before heading back to Pittsburgh. After a sunset cocktail hour and a delicious meal, we were treated to the music of some of the world's finest musicians and funniest personalities.

For the last song, the evening's unofficial emcee, violinist Chris Wu, stood and announced to the crowd that in honor of our wedding anniversary, they would play the Irish tune "Danny Boy," a song Juergen knew to be my favorite. I looked over at my wonderful friend, who gestured at me with clasped hands. By the third line, the corners of my eyes were wet with tears. I put my arm around Carol and squeezed her close to me.

I'd probably heard that tune a thousand times in my life. As it draws near the end, both the arrangement and lyrics open up from its restrained and somber reflection on loss to a wide-open expression of love and inner tranquility. For many years, I related more to the melancholy aspect of it, but for a few moments that night, those beautiful notes brought peace to my soul. That wonderful song capped a month-long renewal of our marriage that made us feel more alive and in love than we'd ever been before.

As I sat there in the hospital with Carol, laughing at Niles Crane's antics, I couldn't wait to do it all over again. In the meantime, I vowed to do something special for our anniversary, which was just a month away. It didn't have to be perfect, but I wanted it to be something that reflected Carol's world.

The next morning, I returned to the seventh floor and engaged with the intercom.

"George for Carol Shannon, Room 711."

Silence. In anticipation of being buzzed through, I gave the door a little tug. Still locked.

This can't be good.

My stomach flipped a couple times, and I felt a little dizzy. I hit the intercom button again and announced my presence.

"Mr. Shannon," a man said. "I'll be right out."

An immediate sweat came over me. *No. No. No.*

The overnight nurse came through the door and offered me a seat in the hallway, but I refused. I remember hoping that I was merely in midst of a horrible nightmare. A family brushed past me to enter the wing, reminding me that this was all so real.

"What happened?"

"She needed more and more oxygen through the night," the night nurse reported. "And we gave it to her. But this morning, when I went in to check on her, she was unresponsive."

I must have been in shock, because I didn't say anything. He told me that Carol had been sent down to the medical intensive care unit on the fourth floor. I bolted for the elevator.

"She seemed like such a great woman, sir," he called after me.

Seemed? I thought, noting with dread how he had spoken

in the past tense.

On the ride down, I texted Chad. He and Catherine had recently moved back to Pittsburgh, and I knew he could be at the hospital within minutes. The elevator opened to the fourth floor just as I finished the message. I flew for the giant entrance to the unit, its automatic doors swinging open and sparing me the task of having to request permission to enter. I found Carol's name next to the first door on the right. Inside, I encountered more machines than I could count, a sight that sent tense flashbacks to those long days and nights leading up to her heart surgery. The difference was that this unit was the hospital's crisis center. The people they brought here faced death. A commanding young doctor in a white coat proved cool under pressure as she scanned the readings on the machines and issued orders to her incredibly responsive staff. It was immediately clear that the doctor's chief concern was keeping Carol's blood pressure up. In any other situation, I would have cut in to ask the details about what was going on, but from the urgency in everyone's actions, I could sense that this was not the time to intrude. The five minutes it took them to stabilize her might as well have been five years.

The crisis unit's entry doors made a prolonged swooshing sound whenever they swung open, and then rattled to a stop. Every time I heard this sound, I would glance out the door, hoping to see Chad. Eventually the sound heralded his arrival, and soon after came Dr. Ismail. Chad immediately started questioning the doctor who had stabilized my wife, and we learned that no one was quite sure why Carol had become unresponsive. My son set his hand on my shoulder to comfort me, then went into the hall to call his brothers.

"I'm so upset that this happened," Dr. Ismail said as she looked me in the eyes. "Your wife has come through too much to be in this situation. I promise you that I will do everything I can for her. I'll be at her side the whole time."

This remains the most heartfelt and direct thing a doctor

has ever said to me. And she kept her word. Dr. Ismail never left Carol's side, and she gave her every chance to live.

Chad returned and informed that Sean would arrive by nightfall, and that Matthew had made a flight reservation for the next morning.

This scenario terrified me well beyond anything she'd gone through; even her heart surgery in 2015 paled in comparison. That time, we'd only been given a sliver of hope for Carol's chances of survival, but even in the bleakest of those hours, I could at least count on that sliver. But now everything felt different. There was an air of finality hanging over the room. It was as if something irrevocable had been set in motion, something that no amount of medical intervention or even the strongest willpower could overcome.

I'd been quite lucky to have spent nearly fifty years with my wife, but I still wasn't ready to see her go, and I worried that she hadn't received all the love she deserved. Sure, I'd poured my love out in the past seven years, but I still had so much to make up for from those times leading up to the strokes. I felt the guilt and shame bubbling to the surface again.

Chad and I sat there all day with our eyes glued to every monitor, looking up only when a doctor or nurse arrived to check on Carol's vitals. Had it really been less than twelve hours since my wife and I had been laughing at some predictable mess that Niles Crane had gotten himself into? At some point, she seemed like she was starting to respond to our voices, but she didn't open her eyes or speak. The good news was that she'd remained stable the rest of the day. By the time Sean arrived that night, she had been sound asleep for several hours, so we all went home to get some rest.

The next morning, we arrived to a pleasant surprise. Carol was awake, though groggy, and clearly trying to speak with us. It was tough to understand most of what she said, but there was one thing she made clear: she didn't want the ventilator.

The number of F-bombs she dropped while tugging on her tubes made it impossible to mistake her meaning. I understand why. That thing plunging down her throat looked painful. I couldn't imagine having to live with something like that. As much as she hated that machine, we weren't yet sure if she would survive without it.

The familiar swoosh and rattle of the door announced Dr. Ismail's entry into the ICU. She arrived with her standard confidence and upbeat tone, but it didn't last long. Carol's blood pressure took another nosedive. Dr. Ismail didn't hesitate to take charge of the situation. She directed nurses, specialists, and other physicians until the intensivist could arrive from working on another patient in critical condition. Moments after the latter doctor arrived, Carol's blood pressure fell through the floor. She had suffered a full-fledged cardiac event. They called for the crash cart and pushed us from the room.

I objected, wanting to be next to that bed so I could beg my wife not to leave. A few minutes later, Dr. Ismail rushed out. They'd saved Carol but needed urgent approval to place a heart pump. Without it, she would pass away. The procedure itself could cause a whole host of complications. The decision seemed obvious. Live to fight another day. Chad and Sean agreed.

I paced and paced for the next sixty minutes. A dozen eternities later, when the surgeon came through those doors and flashed a smile, I let go the longest sigh of relief I'd ever breathed. I hadn't lost my Carol.

The hospital would be moving her to the Cardiac Intensive Care Unit, or CCU, on the eleventh floor. The staff warned that she would likely be staying there for a long stretch. The preceding day and a half had been a whirlwind, and while the inevitability of death hadn't disappeared, at least it had receded.

The heart pump granted Carol's body a chance to heal,

and the medical staff an extension of time to figure things out. "So, I guess Carol decided to throw us another curveball today," Dr. Ismail said with a chuckle.

The curveballs would continue. My wife, bedridden and snaked with more wires than a server room, was doing her best Sandy Koufax impression, just one nasty breaking ball after another.

Most likely because of the trauma of the previous day, the circulation in Carol's left leg suddenly stopped, causing it to blow up like a balloon. The situation became emergent even before we had a chance to settle in and think about it. The next thing I knew, a team of doctors from the vascular surgery department was handing me an onslaught of papers highlighting the benefits of surgery (staying alive), and mundanely rushing through the downside (the possible loss of a leg and the risks of amputation surgery).

I couldn't count the number of times a similar scenario had played out during my wife's care, but no matter how often I'd faced these situations, it always seemed strange that I would need to read a comprehensive legal document and provide a signature while under such incredible duress. Every time, I disregarded the rehearsed words delivered by the doctor or resident and signed my name as quickly as I could. If whatever they wanted to do was going to give Carol a chance, then they could count me on board every time.

Soon after, the doctors were making several deep incisions into Carol's leg, acting quickly to get her veins in working order. In this way, the medical team managed to foul off that first breaking ball.

For the rest of that first week, things seemed headed in the right direction. They'd identified Carol's mitral valve as the likely culprit in causing all the heart problems. Apparently, whenever that valve starts leaking, it can cause all sorts of problems. The initial plan was to see if the picture would improve with time and medicine, and for a few days, it seemed to work. But then came the next big step. Carol would need to wean off the ventilator. Much to everyone's surprise, she met this challenge just a couple days later.

When the nursing staff brought us back in to see her, we swarmed around her bed, all of us eager to hear how she felt.

"Having that tube out's got to feel good, huh?" Matthew said.

"Get me out of here," Carol said.

Totally understandable proposition,, I thought.

"How you feeling, Mama?" Sean said.

We all knew the answer.

"I'm fine," she said.

When I leaned in to give her a kiss, she looked up at me intently.

"Can I go now?"

"They still need to do a little more work," I said.

She snarled playfully as she turned her attention to Chad. "He's just mad because I have a boyfriend."

None of us had any idea who the mysterious interloper could be, but we all had a good laugh.

"I'm serious."

I told her she could have whatever she wanted, which seemed to calm her down. Before we left that night, I kissed her three times on the forehead and told her that the triple kiss would be how she would know it was me. She shot me a fatigued but genuine smile, and gave me a couple long bats of her lashes—a quick flirt, if I wasn't mistaken. I can't properly express how great it was to have her back. I even let visions of us taking on the open roads flash back into my mind. She'd beaten the odds on everything else; why not this one, too?

Less than twenty-four hours later, Carol delivered her next curveball. The staff discovered that she wasn't getting enough oxygen, so the hospitalist was forced to put her back on the ventilator.

The medical team was puzzled as they called for the X-ray

machine. A deep respiratory infection delivered the nastiest curveball yet by filling Carol's lungs with fluid. A particularly insidious complication was that the best chance of improving an infection was to get up and move around—the one thing my wife wasn't anywhere near equipped to do.

With exercise impossible, and with the pills failing to improve Carol's condition, we now found ourselves considering riskier alternatives. Everyone seemed to agree that open heart surgery was completely out of the question, as it would be too much for an already overtaxed body. The last, best hope involved reaching the damaged mitral valve with the use of a catheter guided through her femoral artery. But she would need to get much better before anyone would even consider the measure. So now we had been backed into a wait-and-see approach.

Over the next couple weeks, Carol would send a steady stream of tough pitches at the medical staff, and they would battle her right back to keep the at-bat alive. Just as her infection started to look better, her diabetes roared out of control, hampering her kidneys. Her blood pressure came down, but her body retained fluids. Lasix drained the fluids, but then her blood pressure crept below the low end of normal. No matter what the medical staff did, Carol never seemed to come out ahead.

After three weeks, Carol's doctors started to worry that the ventilator would have to remain in permanently. Although Carol had demonstrated a few moments of mental coherence over the past couple weeks, her speech was becoming rarer and less rational. In her confusion, she would pull at her many lines and tubes. Eventually they outfitted her with wrist restraints. The infection had improved modestly, but it lingered like an unwanted guest. To make matters worse, her unstable blood pressure hung over her like a ticking clock.

Before I knew it, we had rolled into March. Our wedding anniversary was less than two weeks away. By this point, that glimmer of hope I'd experienced after her heart-pump procedure had begun to flicker as if burning out. The thought of road trips landed in the category of wild-eyed dreams. I would have done anything for her to beat this breathing machine situation, to get her feeling half-normal and on to rehab so she could regain some strength. If we could just get her home, I would rearrange everything in our lives to make the best of it—for however long that might be.

Almost every discipline in the Cardiovascular Institute of Allegheny General Hospital had consulted on my wife's case. We must have had a dozen conversations at the foot of her bed or just outside her door. The choice eventually came down to either letting the matter continue in this way, which would mean that she would likely never come off the ventilator and would be permanently bedridden, or we could take the chance for a better quality of life by trying to solve the valve issue. Though her health wasn't ideal, the doctors believed that she was at least stable enough to give her a fighting chance to survive an interventional procedure.

As her healthcare power of attorney, the final decision fell to me.

The only sound as I looked down at her was the steady beat of the ventilator. I'd been married to Carol for nearly fifty years, so I knew that she would want to live, but at the same time, I tried to imagine her riding out her final years in a hospital bed set up in our bedroom. Would she be happy?

Never, I thought.

She hated the walker with a passion, and the wheelchair even more so. Suddenly it seemed so clear. She would want to get back on her feet, or not at all.

On March 5th, I made the decision to move ahead. All we needed was a one good day of stability before the doctors could clear her for the procedure. Remarkably, despite the wide array of potential problems, March 7th went off stunningly well.

Late into the evening, the boys and I took turns at the head of the bed, stroking Carol's hair and whispering our own personal brands of encouragement. Dr. Ismail came into the room and explained the plan for the next day. As always, she finished by checking with Carol. My wife looked at me, and I nodded. Ever the one to go my way, Carol responded to the doctor in kind. After Dr. Ismail cleared out, I asked the boys for a few minutes alone with their mother.

All the delicate talk of death and last-ditch efforts instilled such incredible fear in me. Though the medical facts had been piling up, I remained steadfast against the possibility that she might not survive. At this point, I wanted just one more day at home, to set up her breakfast and pills one last time. I would bargain anything to load her back into the car for a final swing through the doctors' appointments, her comedy routine at rehab, and the largest fucking box of popcorn in the movie theater; one more chance for me to fall asleep watching TV and have her wake me up by asking if I was awake.

When my sons and I got home that night, I somehow managed to fall asleep. According to those big red numbers on the ceiling, it was 1:07 A.M. when my phone rang. I let out a yell as I snapped awake. The number on my phone I recognized immediately as a call from the hospital. There was nothing I could imagine wanting to do less than pick up that line.

An oddly excited man who identified himself as the night doctor told me that Carol had pulled out her ventilator tube. While I'm still not sure to this day whether I felt more dread than confusion over that statement, his next announcement mystified me to the core. She was breathing perfectly fine on her own. No tube. No machine. Nothing.

I sat on the edge of my bed for a long while, trying to wrap my head around what I'd just learned. My first reaction after hanging up was to tell Chad that we needed to go to the hospital because this doctor must have had his facts wrong.

155

Plus, I'd forgotten to ask how she'd done it. We had been told for weeks that Carol couldn't survive without oxygen assistance. We had seen her backslide into respiratory distress at least once on lower levels of support. It just didn't add up, and I wanted answers.

By the next morning, the whole medical staff was abuzz about Carol's feat. Halfway into cleaning up my wife's bedclothes, the night nurse had been pulled from the room on an emergency. Less than three minutes later, all the bells and whistles had sounded from Carol's room. When a group of nurses arrived to address the chaos, Carol had the ventilator mask in her hand, her wrist restraints perfectly strapped.

Then, like the critical scene in a detective picture, all the requisite evidence flashed before my eyes. Fact one: Carol had been stretching her left arm every which way for the past several days, and only now did I realize that she'd been testing the limits of her restraints. Fact two: Carol waited until the perfect moment, when her pillows weren't propping her up and nobody had eyes on her. Fact three: The moment she was alone, Carol had laid herself prone and shimmied down the bed to the point where her hand could reach the tube plunging down her throat.

I have two views on this event, and they aren't mutually exclusive. I'll call the first one the Sinatra Theory. Every doctor on that unit had stood within earshot of Carol as they explained her ongoing medical saga. The ventilator had further hampered an already quiet person, but her mind and hearing had remained needle-sharp. So, just two days prior, when we were all in the hallway putting this risky proposition on the table, Carol decided that she was going to flip that table, with all its delicate medical ideas, right upside down. She'd had enough sutures, procedures, tubes, and machines for a lifetime. If taking away the artificial oxygen supply would end it, then so be it. And just like one of her favorite Sinatra songs, she was going to do it her way.

The second theory, a much more difficult one to verify, operates more like a supplement to the first. It goes like this: Carol and I had built up some goodwill with God, given Carol's lifetime of kindness, our frequent trips to church, and my consistent post-communion discussions from the kneeler. Even to this day, I wonder whether somewhere in her struggle to get hold of the ventilator, Carol was assisted by God. She'd made peace with her Creator and got a little help in fulfilling her desire to remove that cumbersome thing. I can't quote more than a line or two of scripture, have always kept my religion private, and don't know whether I'm going to heaven or hell, but that event made me see faith in a whole new way.

Either way, Carol's great escape was an extraordinary thing. When I was finally able to visit with her, she would only give that feeble little shoulder shrug when I questioned her on what she was thinking. Then it hit me like the proverbial ton of bricks. Carol had effectively delivered her signature move, the left-arm shoulder shrug punctuated by an upturned palm—a blend of "it is what it is" and "you left me no choice."

The longer I sat there, the less I tried to understand her actions, and the more I let myself be amazed by them. Then, in that cleaned slate of my mind, I remembered a self-selected nugget of wisdom etched into my book of quotes:

"The more we feel our lives count for something, the less we fear death."

With her late-night hospital bed acrobatics, Carol had announced that she was ready to let the cards fall where they may. But she had also helped me. She'd let me know that my work was done—that it was okay to let go.

The desire to have one last day with her at home largely came from the deepest part of my heart. I didn't want to lose my soulmate. Some small part of it also came from my lifelong struggle to want things to work out in a perfect little way, to get her home for just one more perfect day. I wanted her to live forever, so I could keep showing her how much I loved her, but she showed me that her life had been full, and that it counted for something. The fear of her death wasn't hers, but mine. If she was willing to let life play out, I needed to be just as willing.

Time is but the stream I go a-fishing in. I drink at
it; but while I drink I see the sandy bottom
and detect how shallow it is.
Its thin current slides away, but eternity remains

– Henry David Thoreau
Walden

CHAPTER ELEVEN
on her own two feet

March 14, 2017

Even though I'd spent almost every waking moment at the hospital, every time I walked into Carol's room, I had to pinch myself. Without the ventilator for almost a week, she was headed to the step-down unit, the next and final step before being discharged. She'd done so well that Sean and Matthew had returned to their regular lives in New York and Montana. When she saw me enter, she offered a little wave and tilted her head in a signal that she wanted a kiss on the cheek. I strolled over and gave it gladly.

Even though it was a day early, I couldn't wait any longer. I pulled the chair next to her bed to tell her about her anniversary gift. But before I could say anything, a doctor I hadn't seen before slipped into the room to announce the next curveball.

"Excuse me, sir," the young man said. "I think one of your wife's teeth has fallen into her lung."

I regarded the doctor a little cross-eyed and went to Carol, who'd already opened her mouth to let me inspect. Dread washed over me as I bent down and examined her teeth like a dentist. I'd been so ready to see my wife take the next step toward getting home, and I knew how desperate she'd become to leave, so a setback on something so unexpected would have been devastating. Just as I was set to quit looking, I noticed a gap, and asked Carol to open wider.

"Well I'll be damned," I said. "There's one missing."

Photo: Carol with George and son Matthew at wedding in Pittsburgh.

Carol would need to head down to the imaging lab to verify the doctor's theory. I agreed to the procedure, and off they went with my wife. I would have to wait to share her gift with her.

Not too long after Carol's strokes, a nonprofit group in Sewickley announced plans to build a little two-screen movie theater in town. My wife was beside herself at this news, and she urged me to get involved with the project. Life had gotten too busy for me to follow up on it. Around the time we moved from the hills back to the village, they'd started excavating the grounds. It was official—our new home would be located less than a hundred yards from an endless supply of popcorn, Diet Coke, and movies.

Finally, eighteen months after breaking ground, the Tull Family Theater (named so after a very generous donation) was set to open in mid-January 2017. Carol counted down the days until the opening, and I couldn't wait to walk her through those doors for the first time. A few small hiccups later, and the opening had been postponed until February 17, 2017, right as Carol had begun her long hospitalization.

I'd felt so bad that she couldn't make the premiere. On the way to the hospital one morning, I swung by the theater with a question for the front office and got just the answer I wanted. My special gift for Carol was in the bag. As I made my way out of the building, a wall full of plaques caught my eye. Those who had contributed money to the project had their names inscribed on these beautiful silver-gray tablets. I turned around, explained the situation to the staff in the office, and one check later, the number of anniversary gifts had doubled.

When they wheeled her into the room after her X-ray session, the doctor confirmed that her tooth was indeed in her lung, and that the bronchoscope would be necessary since that tooth could turn into something of an infection magnet. More risks explained, more papers signed, and we were scheduled for an anniversary day procedure. Compared to many of the twists and turns over the past month, this bend didn't raise too much concern. But considering Carol's fragile condition, I realized that it could be a stumbling block.

Not wanting to wait a second longer, I went back to the bedside. "The new movie theater opened."

"Oh, did it really?" she exclaimed. The little spark I'd seen in her eye returned, the same one I'd seen on the day the theater was first announced.

"They're hiring for certain jobs," I told her. "And the one they need most is ticket-takers. Any interest?"

Carol blinked at me and confirmed her interest. "I'd like that a lot." She gazed into my eyes in a way I hadn't seen in what felt like years.

"Well," I said, laying it on thick, "I can't make any guarantees, but I'm in good with the management there."

She squeezed my hand tight and leveled me with an intense stare. "I want the fucking job."

I laughed, but not entirely because of the profanity. What a relief to hear her string together a coherent five-word sentence. It had been a long time. "I also finally donated to the theater," I said. "Just like you always wanted me to."

I'd stopped by the theater that morning to get a cell phone snapshot of the freshest names on the wall of plaques: Carol and George Shannon. I handed her the phone and helped her hold it up.

"Happy Anniversary."

She took a long look, and with her eyes watering, said, "You're too good to me."

Impossible, I thought.

The next morning, they performed the bronchoscope and removed the tooth without a hitch. The doctor who performed the procedure told me that it was the fastest one he'd ever done, and that it might have beaten the hospital record. She'd thrown her last curveball.

Ten days later, we would be packing up Carol's things and

heading for Villa St. Joseph ("The Villa"), a skilled nursing facility not too far down the Ohio River from where we lived. Over that week and a half, the doctors did they best they could, but some lingering issues remained, like the slowly healing incisions and the quarrelsome respiratory infection. At the time we left the hospital, our biggest hurdle to getting Carol home was the rehabilitation of her significantly weakened body. I'd come to grips with the prospect that if Carol got home, her return would probably be brief, but I hung onto that hope as I followed that ambulance down the highway to the rehab facility.

The Villa resides on the grounds of a convent called the Sisters of St. Joseph motherhouse, an institution in Baden and the rest of Western Pennsylvania for over a hundred years. Within minutes after entering through the front door, I felt an overwhelming sense of warmth and knew that my wife was in the right place.

As they got Carol situated, I wandered the facilities. They were modest, but full of kind and attentive staff members. More than that, I felt a keen sense of peace being in a place full of so many people devoted to their faith. When it came time for me to see my wife, they escorted me into her new room. It was a small and private space that immediately took me right to the spring of 1969, when Carol and I rented our first apartment together.

At the time, Carol was a booking agent with TWA, and we were looking for a place to live as we prepared for our upcoming wedding. We couldn't afford much, and finding inexpensive housing in Pittsburgh was a tough task. We'd looked everywhere from East Liberty to Bethel Park, a large swath of real estate twenty or so miles long. Four months into our search, we caught wind of a one-bedroom for ninety bucks a month in a little town called Pleasant Hills.

On the day of the showing, I arrived first, and the agent and I had to wait on Carol. She would wear these little stub-heels for work, and they made a clicking sound on the floor loud enough for us to hear from down the hall. She strolled in, cig in hand, with a fresh haircut and a new cashmere coat. The agent showed us around the little one-bedroom, which didn't take long, since, apart from the bedroom, there was only a small bathroom off the dining/kitchen/living room combo. The place was maybe a total of eight hundred square feet.

"Well?" the agent said. "What do you think?"

Carol's heels clicked a small circle around the main room as she nodded in approval. Then, she took a long drag from her cigarette and spun a perfect pirouette to face us. "Let's talk turkey," she said, the smoke trailing from her lips.

More than ever before, I knew in that moment that I loved her. That moment was a bottle of the essence of my wife, a bottle from which I still drink every now and then.

We ended up taking the place for the listed price.

I sat next to my wife and stroked her hand while we waited for the care team to explain the plan. In the quietness of those few minutes, I felt deeply comforted by the crucifix I spotted above the door. In our master bedroom, no matter where Carol and I lived, we always hoisted a cross—one that I'd gotten from the church way back when I had rheumatic fever.

The projected course of rehabilitation was that it would last at least a month, and that was just to get her back to the point where she could do the very basic things like sitting up in bed, standing up from a seated position, and walking short distances. They took it very easy for the first couple days, and would end the session after they'd gotten her to sit up on the edge of the bed for a minute. Six weeks in the prone position had caused her body to deteriorate to the point where even her sitting muscles were like gel.

Even the most minimal amount of exertion wore Carol out, which was to be expected considering what she'd gone through. It seemed that all she really wanted to do was sleep. A couple days after her admission to the nursing facility, Chad and Catherine paid her a visit. Even though they'd arrived just after dinnertime, Carol had already zonked out. They taped a small Pittsburgh Penguins flag under her crucifix before they left. The Stanley Cup playoffs were a couple weeks away, and they figured she'd bring the team luck. One week into Carol's stay, on the last day of March, the physical therapy staff started using a machine to help her stand from the edge of the bed. This gadget had a handlebar to grab while she pulled herself up, along with the guiding help of the therapist's hands. Though I hoped for success, I had my doubts, as I'd seen Carol struggle to stand for months, even before her long hospital stay. With the nursing staff firmly supporting her backside, Carol nailed it on her first try. Her tenacity filled me with pride and admiration. Time and again, she'd proved to us that her will had the tensile strength of steel. For the next three days, she made more and more progress, standing for just a few seconds longer. Though she'd never utter a gripe, I could tell it hurt like hell.

On April 4th, she had her biggest day yet. For starters, we were able to get her dressed for the first time since this whole ordeal had begun. Since she had these bright yellow, slip-resistant socks on, I brought in a matching Penguins shirt from the previous year's Stanley Cup Championship. Sean had become such a huge fan over the years, and Carol had gotten caught up in his excitement and had become a fan too. With her standard black athletic pants, she was ready for the first playoff series of 2017, now just about a week away.

As a bonus, Chad had driven out from Pittsburgh to see her before he left for a trip with his father-in-law.

After lunch, the therapy team came into Carol's room with their machine. By this point in the day, she'd been taken out of bed and placed in a bedside chair. When they brought the machine over, she pushed herself to the edge of the chair. Clearly, she wanted this exercise over with as quickly as possible. Device in place, she put her hands around the little bar and pulled herself up about halfway before she stopped cold. We joined the two therapists in their words of encouragement. Her legs shook, and it appeared that she might sit down, but eventually, with a cross face and all her effort, she pulled herself up on her own. For a few wonderful seconds, and for the first time in nearly two months, Carol had gotten back on her own two feet.

Chad and I popped out of our chairs in excitement, practically high-fiving each other. I wanted to hug my wife, but the therapists were in the process of sitting her back down. She vehemently rejected doing another round, and they didn't push the matter. We tried to take her into the television room, but a few minutes later, she asked to be put back to bed.

After they turned out the lights, my son went to kiss his mother on the forehead and told her, "I love you, and don't you ever forget it." The next morning, I met with one of the house doctors to get an update. Just before we went into Carol's room, I told her about how much my wife loved the movies and about the anniversary gifts I'd given her. After her examination, the doctor leaned against the bed and grabbed Carol's hand.

"We're going to get you home," she said. "And you're going to go to that movie theater, get a box of popcorn and a big Diet Coke, and watch as many movies as you want."

To that wonderful personal touch, she added the warmest smile I'd ever seen from a doctor. It was infectious, but Carol's expression remained as steely as her will.

"And I want that fucking job," she blasted as she pointed her finger at me.

My wife and I spent the day together. Night soon fell, and Carol followed suit with her quick trip into sleep. Before I left, I gave her my customary three kisses like I had done every night since I'd almost lost her in the hospital.

I'd come back from the Villa and was having a glass of wine when I received a text from Matthew saying, "Hi, Mom."

Along with the text, he'd attached a photo of himself sitting on his boat, which he'd pulled onto the edge of a beautiful river in Montana, snow-capped mountains in the background. Carol loved nothing more than she loved her children. It would be the first thing I would show her in the morning when I returned.

The phone rang and buzzed, and the reliable red numbers on my ceiling informed that it was 4:15 A.M. Even though Carol had only been a resident for ten days, I already recognized the Villa's number. I knew that I should let that call go to voicemail, and wanted to throw that phone into the trash, because I knew that the news couldn't be anything but terrible.

I will never forget the words of that conversation, but they are too painful to share. The essence was that Carol had been found unresponsive again, and that there was no time to send her all the way down to AGH, so they had to send her to our local hospital in Sewickley, which was about four blocks from our home. I fumbled through getting dressed, but I eventually made it out the door.

For reasons still unknown, I left my car behind in favor of taking the route on foot. I also left my trusty brown bag I'd taken with me on every emergency. At 4:30 A.M., not a single store had opened, and I'd beaten everyone to the sidewalks. Just me and the streets of Sewickley. The only stoplight in town sits at the corner of Beaver and Broad Streets. From that corner, no matter which direction you look, you can see so much of my last thirty-seven years with Carol.

To reach the hospital from where I live, you make a left up the hill at Broad Street until you reach the end of it, which is where the Emergency Room is located. As I hoofed along Beaver and neared the left turn, I heard a vehicle coming up Broad, which connects with the highway that takes you to the Villa. When I turned my head right, I saw an ambulance rolling up the road at a casual rate of speed, with no lights and no signs of urgency. I came to a stop under the traffic light, turned my gaze left, and watched the tail lights of the big white truck until it turned toward the ER.

If I made a right at the light and ran as hard as I could for the next quarter mile, I would come upon St. James Church, where I'd spent many Saturday nights at the pew of negotiations. Maybe the doors would be open, and before the paramedics brought her into the hospital, I could get back down on my knees and make a last-minute deal. There was nothing I wouldn't offer. Instead, I closed my eyes and honed in on the panic that had gripped my heart so tightly. There was nothing I could do to change the outcome.

In that kind of quiet, you can hear the click of the stoplight as it changes. I don't know how many rotations I let pass by before I exhaled the sour fear from my body and took my first steps toward the hospital. The distance from that corner to the sliding emergency doors can't be any more than two hundred yards, but it felt like the longest climb I've ever endured. And it wasn't because of the looming sadness—that would come later. When your brain processes the implications of loss, it sends a flood of memories, perhaps to ease the pain. In the span of two and a half blocks, it's like you've lived forty-seven-some-odd years all over again.

CHAPTER TWELVE
for the rest of my years

For you will bend and tell me that you love me, and
I shall sleep in peace until you come to me!
– Frederic Weatherly
lyrics from "Danny Boy"

June 12, 2017

We laid Carol to rest two months ago. Almost every day since then, I've gotten up first thing in the morning to walk the streets of Sewickley. I make that same left at the corner of Beaver and Broad, but now I go past the hospital on my way to the only land beyond it: the Sewickley Cemetery, a beautiful patch of rolling hills with a view of the Ohio River. Though I don't want to think about it, each time I pass the Emergency Room, my mind takes me right back to that terrible April morning.

In the last seven years, I'd been to the ER a dozen times, but that morning in April was the first occasion on which they took me back as soon as I arrived. For a split second, I'd held out hope that Carol hadn't been the one riding in that unhurried ambulance. But I knew the truth of it almost immediately, because they escorted me to a private sitting room with a couch and a dimly lit lamp—a place that looked like the lounge in a funeral parlor. A minute or so later, the gentlest of doctors broke the news to me. My Carol was gone.

I wish I could say that when I entered the room to say my final goodbye, I was comforted by the peace on her face,

---

Photo: Carol hugging George.

171

a sight I hadn't seen in months. But the truth is that I had to fight back the impulse to ask the medical staff to try at least once more to revive her, to let me hear one last one-liner, see one more shoulder shrug, or have one more chance to tell her how much I loved her. Through my tears, I apologized to her for not showing her more love like I should have, and I waited in vain for the answer to my repeated question of how I could live without her. I stayed with Carol for another two hours, holding her hand as tightly as I could. Before I left, I removed her caged-heart necklace. I have worn it every moment since.

On this morning, I awoke only slightly less than crippled by the heavy sadness I'd been feeling since the day Carol died. For weeks beyond her death, I found myself still gripped with the question of whether I'd done enough for her, and whether I'd made her feel the love to the best of my power. Lately, I'd been able to quell those thoughts with the remembrance of so many moments we'd shared during the rejuvenation of our marriage, or when the doubts lingered, by conjuring up the memory of her voice telling me that she loved her Pogey. This day, the trip up the winding road that connects the edge of the village to the main part of the cemetery felt a little easier.

I enjoyed the shady stroll among the bantering birds, and was calmed by the prospect that in a few short minutes, I would be having my morning conversation with my wife. I couldn't wait to tell her that the Penguins had won the Stanley Cup the previous night, something she rooted for but really wouldn't have cared about at all. Rather, she would have adored the fact that the boys and I kept her spirit alive and fed off an unspoken connection to her during the two months of the playoff run. She would be proud and delighted to know that, even in her passing, she had managed to bring the family closer.

Located in the middle of the cemetery, the stone and glass mausoleum where Carol now resides contains a forty-seat chapel and two walls for entombment. I arrived to find it empty, and entered the still room. As always, I took the chair closest to my wife. I'd chosen an interior tomb because I didn't want her to be cold or get wet, or otherwise be exposed to earth. I wanted her to stay warm and comfortable until I met her in there one day. As I gazed into the clean, white slab where her name had been inscribed, I told myself that she would have liked my choice—but then again, she would've agreed with me no matter what.

My name had also been inscribed on that plaque, just beneath hers, and there was no place that I desired to be more than in my own silver urn touching her matching urn. I knew that if that were the case, then I would get to see her bright smile again, hold that little hand once more, and buy her more boxes of popcorn. Instead, we continued to be separated by a cosmic gap that, since her death, had been filled most often with a sadness proportionate to the profound love that had grown between us over the past seven years.

On each wall of the mausoleum there are forty or so vaults, each with a marble footer separating the tombs from the floor. Under my wife's resting place, I had placed an orchid. Though she loved many different flowers, the orchid was always Carol's favorite. For as long as I could remember, she'd brought that notoriously fussy floral wonder into our home and kept it alive with tender attention and care. Even up to the week before she'd taken her final fall, Carol insisted on being helped around the condo to tend to her orchids. She'd shed them of their dried leaves to keep them thriving, and she always knew when to feed them just the right amount of water.

After I updated her about how she'd kept her grieving family close for the past couple months, I fetched some water for her orchid. Then, like every other time I'd come up to visit her, I sat with my thoughts and memories. I'd traded my place of daily reflection from the edge of the bed in my condo for a seat next to where Carol had been enshrined.

I drifted into this session of deliberation by thinking of Carol's quippish personality. I had often wondered whether her provocative ways were a result of the strokes—that somehow the filter in Carol's mind had been stripped away by the brain injury, which left us with a new Carol. But as the years passed, and as I lightened up, I understood it in an entirely different light. The woman with whom I'd spent these past several years was the true Carol. She had just come into her own. The later-in-life wife of mine spoke her piece, got angry with me, disagreed with me, and even teased me. All the while, this once-unassuming woman who would've rather drowned than speak publicly had developed a keen sense of comedic timing, sharpened her wit, and ultimately captured every room.

Even deeper than what made her so entertaining was that she had become clear in what she wanted. That had manifested itself when she pulled at her first tube in the hospital and had carried through until she yanked out her ventilator weeks before her death. In between, she'd offered sharp opinions about the things important to her, from the size of the box of popcorn to her utter distaste for physical therapy.

Through it all, she'd let her inner self shine, particularly the two qualities that had always defined her: selflessness and tenacity. Though she'd defined boundaries like she never had before, she still deferred to others in matters that weren't important to her, and she never lost sight of the sacrifices that many had made on her behalf. She always acknowledged those sacrifices with a "You're too good to me," or a "Thank you for all you do." With a disability to lean on, it would have been so easy for her to have made her remaining days all about herself, or to wallow in self-pity. Not Carol. She'd gone the opposite way, taking great pains to avoid talking about her condition, and even asking me from time to time whether she'd become a burden. More than anything, she just wanted to live life as she always had.

Our decision to remain undeterred in our daily routine had made our new existence quite public. The slow and steady entrances we'd made wherever we went drew attention from people we knew, and from people we didn't know. I often found myself presented with an honest inquiry or compassionate sentiment about how hard taking care of Carol must have been. These questions and comments had always caught me off guard. From day one, I'd seen my efforts as the critical marriage vow, in sickness and in health, as something honorable, and as something I wanted to do even when it became stressful at times. After years of reflection, it all makes sense to me now. Though I didn't know it back when people would say these otherwise well-intended things to me, this had been my evolution into unconditional love.

Though they could've never known the necessary personal journey to a renewed humility I'd taken to get there, they were simply observing the love between us. By giving my life over to my wife's, I'd knocked out my lifelong defenses and opened myself up to the possibility of unconditional love. Each day I worked to make her happy and get the most out of her life, the more fulfilled my own life became. The better I felt about life, the more I wanted to do for Carol, and the deeper into love I fell.

I'll freely admit that at first it felt like I'd been left in a forest with no map. A lifetime of plans, dreams, and visions of retirement vanished in a single month. My kids and most of my extended family had all moved away, and I lived in a disabled-unfriendly home with no idea about how to be a caregiver. As I stood in that dense forest, I had two choices: sit down and wait for help, or choose one of the many paths and follow it to its conclusion. I decided that my path would be to find the good. When I took my first steps, I had no idea that my trail would lead me to a panoramic view of life itself, with the peaks of unconditional love and valleys of humility. But that ends up being the point, after all. I'd discovered the chance to shower my wife with love, to challenge myself at an older age, and to enjoy many more hearty laughs than I'd ever thought possible.

Of course there is also the community of support that one can have in these situations. Words of encouragement from friends, family, and even total strangers served as critical fuel for my self-esteem as a caregiver. The smiles we received in church after communion, the little affirmative nods in the restaurants we frequented, or the slaps on the back from my closest buddies kept the motors running. In those darker moments, when the flames of fatigue and worry threatened to knock me down, it was the generous compliments that helped me through.

Perhaps the biggest moment of encouragement came from one of the most unexpected places. One day, not long before Carol passed, I ran into Sister Mary Eileen, the former principal of the parochial school my kids had attended, and invited her up to dinner.

During dinner, my feelings of disconnection from the church and guilt over my lack of service grew worse in the presence of this dedicated religious woman. As we moved onto coffee, someone took Carol to the bathroom, and I leaned in to my company to share a thought that had been plaguing me for some time. I was nervous, as the good nun still carried an air of authority, even decades after she'd retired.

"I don't feel as though I'm being a very good Catholic."

Now, all my life, I believed that appropriate worship of a higher being required that I attend church, follow its rules, and give financial help when I could. I lived most of my life that way. But I couldn't count how many Sunday Masses Carol and I had missed after she got sick. And even though we'd make it back, there was nothing routine about our attendance.

The tough but big-hearted nun set her eyes on mine. "What's eating at you, dear?"

"You know," I said, "it really bothers me that I haven't

been to church much over these past few years."

Her gaze grew stern. I imagined how her students must have responded to this, because she certainly captured my attention. Her spine went rigid, and with one sturdy finger, she tapped the table and let me have it.

"You don't worry about that!" She searched my eyes for any confusion about her instruction. "You're doing God's work right here." Her expression warmed as she waited until my gaze met hers.

Just like that, she'd lifted a heavy and self-inflicted burden from my mind. At first, I also felt quite honored that this esteemed woman of the cloth would consider me as having done God's work. Up to that point, I hadn't considered taking care of my wife as something entirely Christian by nature, but it did make sense that I'd have been more effective with the message by helping my wife than I'd have been sitting in a pew once a week for fifty minutes or so.

Sister Mary Eileen's kind words made me feel as though I was making a difference in my wife's life. And it's true, no matter what I've done, I've always pursued meaning. I suspect that if I'd gutted out my first job as a teacher, I'd have found that job to be extremely rewarding. When, as a young man, I finally landed with the right sales job, I loved that territory because it had basically zero sales. I got to make the region grow for twenty-two years before moving on to another challenge.

While Carol's new situation was unfolding, I wanted to make a difference in her life in some way. And as the dust settled, it became clear that the number one thing I could do would be to try to maintain her quality of life. With a purpose in mind, I used that goal as a guiding force in almost every decision, from where we lived, to how we ate, to how we traveled, to what we did for entertainment. Undoubtedly, that's how I'd gotten my start, but that's not how we finished.

Like most other lessons I've learned in life, the real

import of the message that night took a long time to settle in. All along, there was something bigger at work, something I didn't recognize until after Carol was gone. Sure, I'd started out trying to make a difference in her life, and I'm not too humble to agree that, all-in-all, I'd made it an enjoyable ride for those final years. But in her quiet and inconspicuous way, Carol had been the one to take me on the journey, and to transform me into a better man in the process. I'd gone far afield from the enlightened young man ready to take on the world and seek true humility following the St. Paul's retreat. In pouring my entire focus onto Carol, I'd found my way back and discovered an internal peace through living the life of a humble man. In the end, we'd taken care of each other, and in the process, our marriage had reached a serenity we'd never imagined.

The orchid sitting below Carol's crypt had come from one of the many that had been delivered to the funeral home after her passing. On the day of her committal service, I'd brought up a beautiful white one with a faint purple pattern and put it in the same place where it sits today. Nearly every day, I've come up to talk to her and take care of her flower. Though I've tried my best, my thumb isn't nearly as green as my wife's. In the two months since Carol's passing, all but one petal has fallen to the floor. Though that last one's still hanging on, it is dried and curled. Time will soon consume the last moments of the flower's life, and this lingering vestige of my connection to my wife will then be gone. I've wanted nothing more than to see that plant survive until I can join Carol, but lately I've realized that I must let it go. And with the plunge of that last petal, I must also lay down my enduring reservations about whether I'd done enough. Otherwise, I'll risk shading the warm light that those seven years shined upon us.

The last words Carol spoke were with a nurse, who'd dropped in to ask how she was doing. Of course, the answer was, "I'm fine." Those two final and defining syllables contained the biggest lesson I learned from my wife. In living by those words, she embraced her circumstances as they were, and therefore understood humility at the deepest level. It took me the better part of my life to get there, but I am forever thankful that she let me catch up.

Will I still worry about it from time to time? With the way my mind works, yes. I'm not perfect, and never will be. But I'll always have the best seven years of my life, a gift of love and forgiveness that only Carol could have provided. It is a truth that will always outweigh my doubt.

I'd finished talking with Carol for the day, so I leaned in to kiss the white, engraved slab three times. "I love you, honey." I pressed my palm to her engraved name. "I'd stay longer, but I have to go to a meeting." I straightened up. "As of today, I'm officially on the Board of Directors for the cemetery. We have a lot of work to do to keep it looking nice up here."

I'll love you for the rest of my years.

On my way to the door, I scanned the room to see if anything needed to be fixed. Then, I turned back to my wife.

"That's all I'm saying."

the end

acknowledgements

In my lifetime, I never dreamed I would write a book. When Chad suggested that we write one together, I figured it would become what we discussed: lessons I learned in caring for Carol as it pertained to the medical system, insurance companies, caregiving, and therapists. When he returned the first chapter to me in his initial manuscript, I was floored. It wasn't a self-help caregiver's guide; it was a love story honoring the legacy of his mother and how she approached life, and ultimately, death. Chad, I can't thank you enough for what you have given me.

To my daughter-in-law Catherine, my gratitude for being an active participant in Carol's life, all your patience in the times I took Chad away from you to write the book, your professional insight as an author, and for lending your fantastic writing skills to the project.

Thank you to both Sean and Matthew for being the wonderful sons that you are. You supported me and my approach to caring for your mother and always were caring and respectful. You helped in so many ways, but none more than always being there in times when I just needed confirmation that I was not alone. Though you were states away, all your phone calls to check in on us, and your flowers for your mom on all occasions were little things that made a big difference. She felt your love.

Kyle Fager was an invaluable editor and friend from the very beginning. Your professional approach and calm demeanor gave secure and steady passage in developing this story. Also, your knowledge producing the physical book has kept us focused on the final product. Chad and I have been very fortunate to have your expertise available to us throughout.

Thank you to Lori Mross, Judith Thomas, and Mary Jane Platt for reading the early drafts and providing helpful insights and suggestions. You confirmed early on that this is a story worthy of a book.

My friend Dennis Ciccone provided helpful knowledge and insight into the world of publishing. It all seemed very daunting, but you provided guidance and counseling through all your experience in the business. You helped us understand the process in an unfamiliar world.

The photos of Carol and me on the front cover, back cover, and the start of chapter twelve were provided by Pam Ingram of Ingram Portrait Design, Sewickley, PA. You are a wonderful and kind person, Pam, as well as a great photographer.

Thank you, Mandy Stoffel, for your professional approach to the excellent design work for the book. When we started, I wanted a picture of Carol and me on the cover, and through your artistry, I was moved to something deeper. Kyle knew that I would like your work, and he was right.

Thank you to all my friends and family for the kind words of support. Your expressions of love and encouragement that I was doing enough for Carol provided me strength to continue the journey. Every little nod of recognition and pat on the back inspired me. My good friend Roger Entress said to me one day, "Take good care of yourself. You are the only one like you in Carol's life." How profound.

Thank you to Carol's cousin Jodi Jaynes and her husband David, who drove from Columbus, Ohio to be there for our family with each serious episode. They are living proof that just extending love and kindness makes a big difference to the worried patient and caregivers.

On my daily walk, I encountered Jodi Renner, who helped me talk through my disappointment that God wasn't present in my life to help ease my burden. Jodi explained that I was looking in the wrong place. As she said, I shouldn't be looking

acknowledgements

for God to help me, but rather, I should understand that God was present in me so that I could help Carol. Simple but enlightening.

Thank you also to my friend Tex Enoch, who visited with us at our home and said upon leaving, "Carol is the little engine that could." Those words spoke volumes.

My cancer is present but very much under control thanks to the good care of Dr. Shifeng Mao and his team at Allegheny General Hospital. He is a warm and caring doctor that takes his responsibilities personally.

And, finally, I have a chance to say I'm sorry to Doc Bartruff. Rest in Peace, Doc. You were a good man.

please visit

BESTSEVENYEARS.COM

for more information about
speaking engagements, book signings,
and to get in touch with the authors.

about the authors

GEORGE SHANNON lays claim to the story behind *The Best Seven Years of My Life*, but he leaves the writing credit to his son Chad. George enjoyed success throughout his career as a sales and marketing executive. He applied those learned skills to navigating the healthcare system as Carol's advocate.

While George was taking care of Carol's health, Carol was quietly showing the way to a humble and loving relationship. The entire experience transformed George's approach to accepting himself as he is, the circumstances as they are, and those around him as they are. Humility and unconditional love were the result.

CHAD PATRICK SHANNON is a freelance writer, story consultant, and attorney. He has written articles, film scripts, comedy sketches, plays, and historical/legacy pieces, but he couldn't have asked for a better subject for his first full-length book, *The Best Seven Years of My Life*.

In addition to his own writing, Chad consults with writers, attorneys, and healthcare organizations to develop story structure and narrative techniques. He has also written and directed three award-winning short films. He lives in Pittsburgh with his wife and creative better half, Catherine, along with their dog, Stella.

LA LOVE

DE LA MÊME AUTEURE

Le Désert des mots, Le Buisson ardent, Amay, Belgique, 1991.

La 2ᵉ Avenue, Éditions du Noroît, 1990.

La Minutie de l'araignée, Éditions de la Nouvelle Barre du jour, 1987.

La Catastrophe, Éditions de la Nouvelle Barre du jour, 1985, en collaboration avec Élise Turcotte.

Les Verbes seuls, Éditions du Noroît, 1985.

Petite Sensation, Éditions de l'Estérel, 1985.

Rouges chaudes suivi de *Journal du Népal*, Éditions du Noroît, 1983.

LOUISE DESJARDINS

LA LOVE

roman

LEMÉAC

Mise en pages : Mégatexte

ISBN 2-7609-3153-6

© Copyright Ottawa 1993 par Leméac Éditeur Inc.
1124, rue Marie-Anne Est, Montréal (Qc) H2J 2B7
Dépôt légal — Bibliothèque nationale du Québec, 2e trimestre 1993

Imprimé au Canada

À Renaud et à Simon

Certains jours, le gaz de la mine envahit le ciel de Noranda et nous fait tousser. Une odeur âcre nous arrive dans le nez et nous donne envie de vomir. À Rouyn, c'est pire, disent les gens de Noranda, toujours pire, parce qu'il y a des hôtels, de la débauche et du péché. Pour s'y rendre, rien de plus facile : il faut longer le lac Osisko, en face de l'hôpital, tourner à gauche et s'engager sur la *Main*. La vie se met à vivre dans le rouge des néons et dans le sous-sol de l'hôtel Radio, au Radio Grill. À Noranda, c'est plate à mort.

Je vais souvent prendre un coke au Radio Grill, un des quatre restaurants chinois de la ville. Ma mère ne veut pas que j'y aille après l'école parce que c'est commun, dit-elle. Des après-midi d'extravagance, quand me prend un goût d'interdit, je m'offre une patate sauce en lorgnant les plats de poulet aux amandes que mangent des adultes un peu soûls, bien assis sur leurs banquettes vert émeraude capitonnées. Ils se dégrisent un peu avant de retourner dans le lounge, juste à côté. Je mets des dix cents dans le sélecteur de table du juke-box et je fais jouer la même chanson, toujours : *Love me Tender.*

Des filles plus âgées que moi parlent haut et fort dans ce restaurant. Sandra Dubreuil, entre autres, raconte en détail ses expériences amoureuses avec un sans-gêne qui m'attire beaucoup. Ses discours sur les French kisses et les 69 m'intéressent bien plus que les sermons du curé et constituent pour moi la représentation ultime de la luxure.

Je cherche à savoir. Ma mère passe son temps à dire que l'amour est la chose la plus importante dans la vie. Pour moi, l'amour, c'est comme l'amour du bon Dieu, l'amour de ses parents, l'amour de son prochain : quelque chose qui se passe au ciel entre les anges. Par contre, quand on regarde des revues d'acteurs et qu'on voit un homme et une femme qui s'embrassent, mes frères et moi, on appelle ça de la love, une chose mystérieuse qui se passe entre un homme et une femme et qui a un rapport avec un des sept péchés capitaux, la luxure, ou avec un des dix commandements, l'œuvre de chair en mariage seulement.

À part quelques films de love et le livre *Toi qui deviens femme déjà,* que ma mère m'a donné pour mon treizième anniversaire, Sandra est ma seule source de renseignements. À dix-sept ans, elle a les cheveux teints au peroxyde, une peau de riche, sans boutons, jamais grasse.

Les filles ont toutes des chums. Moi non. Pas encore. Parfois, en jouant au base-ball avec mes frères, je fais la vache et Ronnie Turner m'entraîne avec lui pour chercher la balle derrière les traques, dans le fossé. Les traques sont juchées sur un long trassel toujours encombré de wagons de minerais qui avancent et qui reculent. J'ai l'impression qu'ils ne vont jamais nulle part. Quand on cherche la balle, Ronnie et moi, on fait semblant de ne pas la trouver et on s'accroupit sur la moque. Là, parmi les quenouilles, on s'embrasse comme dans les films de love. Je trouve ça très agréable. La moque sent la rouille sous nos pieds. La rouille ou les égouts. Mon père, qui sait tout, dit que les déchets de la mine forment cette croûte épaisse. Ronnie met sa langue dans ma bouche, on mélange nos langues. Il m'apprend que «moque» s'écrit *muck*, que c'est un mot anglais. L'autre jour, il m'a révélé que le mot «trassel» s'écrivait *trestle*, et ça m'a bien déçue aussi. Chaque fois que j'apprends qu'un mot s'écrit d'une façon différente de celle que j'avais imaginée, c'est comme s'il m'échappait et ne m'appartenait plus. Par exemple, depuis que je suis toute petite, je pense que les ponts de métal sur lesquels passent les trains s'appellent des «trassels» et je croyais dur comme fer que ce mot s'épelait T-R-A-S-S-E-L. Maintenant, je ne sais plus comment dire ça en français. Il doit pourtant y avoir un mot. Personne ne le connaît. Même pas mon père, qui est pourtant un parfait bilingue.

Quand Ronnie me parle doucement et qu'il m'embrasse, j'ai l'impression d'être une vraie fille. Mais je n'ose pas rester trop longtemps cachée dans les quenouilles derrière les traques. J'ai peur que mes frères ne s'en aperçoivent. Ils me surveillent tout le temps, surtout Coco et Bernard, au cas où je ferais une bêtise. Eux, ils font beaucoup de mauvais coups, et je suis toujours là quand ils les font. Je dis tout à ma mère. C'est elle qui décide si, de son côté, elle va tout raconter à mon père. Elle mesure toujours la portée de ses paroles, ma mère. Si mon père a trop mal à la tête, elle ne dit rien. S'il arrive de bonne humeur, alors elle peut se permettre de lui annoncer tranquillement que Bernard a cassé une vitre ou que Coco a perdu vingt dollars en allant faire des commissions. Ils font tellement de bêtises, mes deux grands frères, qu'elle a l'embarras du choix quand mon père arrive. Heureusement, elle ne raconte pas tout. Elle dit qu'il faut user de diplomatie, qu'on doit s'arranger pour que mon père ne soit pas trop trop fâché. D'une manière ou d'une autre, mon père est presque toujours soucieux. Il a des gros plis creusés entre ses sourcils derrière ses lunettes. Il a son mal de tête : ma mère dit qu'il travaille trop fort, qu'on est trop tannants, qu'il digère mal. J'ai très peur de lui, et mes frères aussi. Ma mère est la seule à ne pas avoir peur de lui. Du moins, elle fait comme si elle n'avait pas peur. Elle seule sait lui parler, le soir, dans la chambre à coucher. On les entend chuchoter, puis après, plus rien.

Danielle Dusseault trouve que mon père est très drôle, qu'il ressemble à Cary Grant. Mais ce qu'elle ignore, c'est qu'il est drôle seulement quand il y a de la visite. Autrement, entre nous, il a ses yeux de mal de tête. Il ne se gêne pas pour donner des volées à mes frères (une chance que moi, il ne me touche pas), et ma mère lui donne entièrement raison : elle ne dit rien ou bien, quand tout est fini et que le silence s'écroule sur notre peine, elle ramène les choses à l'ordre en disant qu'ils la méritent, la volée, que ce sont des garçons, qu'il faut les dompter. Et mon père va lire son journal, tout apaisé. Je reste dans ma chambre le plus longtemps possible. Si mon père me frappait, j'en mourrais. Je fais tout pour qu'il m'oublie. Je me retiens parfois de respirer.

12

Mes frères sont plus braves que moi parce que même s'ils savent qu'ils auront la volée, ils ne se gênent pas pour faire des mauvais coups. Mais ils s'arrangent pour rester le moins possible dans la maison et pour ne rentrer qu'à l'heure des repas.

À table, on s'assoit toujours à la même place : mon père, à un bout, ma mère, à l'autre bout, Jacques (dit Coco) et Bernard, les deux plus vieux, d'un côté, Lucien et moi de l'autre. Lucien est juste un peu plus jeune que moi et c'est mon frère préféré. Il est le seul à ne pas me traiter de femelle, à ne pas menacer de me battre. Maurice, le bébé, est dans sa chaise haute, près de ma mère, et il s'endort régulièrement dans son bol de soupe. On mange dans une véritable cacophonie et on s'arrange pour sortir de table au plus vite. Parfois mon père est en forme et il crie : « Silence ! », puis il se met à réciter des poèmes en anglais, qu'il a appris au collège de Sudbury. On dirait que ces poèmes-là sont gravés dans le granit de sa mémoire. Les mots *sweet* et *love* reviennent souvent et on voit bien qu'il s'agit de grandes amours. Ma mère, qui ne sait pas l'anglais, sourit et soupire un peu en ramassant la vaisselle. Il raconte aussi des histoires de bois, interminables et belles, avec des ours, des loups, des lacs gelés. Il réussit à vaincre tous les dangers, et je l'admire un instant. On écoute poliment. Puis quelqu'un (habituellement Coco) renverse un verre de lait ; mon père revient alors dans son état naturel et fronce les sourcils en criant « maudit bâtard de viarge ». Ma mère s'arrange pour tout ramasser à la vitesse de l'éclair, et un silence de plomb nous fige tous.

Mes frères me traitent de « plus grande bavasseuse de la terre ». Ils voudraient bien me malmener davantage, mais ils n'osent pas parce que je raconte toujours tout. C'est mon arme contre Coco et Bernard, et ils me détestent. Ça tombe bien, je les déteste moi aussi. J'aime mieux mes deux petits frères, Lucien et Maurice. Mon père, spécialiste des surnoms, les appelle Lulu et Momo. Quand son mal de tête le délaisse un peu, il fait des blagues qu'il trouve très drôles. Une de celles-là, c'est mon surnom : la Suffragette. Je ne vois pas ce qu'il y a de comique là-dedans, mais la visite rit beaucoup de mon surnom. Surtout ma tante Alphonsine.

Quand Ronnie m'embrasse, j'ai très peur parce que je sais que c'est défendu. Au fond, j'ai peur d'être enceinte. Je pense que «frencher» veut dire «faire l'amour» et que les bébés viennent quand on les veut, comme ça, par un acte de volonté pure et simple, en s'embrassant. Cette méthode de fertilisation concorde parfaitement avec la théorie de l'opération du Saint-Esprit.

Depuis quelque temps, j'ai l'œil sur Eddy Goldstein. Sandra passe son temps à dire qu'il est sexy parce qu'il joue de la guitare. Du western et du rock'n'roll. Elle dit que, quand il gratte les cordes de sa guitare, c'est comme s'il la chatouillait. Je la trouve un peu folle, mais ses histoires me font rêver. Des doigts qui inventent des airs et qui caressent... J'aime la musique, surtout le rock'n'roll. J'apprends le piano, mais je ne joue que des sonates, des fugues et des menuets. De la musique de l'ancien temps. Du

Clementi, du Czerny. Ma mère aime le classique, le vrai. Du Bach, du Rachmaninov. Mon père aime *Mantovani and His Orchestra, La Méditation de Thaïs*, les vraies belles chansons d'amour et le western western. Quand je fais mes gammes, ça lui donne mal à la tête et il crie : « Mais c'est-tu plate c'te musique-là. » Ma mère vient me demander gentiment d'arrêter, ce qui fait drôlement mon affaire.

J'imagine qu'Eddy sera mon premier vrai chum. Il vient lui aussi au Radio Grill avec ses amis du High School, et j'ai remarqué qu'il me reluque. Je veux lui téléphoner et j'ai fini par obtenir son numéro par Danielle Dusseault, qui a des amis anglais. Je l'ai transcrit sur un bout de papier que je triture dans le fond de ma poche et c'est comme si je touchais un peu Eddy du bout des doigts.

Mes parents sont partis à la messe de cinq heures avec Bernard et Lulu. Je garde Momo et, pendant qu'il dort, je décide d'appeler Eddy finalement. Sa mère répond, mais je suis trop timide pour lui parler en anglais. Je m'étais pourtant exercée à poser la question : « *May I speak to Eddy, please ?* » Au début, j'avais pensé dire : « *Can I speak to Eddy ?* » puis, après avoir vérifié dans mon livre d'anglais, j'ai opté pour le *May I*, plus psychologique, moins physique. Je m'essaie une deuxième fois, mais je dois raccrocher avant d'ouvrir la bouche : Coco, que j'avais complètement oublié, a fait irruption dans la cuisine. Il dit : « Ah ! Ah !, c'est comme ça que je te pogne ! » puis il file dehors sans que j'aie le temps de lui crier des bêtises par la tête. Au troisième essai, je peux enfin parler à Eddy, car c'est lui qui répond. Je sais qu'il parle français, je l'ai entendu au Radio Grill. Je dis d'une traite :

«Veux-tu venir danser au Teen Beat Club avec moi vendredi soir?»

— Qui parle?

— Claude Éthier.

— Claude, c'est pas une nom de fille ça.

— Tu sais... je vais au Radio Grill, prendre un coke après l'école.

— Ah oui! Les filles français, répond-il en tournant son *r* dans la bouche d'une manière très anglaise.

— Oui!

— Hum... tu es comment?

— J'ai les cheveux blonds.

— Avec des lunettes?

— Oui, mais j'les mets pas pour sortir.

— Ça fait rien, c'est drôle les lunettes. J'en ai moi aussi.

Je n'en peux plus, mes tempes battent très fort. Ouf! Je raccroche. Quinze minutes plus tard, je me dis qu'Eddy n'a ni mon numéro de téléphone ni mon adresse et qu'au fond il ne m'a rien promis. Je prends mon courage à deux mains et je le rappelle pour savoir s'il veut m'accompagner.

«Oui!» dit-il, en me demandant mon adresse cette fois.

— 122, 2e avenue.

— À quelle heure?

— Sept heures.

Tout est consommé. Je me sens rouge et chaude comme après avoir couru longtemps. Il faut que je garde le secret. Les filles n'appellent pas les garçons. C'est laid, une fille qui appelle un garçon. Très laid. C'est parce que j'ai des lunettes que je suis obligée d'appeler un garçon. Quand mes parents reviennent de la messe, rien ne paraît, le souper est prêt, et ma mère me félicite parce que j'ai bien disposé les sandwiches dans une grande assiette, après en avoir enlevé toutes les croûtes.

Pendant la semaine, je n'arrête pas de penser à Eddy et je me demande s'il m'oubliera. Je le vois au Radio Grill et il me fait un petit sourire, sans plus. Personne ne peut s'apercevoir qu'on sortira ensemble vendredi soir, et j'en doute moi-même jusqu'au jeudi soir après l'école : il me fait un grand clin d'œil en passant devant notre table, et Sandra ne manque pas de passer la remarque : «Ouais, Claude Éthier, on dirait qu'Eddy Goldstein a un kick sur toi!» Je rougis jusqu'aux oreilles et je pars en vitesse, assurée qu'Eddy tiendra sa promesse. Tu peux toujours niaiser, Sandra Dubreuil, tu vas avoir la surprise de ta vie.

C'est vendredi soir, je n'ai pas écouté un mot de ce que la sœur a enseigné aujourd'hui. J'ai passé la journée dans un rêve ouatiné. Eddy vient me chercher pour m'emmener danser à la salle des Canadian Corps. Je me suis habillée rock'n'roll : blouse transparente, jupe à crinoline, *bucked shoes*. Prête à tous les frissons. Je surveille à la fenêtre et dès que je le vois au coin de la 2ᵉ avenue, je crie bonsoir à ma mère.

Elle n'a rien vu. Je sors en coup de vent et la porte se referme sur une vague fin de phrase :

— ... pas plus tard que onze heures...

C'est vrai, tout se passe exactement dans mon rêve jusque-là. Mais je n'avais pas prévu qu'Eddy cacherait l'auto de son frère en bas de la côte. Une belle Studebaker rouge décapotable. Il est très fier de son coup. Je ne sais pas quoi faire. Ma mère me tuera si elle sait que je monte dans une auto avec un garçon, et ma paire de grands frères risque de venir au Teen Beat Club, comme tous les vendredis soirs. Ils vont me dénoncer s'ils me voient en auto. Je ne peux pas prendre un tel risque.

— Viens... on va y aller à pied. Je bégaye un peu.

— Pourquoi, mon char est pas assez belle ?

— Non, c'est pas ça, mais ma mère veut pas que j'aille en auto avec un gars. A veut vraiment pas.

— Ton mère le saura pas.

— Mes frères vont y dire, voyons.

Eddy fait claquer toutes les portes de son auto. Il prend son temps. Il vérifie tout. Il n'a pas l'air très content. Je l'attends sur le trottoir et j'ai peur qu'il soit fâché et qu'il me laisse tomber. Mais non, il me prend machinalement par la main, et on marche tranquillement sur la rue Murdoch jusqu'à la 7e rue. Comme si on sortait steady depuis longtemps. En passant devant le magasin Buckovetsky, je me retourne pour regarder la vitrine parce que ma tante Alphonsine descend les grands escaliers de l'église en face. Je ne veux pas qu'elle me voie. Des huit sœurs de ma mère, c'est la plus grande téléphoneuse.

On fait la file pour entrer dans la salle des Canadian Corps. Toute la gang du Radio Grill est là. Sandra Dubreuil est toute seule, stag, Danielle Dusseault est avec son chum steady André Savard, Nicole Gauthier avec Gerry Lalonde et Yvonne Théroux avec Élie Bucovetsky. On va s'asseoir à leur table et tout le monde me regarde comme si j'étais une étrangère. Revenez-en! Il faut dire que j'ai moi-même la sensation d'avoir accompli un exploit, un vrai.

L'alcool est strictement interdit au Teen Beat, c'est pourquoi ma mère me permet d'y venir. On boit du coke, et Eddy nous verse du rhum dans un verre sous la table. Il a un petit flasque dans un sac de papier brun camouflé sous un jacket des Copper Kings. Son grand frère, celui qui lui prête la Studebaker, joue pour les Copper Kings, notre équipe locale de hockey. Les garçons parlent musique : rock'n'roll, rock'n'roll. André Savard joue parfois avec Eddy dans son sous-sol et ils se cherchent un bassiste pour former un groupe. Bernard joue du piano à l'oreille et voudrait bien se joindre à eux, mais il n'ose pas. Tout le monde pense que jouer du piano, pour un garçon, ça fait tapette.

Mes grands frères s'assoient toujours à une table assez éloignée de la mienne pour pouvoir me surveiller sans que ça paraisse. Ils font comme s'ils ne me connaissaient pas. Ils veulent avoir quelque chose à raconter, qui ferait fâcher mon père et mettrait beaucoup d'huile sur le feu, qui ferait éclater peut-être son mal de tête.

Mais ce soir je suis dans les bras d'Eddy, et rien ne peut m'arriver. Mon père et ma mère, je les ai loin, comme dirait Bernard. Le slow est plus chaud que chaud, et Eddy fait voyager ses mains autour de mes hanches et de mes épaules. On s'embrasse avec maladresse dans les petites lumières bleues, rouges et jaunes. Eddy m'offre un coke entre les danses et il n'oublie pas les sips de rhum. *You Are My Destiny* résonne dans la salle comme une élégie brumeuse. J'aime aimer en anglais, comme dans les films. *Love me Tender*, la langue d'Elvis me colle au corps.

Les filles n'arrêtent pas de me regarder. Toutes les autres filles du couvent vont savoir que j'ai un chum lundi matin. Mes frères le savent. Ma mère va le savoir. Mon père aussi. Le monde entier va le savoir. Ça me donne le vertige, et je me laisse aller à *djiver* avec Eddy. Il est très patient avec moi parce que je perds souvent le rythme. « Laisse-toi mou, dit-il, suis-moi. » Parfois Sandra vient s'interposer en me disant : « J'te vole ton chum une minute si ça te fait rien. »

Sandra Dubreuil s'accroche à Eddy comme un morceau de puzzle Jigsaw. La suffragette en moi a le goût de faire une scène, elle se retient, pour ne pas déplaire à Eddy. Danielle et André sont toujours assis dans un coin, à necker. Ça fait longtemps qu'Élie et Yvonne sont agglutinés. Nicole Gauthier est partie dehors avec Gerry, comme tous les vendredis soirs. On ne les a presque jamais vus danser, ces deux-là. Nicole se vante de faire l'amour souvent. Elle est très avancée pour son âge. Je tète mon coke en regardant les autres danser et j'ai peur de me mettre à pleurer d'une seconde à l'autre. Je garde mon calme en apparence, mais mon cœur veut éclater. Je devrais m'en aller en courant, mais je reste rivée à mon coke. Finalement, Eddy revient me chercher pour le dernier slow. Toutes les lumières s'allument, c'est le temps de s'en aller. Sandra colle encore un peu, mais elle finit par comprendre et décide de partir avec Élie et Yvonne.

Eddy me reconduit jusqu'à son auto et il m'invite à monter. Je suis sûre qu'il veut faire un peu de necking. Ça me tente, mais je me sauve en courant parce que j'ai peur d'être en retard. Quand je rentre chez moi, ma mère m'attend dans la cuisine, comme toujours, mais cette fois-ci elle me dit simplement bonsoir parce que je suis à l'heure. Je me glisse mouillée dans mon divan-lit, à cause des caresses d'Eddy. Je suis exténuée, mais follement excitée. Je ne veux pas que ma mère sache que j'ai dansé avec Eddy. Elle le saura, à cause de mes bavasseux de frères. En attendant, j'aime croire qu'elle ne le sait pas, qu'elle ignore tout de ma vie et même de mon existence.

Eddy vient parfois parler avec moi devant la porte après souper. Il n'entre jamais dans la maison. Ma mère voudrait bien qu'il vienne jaser avec elle au salon, mais je refuse, parce qu'on ne pourrait plus rien se dire. Dans l'esprit de ma mère, Eddy a deux défauts : il est juif et il a une auto. Moi, ces deux choses-là me séduisent beaucoup. Mais ce qui m'attire encore davantage, c'est son petit côté bum de grande famille.

Le père d'Eddy, monsieur Goldstein, est propriétaire d'un grand magasin de musique où ma mère a acheté son piano.

«C'est-tu de valeur qu'y soit juif, dit ma mère, c'est pourtant un grand musicien, c't'homme-là. J'ai quand même fait une bonne bargain.»

La mère d'Eddy est une juive d'origine russe, mais elle ne va pas à la synagogue. Ma mère dit, comme le curé, que seuls les vrais catholiques vont au ciel : «Hors de l'Église, point de salut.» Quand je vais chez Eddy écouter la band dans son sous-sol, sa mère me lance un petit *Hello* sec. Elle a un léger accent russe, mais pour le remarquer il faut savoir qu'elle n'est pas une Anglaise pure laine. Elle a l'air de n'importe quelle mère parce qu'elle porte un tablier et qu'elle a les yeux sévères. Parfois on l'entend rouspéter dans la cuisine et on ne comprend pas ce qu'elle dit. Alors, les gars jouent un peu moins fort.

Eddy a une qualité : il a du discernement. Il ne téléphone jamais à la maison, car il sait que mes frères se moqueraient de moi. Coco surtout, qui ne respecte absolument rien. L'autre jour, à table, il a demandé à Bernard de faire une phrase avec Eddy en me regardant dans les yeux. «Viens m'*aider* à faire la vaisselle», a-t-il dit en imitant ma voix. Ah! Ah! Ah! Tu te penses bien drôle, Coco Éthier! Tout le monde a ri parce que j'ai rougi jusqu'au cœur. J'aurais pu le tuer. Je suis partie en pleurant dans ma chambre. Un jour, je vais tous les tuer. En attendant, je pense à Eddy, et ça m'aide à vivre.

Heureusement qu'il y a le Radio Grill. Eddy et moi, on s'y installe avec les autres pour manger une patate sauce et boire notre coke. Sandra parle moins fort, par respect ou peut-être par jalousie, et je l'ai vue mettre son dix cents dans le sélecteur de table du juke-box avant que les paroles moelleuses de *Are You*

Lonesome Tonight parviennent à nos oreilles. Je suis devenue la vedette de la classe, cette fois, non pas parce que j'ai des bonnes notes, mais parce que je suis une petite morveuse à lunettes qui a décroché le mâle le plus exotique en ville. L'orgueil me sort par les pores. J'en oublie mes lunettes.

Je pense tout le temps à Eddy. En faisant des équations, en traduisant Cicéron, en marchant dans l'odeur moite de la neige collante, en piochant sur mon Czerny. J'apprends un concerto de Mozart avec Danielle Dusseault. On compte les demi-pauses, les doubles croches et les soupirs. À la fin des pratiques, on arrête au Radio Grill et on se parle de nos chums. Eddy par-ci, Eddy par-là. Danielle me parle d'André, mais sans enthousiasme; c'est vrai qu'il n'est pas nouveau dans sa vie. Nicole Gauthier est toujours là avec son Gerry et elle ne me parle presque plus. Je suis devenue son égale et ses séances de necking ne m'impressionnent plus. Finie la poudre aux yeux.

Eddy Goldstein tamise toutes les heures. Même mon père me fait moins peur pour la simple raison que je ne regarde plus ses sourcils froncés. Passer l'aspirateur et laver la vaisselle sont devenus des oasis de rêverie. Ma mère me vante au téléphone : Claude est serviable ces jours-ci, une soie, Claude rentre à l'heure, Claude par-ci, Claude par-là... À la maison, seuls Coco et Bernard savent que je me tiens au Radio Grill après l'école. Ils gardent ce secret pour faire du chantage au cas où je les dénoncerais. De mon côté, je dois dire que le nombre de cigarettes qu'ils fument en cachette en attendant l'autobus ne m'intéresse même plus. Entre mes frères et moi, c'est la trêve.

Sandra décide d'organiser un party au chalet de ses parents samedi prochain, le premier samedi du mois de juin. Génial. Pour la première fois, j'ai le droit d'être invitée à un party des filles du couvent, parce que j'ai comme chum le plus beau six-pieds des deux villes.

Ma mère ne doit pas savoir que ce party aura lieu dans un chalet. Un chalet, c'est loin dans le bois et, dans le bois, on peut se cacher pour s'embrasser en pleine liberté. On ne peut cerner la forêt. Dans la forêt, tout peut arriver, le soir surtout. Pourtant mon père dit toujours que le bois est moins dangereux que la ville: «Les animaux sont pas méchants si on les dérange pas.» Mais ça ne convainc pas ma mère. Moi non plus.

Je fais des exercices de mensonge. Je me ferme les yeux et je me dis en me concentrant: «Je vais à un party chez Nicole Gauthier. En ville.» Je répète cette phrase jusqu'au moment où je me sens capable de la sortir tout d'une traite, comme «Rien ne sert de courir, il faut partir à point» ou bien «Qui trop embrasse mal étreint» et toutes ces phrases usées que ma mère répète à tout bout de champ. Elles sont gravées dans mon cerveau et je pense que je me les rappellerais même si j'étais à moitié morte et para-lysée. La force de ma mère, c'est qu'elle peut citer des phrases célèbres et incontestables de ce genre. Quand elle fait répéter les leçons à Coco, par exem-ple, elle dit toujours: «Ce qui se conçoit bien s'énonce clairement et les mots pour le dire arrivent aisément.» Un jour, Lulu et moi, on a retrouvé toutes ses maximes dans les pages roses du dictionnaire Larousse. Avec des phrases en latin en plus, les mêmes que mon père nous déclame et auxquelles on ajoute *amen,* pas trop fort, pour qu'il ne nous comprenne pas : *Tempus fugit. Carpe diem. Alea jacta est.*

Je suis penchée sur le clavier du piano et je lave une à une les touches d'ivoire un peu jauni. J'annonce à ma mère en rougissant jusqu'à la racine des cheveux que je vais à un party chez Nicole Gauthier. En ville.

— Qu'est-ce que tu dis, Claude ?

— Chus-t-invitée à un party samedi prochain, c't en ville.

— Chez qui ?

— Chez Sandra Dubreuil... Non, chez Nicole Gauthier.

— Chez le juge Gauthier ? Ton père ira t' chercher à minuit.

— Non, non, laisse faire, son père a dit qu'y viendrait tout' nous reconduire après.

— Bon, comme tu veux.

Je l'ai échappé belle. Je ne dis plus rien. Ma mère ne m'a rien demandé au fond, elle ne m'a surtout pas demandé avec qui j'y allais. C'est bien ainsi, je m'arrangerai avec Eddy pour qu'il vienne me chercher à six heures au coin de la 2e avenue et de la Murdoch. Je lui demanderai de m'attendre dans l'auto.

Je ne pense qu'à ça : j'irai dans le bois ce soir-là, derrière le chalet de Sandra Dubreuil. Eddy m'embrassera sous les épinettes, je lui résisterai à peine. Je ferai tout jusqu'au bout, comme Nicole Gauthier avec Gerry. J'irai jusqu'où il voudra, comme ma grand-mère avec mon grand-père le jour de ses noces. Elle répète à qui veut l'entendre, ma grand-mère, que sa mère l'avait ainsi informée des choses de la vie avant de se marier : « Tu feras ce que ton mari te dira de faire. » Mais j'ai peur d'aller jusqu'au bout. Je ne sais pas où ça bascule, où se trouve le péché qui fait qu'on tombe enceinte. J'ai peur de tomber enceinte. J'ai encore plus peur d'être maladroite, de ne pas savoir comment faire. Tout faire et ne rien faire. Comment savoir comment ?

Je fais des recherches dans le dictionnaire. *Enceinte. Coït. Organes génitaux. Soixante-neuf.* Je ne suis pas plus avancée. Je veux en parler à Sandra, mais j'ai peur d'avoir l'air niaiseuse. J'ai beau chercher une façon d'aborder le sujet, je n'en trouve pas. Inutile d'en parler à Danielle Dusseault, elle est aussi ignorante que moi. Je ne peux rien dire à ma mère parce que j'aurais l'impression d'aller avouer une grande faute à la confesse. Ma mère ne pense pas que je pense. Moi je ne pense pas qu'elle puisse même embrasser mon père autrement que sur la joue quand elle le remercie de laver la vaisselle. C'est rare que ça arrive, mais des fois, le dimanche soir, quand il a fait une bonne sieste l'après-midi, il dit : « Laisse faire, Honey, va jouer du piano, j'vas la laver, la vaisselle. » Et pendant qu'elle joue *Plaisir d'amour*, il chante à tue-tête. Mais il n'y a aucun mystère là-dedans, c'est l'amour pur et simple des parents qui ont des enfants. Ça n'a rien à voir avec la love. Non, vraiment pas.

Tous les jours, je fais une répétition générale du party. Je m'enferme dans ma chambre avec ma crinoline, mes bas de nylon, ma gaine-culotte, mon soutien-gorge, mon petit foulard à pois, ma robe rose, ample, mes souliers à talons hauts. J'essaie de me faire une queue de cheval : mes cheveux trop fins n'arrivent pas à tenir dans l'élastique. Je mets plein de bobby pins.

Ma mère coud tous mes vêtements, sauf mes jeans. « C'est trop compliqué, les braguettes », dit-elle. Pour coudre, elle n'achète pas de tissu, elle se sert de vieilles robes que ma tante Alphonsine lui donne. Elle dit qu'elle coud dans « du vieux » et elle en est très fière. Après avoir décousu minutieusement les robes, elle replace le tissu dans le droit fil, le taille selon un patron Vogue très difficile, faufile et coud une nouvelle robe. À la fin, elle la garnit de dentelle pour que ça fasse « robe achetée ». Mon rêve, c'est d'avoir une robe toute faite qu'on choisit dans un magasin, pareille à celles des autres. Je porte toujours des jeans et je laisse mes robes moisir dans la garde-robe au grand dam de ma mère qui voudrait que j'aie l'air d'une vraie demoiselle. Pourtant, elle m'a donné un nom plutôt garçon, Claude, et je le déteste tout autant que les robes faites à la maison. Noyée dans les garçons comme ça, j'ai l'impression de ne pas être normale, d'être un peu infirme : chaque fois que je fais une chose de fille comme repasser une robe, mettre du rouge à lèvres ou des souliers à talons hauts, je me fais traiter de femelle par Coco. Il en profite pour retrousser sa manche, durcir ses biceps, et il dit : « Touche à mes *muscles*, ça c'est de l'homme. » Il prononce *mussels*, en anglais, et tout le monde rit. C'est vraiment ridicule d'être une fille.

Dans ma classe, toutes les filles ont les cheveux bien peignés, jamais gras, les ongles longs, pas rongés, les mains blanches, pas tachées. Tout cela tient du mystère, un mystère que j'associe à la richesse. Ces filles, même myopes, arrivent à ne pas porter leurs lunettes. Comment font-elles pour se sentir à l'aise et ne rien voir? Je me sens bien laide avec mes lunettes, mais je tiens à tout voir. Tout, dans les moindres détails, et que rien ne m'échappe! Ma mère soupire souvent en disant: «Pauvre p'tite, toute défigurée avec tes lunettes. Pis, arrête de te manger les ongles, c'est pas beau, c't un signe de jalousie. Regarde, Danielle Dusseault, elle, a se mange pas les ongles.»

Danielle Dusseault, c'est ma grande amie. Elle joue du piano, et son père est médecin. Ma mère l'aime beaucoup, elle la trouve très jolie et ne se prive pas pour s'extasier devant ses cheveux ondulés, ses belles manières et ses grands yeux bleus. Quand on revient ensemble de l'école, Danielle me dit à peu près tout ce qu'elle fait avec André Savard dans son sous-sol quand ses parents sont au salon à regarder la télévision. Danielle est la seule qui a la télévision chez elle, un gros appareil combiné avec un tourne-disque et un radio. Je l'envie beaucoup d'avoir la télévision, mais je ne l'envie pas du tout d'être amoureuse d'André parce qu'il n'est pas mon genre. Il est plutôt freluquet et bas sur pattes. Et surtout, il a toujours l'air de tout savoir.

Après l'école, je m'arrête parfois chez Danielle, qui habite une vraie maison à deux étages sur le chemin Trémoy, une rue très sélect avec des grands arbres et des grosses maisons en bordure du lac Osisko. Chaque fois que j'entre chez elle, j'ai un pincement de cœur en voyant comme c'est beau, grand et propre. Les divans fleuris du salon creusent profondément quand on s'y assoit et, dans la grande fenêtre à carreaux, on a une vue magnifique sur le lac. Chez nous, on ne voit pas le lac, on est plutôt collés sur les cheminées de la mine et le trassel. Chez Danielle, il y a même un foyer véritable, et le tapis dans les escaliers est si épais qu'il absorbe le bruit des pas. Les chambres à coucher sont toutes meublées en vraies chambres à coucher, avec des couvre-lits assortis aux rideaux et des commodes toutes pareilles. Quand on arrive dans la maison, Danielle ouvre le frigidaire et nous sert un jus de raisin Welch véritable qu'elle mélange avec du ginger ale. Après, on change l'eau de son poisson et ensuite je rentre souper en rêvant d'habiter un jour dans une grande maison qui donne sur un lac, avec un mari très riche, exactement comme dans les photo-romans que je lis chez ma tante Alphonsine.

Danielle veut toujours être invitée chez moi. Pourtant notre maison est très ordinaire et très petite, c'est à peine si elle peut nous contenir tous. Je veux toujours aller chez les autres. Mais peut-être que Danielle se sent admirée par ma mère. Peut-être qu'elle a un œil sur Coco ou sur Bernard. Ou peut-être qu'elle aime les repas de famille mouvementés. Elle trouve que ma mère fait bien la cuisine, elle n'arrête pas de dire : «C'est bon, madame Éthier, votre pâté chinois, votre tarte au sucre, votre bouilli aux légumes.» Nous autres, on la regarde et on la trouve un peu niaiseuse, parce que du pâté chinois, de la tarte au sucre et du bouilli aux légumes, on en mange souvent. Mais on n'a jamais de jus de raisin Welch véritable et encore moins du ginger ale. Du lait, c'est tout. C'est bon pour la santé, la vitamine D. C'est plate, les vitamines.

Tout baigne dans l'huile aujourd'hui, jour J du party au chalet de Sandra. Ce matin, j'ai fait le ménage dans une envolée lyrique; la poussière s'évanouissait, docile, sous le balai de l'aspirateur. Je chante *Love me tender, love me true, never let me go.* Rien ne m'atteint plus, ni les quolibets de Coco, ni le front sourcilleux de mon père, même pas les conversations interminables de ma mère au téléphone avec ma tante Alphonsine. Je suis blindée de bonheur.

Il est trois heures de l'après-midi, et je monopolise la salle de bains depuis une bonne demi-heure. On frappe à la porte, je crie que je suis à la toilette. Mais au bout d'un certain temps, quand la pression devient trop forte, je range en vitesse mon rouge à lèvres, mon mascara et mon spray net. En me penchant très vite, je m'aperçois que je commence à être menstruée. Je prends trois Midol coup sur coup.

C'est le mois de juin et pourtant, ce matin, il y avait un petit tapis de neige sur la galerie. On dit «galerie» chez nous. Ma tante Laura de Montréal a importé le mot «balcon», mais pour moi, un balcon, c'est une petite galerie de Montréal sur laquelle les gens passent l'été à se bercer. La grosse voisine, madame Turner, dit «perron», et ma mère trouve cela très vulgaire, à cause de Dominique Michel, qui chante *En veillant su'l' perron* avec une voix western. J'ai fait quelques pas de danse sur la galerie et mes traces avaient l'air des pistes un peu folles d'un animal traqué.

Il fait très froid. Je ne pourrai pas porter ma belle robe neuve usagée rose fille. Même s'il avait fait chaud, je ne l'aurais pas portée, à cause des maringouins qui raffolent des dessous de crinoline. Et puis, les autres filles ne portent pas de robes. Elles n'ont pas besoin de ça pour se distinguer des garçons.

J'enfile donc mes jeans et j'emprunte à mon père, sans qu'il le sache, une chemise blanche, très empesée, que je froisse suffisamment pour qu'elle fasse blousante. Les sourcils bien noirs, les lèvres bien rouges, j'ai enfin réussi à faire tenir ma queue de cheval grâce à de nombreuses bobby pins et beaucoup de wave set. Je chausse mes *bucked shoes* blanc et bleu et je me déclare prête à l'attaque.

Quand j'arrive, triomphante, à la cuisine, ma mère me dit :

— Comment, t'es pas encore habillée ? Quand même, tu vas pas porter des salopettes pour aller chez le juge Gauthier.

Ma tête se met à tourner. Je ne peux plus contrôler ni ma langue ni mon cœur. Je bafouille :

— M'man, arrêtez d'appeler ça des salopettes, c'est des jeans. Pis Nicole Gauthier, c'est elle qui nous a dit de nous habiller en jeans. Toutes les filles sont en jeans. Personne porte pus ça, des robes.

— Mon Dieu Seigneur, dépêche-toi de partir avant que ton père te voie.

J'ai peur qu'il surgisse dans la cuisine, que sa colère éclate, à cause de sa chemise qu'il reconnaîtrait, de mes lèvres Marilyn Monroe, et je m'efface. Au moment où je tourne le coin de la Murdoch, je vois Coco et Bernard qui traînent Lucien en revenant du terrain de base-ball. Je pense que je devrais rebrousser chemin, mais je me ravise et je me mets à courir. Eddy est là qui m'attend près de la Studebaker de son frère. J'arrive à bout de souffle en criant : « On part ! »

Eddy comprend très vite quand il voit mes trois frères au bout de la rue. On saute dans l'auto. Je me colle tout au fond de la banquette, juste à temps pour éviter mes frères, puis l'auto démarre en trombe vers le lac Fortune.

Le ciel est bas. On dirait qu'il va neiger de nouveau. Eddy me serre la main de temps en temps. La route de gravier me donne un peu mal au cœur, surtout en descendant les côtes. J'ai parfois des petites crampes, mais j'essaie de ne pas y penser. Je me concentre pour que le mal ne m'atteigne pas, et ça marche. On se dit des banalités : « Y fait pas mal froid pour le mois de juin. À quelle heure que ta mère veut que tu reviennes ? » J'ai peur d'avoir l'air niaiseuse. Mais Eddy me met vite à l'aise, puis soudain on rit, pour rien, puis on arrête de parler et on devient graves et silencieux. Eddy prend les virages de façon à ce que je tombe un peu contre son épaule. On arrive au chalet de Sandra Dubreuil sans qu'Eddy ait hésité une seule fois sur la route à suivre.

Le père de Sandra est un gros vendeur de chars. Il nous accueille avec sa voix grasse et sa montre plaquée or. « Parquez-vous là », dit-il en ronflant un *r* à l'anglaise et en faisant des gestes majestueux de policier. De madame Dubreuil je ne vois que les bagues à diamants, les cheveux flamboyants et le rouge à lèvres qui dessine ses lèvres en forme de cœur.

— Bonjour, mon petit Eddy, t'es le premier arrivé. Sandra est en train de finir les sandwiches dans' cuisine. Assoyez-vous.

Elle a dit tout cela sans me regarder. Je me dis que ma mère n'aurait quand même pas dit «assisez-vous». Sandra arrive très vite dans le salon. Tout de suite, elle se colle près d'Eddy sur le fauteuil crapaud. Je m'installe sur une chaise droite et j'observe les murs en faux *nutty pine*, le fer forgé du foyer et les miroirs fumés du bar. Je trouve que les Dubreuil sont vraiment des gros riches. On dirait que tout se convertit en signes de piastre autour d'eux.

Sandra et Eddy se parlent en anglais et ne me regardent même pas. Une boule se forme tranquillement tout au fond de ma gorge. Dans un coin près d'une fenêtre qui donne sur le lac, il y a un tourne-disque et une pile de 78 tours. Eddy met un disque. Sandra me regarde enfin et elle me donne un coke en disant distraitement : «Ça va, Claude?» Elle n'attend pas la réponse et continue de parler à Eddy, de très près.

Puis les autres arrivent, par couples. Ils sont tous là qui rient beaucoup et qui parlent moitié français, moitié anglais. Sandra ne laisse pas Eddy d'un pouce. Ça résonne très fort. Les gars cachent leur bière dans les recoins et sortent leur guitare. Je fixe les doigts d'Eddy qui vont et viennent en pinçant les cordes. Un petit air western m'éclaire le cœur un instant, comme le lac devant moi, tout noir, traversé d'un rayon de lune. D'une voix nasillarde, il prononce à l'anglaise des phrases de tous les jours qui deviennent belles à cause de la musique, mais qui, dites comme ça, seraient bien fausses et bien plates : *un coin du ciel, ma petite maman chérie, donne-moi ton cœur.* L'atmosphère s'alourdit et Sandra se lève soudain du divan de velours rouge vin en s'exclamant : «C'est fini le braillage, on danse! Réveillez-vous, envoye Eddy, fais jouer *Blue Suede Shoes.*»

Je me mets à danser, mais quelque chose ne va pas. Quand on fait tourner *Love me tender*, les couples s'agglutinent. Ça dure une éternité et je reste seule près de la fenêtre embuée avec le rayon de lune sur le lac. Mon mal de ventre devient de plus en plus aigu. Je décide d'aller aux toilettes pour passer le temps. Quand je reviens, ils sont toujours sur le même slow, comme si l'aiguille était rivée dans le disque. Un slow, c'est bien connu, ça se danse à deux. J'attends dans mon coin, les yeux dans l'eau, que finisse *Never let me go.*

Le reste de la soirée se passe dans une brume de bière, de coke, de chips, de rock'n'roll, de sueurs. Eddy danse, rit, boit, mange et j'attends patiemment qu'il soit onze heures et demie. Je suis redevenue une fille à lunettes, calée dans mon fauteuil à observer Sandra et Eddy, Yvonne et Élie, Danielle et André, Nicole et Gerry. J'aurais le goût de partir en courant, de les tuer tous, mais je reste là, figée dans mon fauteuil, incapable de me lever, incapable de réagir. Toutes sortes de phrases traversent mon cerveau à une vitesse vertigineuse : «Sandra Dubreuil, lâche mon chum, chus pas assez niaiseuse pour pas m'apercevoir que tu veux me le voler, mon chum. Pis toi, Eddy, tu vois pas que t'es-t-en train de t' faire enjôler par la belle Sandra?» Mais rien ne sort, tout reste collé au fond de mon ventre, tiraillé dans mes crampes. Ma peine pèse trois tonnes dans le chalet du lac Fortune.

À onze heures, je ramasse mes esprits et je finis par dire à Eddy de me raccompagner. Peine perdue.

Je le supplie et, en dernier recours, je lui avoue que j'ai mes règles. « *What's that?* » me demande-t-il. Je n'arrive pas à trouver le mot anglais pour le lui expliquer, pourtant je le sais, « *I have my period* », mais ça ne sort pas. Blanc de mémoire, rien à faire, « *Never mind*, reste là avec Sandra », et il reste accroché à son bras. Je décide de revenir avec les parents d'Yvonne, qui me posent des questions sur mes études, sur mon avenir, sur toutes ces choses qui n'ont plus la moindre importance pour moi. Élie ne dit pas un mot, Yvonne non plus. Il n'y a que ma voix qu'on entend. Je réponds pour être polie, c'est tout. J'ai froid, et la lune, très jaune, accompagne ma peine dans la nuit.

Le père d'Yvonne fume comme une cheminée et ça sent le gaz dans l'auto. J'ai envie de vomir, comme quand j'étais petite. J'ai honte d'avoir mal au cœur dans l'auto, ça dérange tout le monde. Ça me met sur les nerfs, je ne pense qu'au moment précis où il faut avertir, le moment exact qui précède la minute où je vais vomir, pas trop tôt, pas trop tard. Quand j'étais petite et qu'on allait à Notre-Dame-du-Nord chez ma grand-mère Éthier, je faisais parfois arrêter l'auto. Je descendais prendre une bouffée d'air et j'entendais mon père gueuler. Je mettais un doigt au fond de ma gorge pour vomir. Parce que si je ne vomissais pas, il gueulait encore plus fort, et souvent, la chicane prenait entre mes frères sur le siège arrière. Quand je revenais dans l'auto, tout le monde disait que je sentais le vomi. Pour l'instant, je me retiens, et ça m'empêche de trop penser à Eddy et à Sandra qui sont en train de s'embrasser. J'aimerais qu'on frappe un orignal, qu'on prenne le fossé, qu'un train nous coupe en deux. Quand je serai morte, il faudra bien qu'on s'occupe de moi.

À la maison, ma mère m'attend, furieuse; elle s'est obstinée à venir me chercher à minuit chez le juge Gauthier. Je n'y étais pas. Évidemment, personne n'y était. Je décide de tout lui dévoiler. Ses réprobations ne m'atteignent pas, je suis trop fatiguée, trop malade, trop pleine de peine; je vais directement dans les toilettes, je vomis tout mon soûl, puis je me couche en zombi. J'avale deux des grosses pilules que mon père prend pour son mal de tête et je me cale dans le néant du sommeil.

Eddy ne me rappelle pas. Moi non plus, je ne le rappelle pas, car après tout j'ai mon honneur. Je sais par les filles qui sont retournées au Radio Grill que Sandra et Eddy sortent steady. C'est chose faite. Je pense toujours que j'aurais dû m'interposer, m'imposer, garder mon territoire, le rappeler, lui dire des bêtises, à lui et à Sandra Dubreuil. C'est ce qu'ils font dans les films de love, mais tout ce que je réussis à faire, c'est de laisser mijoter ça dans mon cerveau. J'en parle souvent avec Danielle, et elle dit que l'amour ne se force pas. Qu'André l'aime à la folie sans qu'elle ait même à lever le petit doigt. Qu'est-ce qu'elle a, elle, de plus que moi pour qu'un gars l'aime à la folie? C'est vrai que même si André m'aimait à la folie, ça ne me ferait pas un pli.

L'été passe et je me prépare à partir pour le pensionnat. Il faut que je m'exile à Ottawa pour terminer mes études parce qu'à Noranda, après la onzième année, les filles n'ont pas le droit de fréquenter le collège de Rouyn, le seul en ville, pour garçons seulement.

Contrairement à Coco et à Bernard, j'aime l'école parce que c'est le seul endroit où je suis heureuse. Le couvent du Saint-Esprit, où je fais mes quatre premières années de classique, est une sorte de vieille maison au toit en déclive située à Rouyn, en face des cheminées de la mine, juste au bord du lac Osisko, bien vert et bien puant. Ce couvent abrite deux salles de classes, cinq fougères, une chapelle, plusieurs sœurs et dix pianos. Le midi, après le dîner, toutes les filles pratiquent en même temps et ça fait une joyeuse cacophonie dans les couloirs. Il y a en tout cinquante filles là-dedans, et presque toutes apprennent le piano. Je suis nulle en piano, mais ma mère tient mordicus à ce que je l'apprenne. Elle est musicienne dans l'âme, ma mère. Elle dit « la musique adoucit les mœurs » et elle fredonne *Un Canadien errant* toute la journée, en faisant des gâteaux. Ça fait partie du bonheur de la maison. Moi, je ne fredonne jamais parce que je n'arrive pas à me souvenir d'un seul air de chanson. Ma force à moi, c'est que je suis bonne à l'école et que j'ai la mémoire des mots.

Ma mère a réussi à me convaincre de faire une maîtresse d'école à force de me répéter que j'étais vraiment faite pour ça. À cause de mon caractère de suffragette. Avant même d'aller à l'école, je jouais à l'école avec Lucien. C'était moi la maîtresse parce que j'avais beaucoup de patience pour lui montrer à lire *Léo et Léa*. Mon père disait souvent : « Tais-toi, la Suffragette, tu parles trop, tu parles trop fort. » Évidemment, il me gâchait tout mon plaisir. Puis on se mettait à jouer à l'autobus, pour changer, et pour que Lulu puisse faire ses vroum vroum. Ça, ça rassurait mon père.

Avec le temps, mon père a abandonné ce surnom détestable de Suffragette. Dans des moments d'épanchement très rares, il m'appelle Chouchoune. Mais je ne mérite ce surnom que lorsque je suis très fine, c'est-à-dire lorsque j'écoute sans broncher les histoires qu'il raconte à table ou que je ne dis rien même si je ne suis pas d'accord avec lui. Depuis que je suis devenue «grande fille», il n'ose plus m'appeler Chouchoune. À vrai dire, il se sent plutôt désemparé devant moi. Il me dit souvent que je lui fais penser à sa mère. Et sa mère, je ne suis pas sûre qu'il l'aime tant que ça. En tout cas, ma mère a discuté longtemps avec lui au sujet de mes études, et il a fini par accepter que j'aille à Ottawa, au pensionnat, parce que j'ai des bonnes notes et qu'au fond il veut bien que je sois instruite. Il est fier de mes notes et, de cela je suis certaine à cause de l'éclair dans ses yeux quand il ôte ses lunettes pour scruter mon bulletin. Ma mère dit que l'instruction c'est la liberté. Moi, je crois qu'elle pense que cela augmente mes chances de rencontrer un aspirant-médecin, genre André, d'avoir accès un jour aux premiers bancs de l'église le dimanche et de faire de grands voyages.

À Noranda, les toutes premières rangées de l'église sont occupées par le notaire, les avocats et les médecins qui écoutent attentivement le curé qui va souvent en Europe et qui se sert du sermon pour raconter ses voyages. Les femmes des gens «honnêtes», comme les appelle mon père, s'habillent à Montréal. Elles sont les princesses d'Abitibi. Elles font penser aux photos rêvées du *Life*. On parle de leurs infidélités conjugales, des cinq à sept qu'elles organisent, de leurs enfants malheureux. On va jusqu'à prétendre que certaines d'entre elles sont des fifines, qu'elles boivent. En observant les grands chapeaux, les manteaux de vison de ces dames du Nord, j'imagine ce luxe qu'elles déploient dans leur maison à deux étages après souper : leurs pyjamas de satin, leur voix feutrée, leurs belles manières. Comme Lana Turner dans *Diane de Poitiers*.

Assis dans les derniers bancs ou au jubé, les mineurs s'efforcent d'être généreux avec cet homme qui les représente si bien à l'étranger. À la fin de ses récits de voyages, il fait toujours une remontrance sur notre manque de générosité. Puis, avec une transition qui tient de la magie, il passe aux mauvaises pensées en mettant en évidence les broderies de son surplis empesé. Voyages, argent, péchés de la chair. Le mot «chair» sonne «chère» dans ma tête. Œuvre de chère. J'aimerais aimer la religion, mais j'ai toujours une barre dans mon cerveau qui m'empêche de m'abandonner complètement et d'avoir la foi, la vraie, celle qui déplace les montagnes.

Au fond, j'aime la messe comme l'école, parce que je peux y être seule et tranquille. La messe est un temps de rêve absolu, de jouissance solitaire, de baisers de longue durée. Eddy me lèche les lèvres, langoureusement. Ou bien est-ce Pat Boone, avec sa peau de bébé? Dans la paix du sermon, une lumière blonde traverse les vitraux et caresse les bancs de chêne. *Love Letters in the Sand* rejoue dans ma tête, à l'infini.

Eddy ne va pas à la messe. Ça se comprend, il n'est pas catholique. Il ne va pas à la synagogue non plus, il me l'a dit. Il ne croit en rien et trouve que la religion, c'est ridicule et qu'au lieu d'unir les gens, ça les sépare. Que ça justifie toutes les guerres. Je ne comprends pas trop trop ce qu'il veut dire, mais je pense qu'il y a là une sorte de vérité.

Ce que j'aime le plus au monde, c'est lire. J'ai déjà lu tous les livres de la comtesse de Ségur et de la bibliothèque de Suzette. Depuis que je sais lire, j'en ai reçu en cadeau d'anniversaire de ma tante Alphonsine, qui a une étagère pleine de livres de Pierre Loti et de Delly, bien couverts et bien classés par ordre alphabétique. Elle m'offre maintenant des *Brigitte* de Berthe Bernage. *Brigitte jeune fille, Brigitte maman, Brigitte aux champs,* etc. Dans ces romans, le personnage principal est une belle jeune fille, française, catholique pratiquante, riche et parfaite. Tout le monde l'aime, son fiancé, son père, sa mère, ses beaux-parents. Il y a des petits malentendus dans leur amour, mais ça finit toujours par s'arranger dans un froufrou de robes blanches.

À part les livres, j'aime bien le cinéma. Il y a plusieurs salles de cinéma dans les deux villes, sept peut-être. Je n'ai pas tout à fait seize ans et en principe je n'ai pas le droit d'y entrer. Mais j'y vais souvent avec Danielle et Yvonne. On se met beaucoup de rouge à lèvres et on emprunte les souliers à talons hauts de nos mères. Les gars y vont de leur côté. Eddy ne m'y a jamais emmenée, mais je l'ai vu l'autre jour avec Sandra, quand je suis allée voir *The Eddy Duchin Story.* Ils ont necké pendant tout le film. Dans le noir, je ne savais plus si j'avais de la peine à cause de Tyrone Power quand il apprend que Kim Novak est morte en accouchant ou à cause d'Eddy Goldstein qui entourait de ses grands bras les épaules de Sandra Dubreuil. C'était comme si je voyais un film dans le film et je pleurais doublement à chaudes larmes. Danielle me donnait des Kleenex et, à un moment donné, ils se sont ratatinés en petits tapons mouillés qui n'absorbaient plus rien. Danielle n'arrêtait pas de me dire à l'oreille :

— Fais-toi-z-en pas, c'est juste un film. C'pas vrai, c'est juste une histoire, voyons donc.

J'avais les yeux rouges quand je suis rentrée à la maison et Coco n'a pas manqué de le remarquer :

— Encore la p'tite femelle qui braille pour rien. Tu vois, t'es trop jeune pour aller aux vues.

Il est comme ça, Coco. Il réussit toujours à décocher une flèche là où ça me fait le plus mal : c'est un archer du cœur. Il ne veut pas que je marche du même côté de la rue que lui. Même quand il est avec Bernard, il me demande toujours de traverser. Ils ont honte d'être avec leur sœur, parce qu'ils ont honte d'être avec une fille. Coco et Bernard m'appellent «femelle» parce que je n'aime pas les films de cow-boys qui me donnent des cauchemars la nuit. Il m'arrive de rêver que je suis une belle Indienne aux tresses noires tapie au fond de sa tente, que de gros cow-boys aux jambes arquées menacent avec leurs fusils. Parfois mes cris au secours débordent du rêve et réveillent tout le monde dans la maison. Mon père vient alors me secourir et je pleure dans ses bras pendant qu'il m'appelle Chouchoune. Il a ce bon côté, mon père : il est protecteur quand on est mal pris. On peut toujours compter sur lui et on oublie une minute qu'il nous fait peur.

Coco et Bernard considèrent qu'il n'y a que deux sortes de films, les films de cow-boys et les films de love. Ils aiment mieux les films de cow-boys à la condition qu'ils ne soient pas trop infestés de love. Moi, j'aime les films de love en couleurs, les films qui suintent la passion. J'adore ça, même si je pleure et que je sors avant la fin. C'est la troisième fois que je vois *The Eddy Duchin Story* et je suis prête à y retourner n'importe quand.

Hier, Coco et Bernard n'ont pas pu entrer au Capitole. Ils ont plus de seize ans, mais ils ont l'air d'en avoir douze. Je faisais la queue et ils sont venus me supplier d'acheter les billets pour eux. J'ai refusé net et j'ai donné mon ticket au placier, du haut de mes talons hauts. Il y avait à l'affiche un film historique érotique : *Land of Pharaohs*. Heureusement que c'était biblique, parce que Joan Collins se promenait les seins presque nus dans des scènes pas mal osées. Sûrement de quoi faire un péché véniel. Mais Joan Collins a été bien punie quand elle s'est fait enfermer vivante près du sarcophage de son pharaon de mari. Elle voulait toutes ses richesses, elles les a eues, mais elle en mourra. Son cri de détresse traverse de bord en bord l'écran de cinémascope.

Ma mère ne veut pas que j'aille au cinéma. Je dois lui conter des mensonges quand j'y vais. Par exemple, hier, je lui ai dit que j'allais chez Yvonne Théroux pour passer l'après-midi. Quand je suis revenue à la maison, j'ai tout de suite compris que Coco et Bernard lui avaient tout raconté. Comme d'habitude, elle a été très polie en surface.

— Tu m'avais dit que tu allais chez Yvonne.

— Oui, j'suis allée chez elle, mais elle était pas chez elle, puis j'ai décidé d'aller voir un film historique.

— Un film historique ! Pour dix-huit ans et plus !

— Coco pis Bernard ont essayé d'entrer eux autres aussi, mais y ont pas pu.

— Laisse faire Coco pis Bernard. C'est de toi qu'on parle. Moi qui avais tellement confiance en toi. J'pourrai pus avoir confiance.

— O.K., j'ferai pus ça.

— Pis regarde-moi donc comme il faut. Depuis quand que tu mets mes robes pis mes souliers, pis ôte-moi ton épaisseur de rouge à lèvres. Ça fait commun.

Coco et Bernard ont vu toute la scène sans broncher. J'ai fait claquer la porte de ma chambre. Je jure de retourner au cinéma voir n'importe quel film dès que l'occasion se présentera. Je rêve que j'appelle Eddy pour qu'il m'accompagne. Personne n'en sait rien. Je veux qu'il m'offre un gros pop-corn et qu'il me tienne la main tout le long du film. Eddy, mon bel Eddy, qu'est-ce que tu peux bien lui trouver à Sandra ?

En attendant, je prépare ma valise pour le pensionnat. Je brode des taies d'oreiller. Ma mère me montre comment faire du petit point. Elle a déjà brodé des nappes et des serviettes avant de se marier et elle aimerait bien que je puisse faire comme elle. Je n'en vois pas l'utilité. Ma mère non plus, mais elle trouve que c'est un bon exercice de patience et de perfection. Je garde souvent mon petit frère Momo, et ça m'exerce assez bien la patience, merci.

Je n'ai pas vu Eddy depuis longtemps. J'aime autant ne pas le voir. Je ne sors pas tellement : j'ai peur de le croiser. Si je le voyais, je mourrais. J'aurais l'air d'une vraie niaiseuse. Je me connais : j'aurais des tonnes de bêtises à lui dire, qui resteraient là, dans ma tête, à se déplacer comme un typhon sans fond. L'été avait bien commencé mais il finit mal cette année.

Enfin le début de septembre, enfin je peux partir. Il fait beau et je prends l'autobus de l'Abitibi Coach Lines, seule, avec une valise énorme qui contient tout mon trousseau : des draps, des serviettes, des uniformes, des cahiers, mes petits calepins noirs dans lesquels j'écris mon journal. Je n'écris pas tout, évidemment, parce que mes frères viennent parfois fouiller dans mes affaires et je ne veux pas qu'ils lisent des choses qu'ils pourraient utiliser contre moi.

Avant de partir, j'ai rencontré Eddy, au coin de la Gamble, sur la *Main*, juste en face du Kresge. J'étais surprise de le voir tout seul, comme ça. Il a même fait un grand sourire en me voyant. C'est là qu'il m'a appris la nouvelle : il a cassé avec Sandra. Je l'ai écouté attentivement et, à ma grande surprise, les phrases qui bourdonnaient dans ma tête depuis le fameux party au chalet de Sandra ont disparu. J'avais beau les chercher, je ne les trouvais plus. Pas le moindre mot. Je lui ai même souri, sans y penser. C'est tout ce qu'il attendait. Les yeux fermés, il s'est penché pour m'embrasser sur la bouche. Je l'ai laissé faire. Il a promis d'écrire et je l'ai cru sur parole. Je suis repartie la tête haute, comme un grand pin blanc émergeant d'une sapinière chétive.

Le voyage de Rouyn à Ottawa dure dix heures. Je ressasse cette promesse en lisant une pile de vieux photo-romans et de vieilles revues d'acteurs que ma tante Alphonsine m'a refilés. Je lis les méchancetés que Louella Parsons déblatère sur Elizabeth Taylor et Eddy Fischer. Pour une fois, je les trouve tous moins chanceux que moi. Quand ça devient trop mélo mollo, je regarde le paysage.

J'aime la réserve du parc La Vérendrye. J'ai l'impression de courir un danger sur cette route déserte qui n'en finit plus : pas de maisons, pas d'églises, pas de monde, beaucoup de gravier, beaucoup de poussière, beaucoup de conifères, beaucoup de lacs. Un gros ours surgit du bois et l'autobus s'arrête. Le chauffeur dit que la nuit, il y a des orignaux qui traversent et qu'il faut être très prudent si on ne veut pas les frapper. Mon grand-père est mort comme ça, à l'aube, entre chien et loup, après avoir heurté un orignal. Mon père a raconté mille fois cette histoire, comment son auto avait été défoncée par l'animal gros comme un cheval. Il avait fallu des tenailles pour sortir mon grand-père de l'auto tant elle était écrasée et il y avait du sang et des tripes partout sur la route. C'est la seule histoire vraiment morbide qu'il raconte. Rien à voir avec les quelques vers de Hamlet qu'il nous récite quand le mot «Shakespeare» est prononcé, ce qui a pour effet de le remonter comme un automate.

Passé le parc La Vérendrye, l'autobus s'arrête à Grand-Remous pour le dîner. Les remous bouillonnants de la rivière Gatineau me fascinent, de même que les billots qui virevoltent au-dessus de l'écume comme s'ils n'étaient que broutilles. On reprend la route aussitôt après le repas. Près de Maniwaki, les arbres commencent à montrer leurs couleurs et les collines sont aussi rondes que celles de Notre-Dame-du-Nord, chez grand-maman Éthier. Les plates étendues de l'Abitibi que j'ai laissées derrière moi, avec leurs épinettes rabougries et leurs pins isolés parmi quelques bouleaux, me semblent ternes et sèches. Je me dis qu'au fond, l'Abitibi, c'est bien laid.

Il n'y a vraiment que ma mère pour penser que c'est beau. Elle dit que c'est beau parce que tous les étés des Américains s'y installent avec l'air insouciant des riches qui s'ennuient. L'hiver, personne ne les revoit et tout le monde rêve de les rejoindre en Floride. Mon père dit qu'il est bien chanceux d'être payé pour aller dans les bois d'Abitibi alors que les touristes sont obligés de payer pour y pêcher. Je les trouve bien stupides, ces touristes, de payer pour se faire manger par les mouches noires en attendant que le poisson morde.

À Maniwaki, plusieurs filles montent dans l'autobus. Elles se connaissent toutes et elles vont au couvent d'Ottawa elles aussi, d'après leurs dires. L'une d'entre elles s'appelle Annie. Ses cheveux noirs et son teint d'Indienne contrastent avec ma peau blanche et mes petits cheveux blonds. J'ai l'air malade à côté d'elle. Elle rit facilement, parle avec une voix rauque et plisse ses yeux noirs pour rire entre chaque phrase. Je lui souris, et elle vient s'asseoir près de moi.

— Comment tu t'appelles?

— Claude. Pis toi?

— Annie. D'où tu viens?

— De Noranda.

— Wow, c'est loin. Où tu t'en vas?

— À la même place que toi, au couvent Sainte-Marie.

— Ah! c'est le fun...

Elle éclate de rire et elle dit très fort aux autres filles que je suis une nouvelle de Noranda. Elles me regardent de la tête aux pieds. Je me sens rassurée de connaître des filles avant même d'arriver.

Elles racontent que leurs chums vont les attendre au terminus. Elles semblent plus vieilles que moi et elles parlent des garçons, des partys qu'elles ont eus pendant l'été et de ceux qu'elles auront pendant l'année. Elles ont l'air de se connaître depuis bien longtemps et je les envie d'être si joyeuses toutes ensemble. Moi je n'ai qu'une vraie amie, c'est Danielle Dusseault. Sandra, Yvonne et Nicole, ce ne sont pas de vraies amies. Pas Sandra en tout cas, je ne peux plus la voir en peinture. Je ne sais même pas où elle ira à l'école cette année. Danielle est à Ottawa, mais dans un couvent très huppé. Yvonne et Nicole sont parties à Québec dans un grand couvent renommé, elles aussi, au collège Bellevue, si je me rappelle bien. Ma mère dit que tous les couvents se valent.

Alors pourquoi les filles de riches vont-elles ailleurs que moi? Elle n'a pas de réponse à ça.

J'entre dans un édifice de pierres grises entouré d'une énorme clôture de pierres tout aussi grises. La sœur qui m'accueille s'appelle sœur Dorothée-de-la-Passion et elle m'assigne un des cent lits blancs du dortoir. Annie vient me rejoindre presque aussitôt. Je me familiarise peu à peu avec ce que ma mère appelle «les êtres de la maison»: les toilettes, les baignoires, le réfectoire, la salle de récréation, le parloir, le bureau de la directrice. Tout est en rang d'oignons. Ça sent le savon de Castille. J'ai l'impression de me promener dans des dédales, mais je me sens libre malgré tous les règlements affichés un peu partout: me voilà enfin débarrassée de Coco et de Bernard. Je sors de mon monde de garçons, je n'aurai pas à surveiller mes frères, ni à me faire surveiller. Je commence une nouvelle vie. Personne ne me connaît. Je me sens importante, je suis quelqu'un, une fille parmi les filles.

Les fins de semaine, les autres partent chez elles à Maniwaki, à Notre-Dame-du-Laus ou à Gracefield, et je reste seule avec les sœurs à hanter les grands couloirs aux planchers cirés clair. L'après-midi, je vais voir un bout de film interdit; la nuit, je lis une partie de roman dans les toilettes en fumant des bouts de cigarettes. Le dimanche, je bois la moitié d'une bouteille de coke dans le dortoir où il est strictement interdit d'apporter de la nourriture. C'est plate à mort. Au moins, je peux écrire tout et n'importe quoi dans mes petits calepins noirs et je n'ai pas peur que mes frères découvrent ce que j'invente à propos d'Eddy.

Beau temps, mauvais temps, comme toutes les filles du couvent, j'assiste à la messe de six heures et demie du matin, ce qui me fait vomir tout reste de religion. La chose que je déteste le plus au monde, ce sont les sermons, et ici j'ai droit tous les jours à d'interminables histoires d'Évangile. Je compte les fois où le mot Jésus est prononcé et ça me donne le vertige. Je me ronge les sangs et les ongles et je n'écoute rien sauf quand l'aumônier parle des mauvaises pensées. Les filles disent tout bas qu'il a une blonde à Paris. En tout cas, il y va souvent et il en revient tout guilleret. J'attends la communion. Ça me permet de bouger un peu et de ne penser à rien.

Une fois je me suis évanouie, parce que c'était le début de mes menstruations. La surveillante m'a ramassée, m'a ramenée à l'infirmerie et m'a donné une bouillotte en disant tendrement : « Pauvre petite fille, c'est dur d'être une femme. C'est ben dur. » Le docteur a prescrit des pilules très fortes qui me droguent pendant plusieurs heures. Quand le pire est passé, je me relève en pleine forme, et personne ne pourrait dire que je viens de me tordre de douleur. J'oublie tout ça pendant quelques jours et tranquillement la hantise de la prochaine fois revient. Le docteur a assuré ma mère que tout rentrera dans l'ordre un jour quand j'accoucherai de mon premier enfant. C'est héréditaire, paraît-il, parce que ma tante Laura a eu les mêmes maux de ventre. Comme tout le monde pense que c'est pour ça qu'elle est restée vieille fille, ça me fait bien peur.

Je vais plus souvent qu'à mon tour à l'infirmerie et j'y ai presque installé mes pénates. Il y a une chambre de bains attenante et j'en profite pour y fumer quelques cigarettes en cachette en ouvrant très grand la fenêtre. Annie vient m'y rejoindre et on parle pendant des heures. L'autre soir, très tard, on s'est fait prendre, et la surveillante nous a dit qu'elle allait nous dénoncer à la directrice.

— Malade, pas malade, retournez au dortoir, a dit sœur Dorothée-de-la-Passion avec sa voix haut perchée.

Je n'ai plus le droit de retourner à l'infirmerie et j'écope du ménage de la bibliothèque. C'est dommage, il n'y a aucun livre qui m'intéresse dans la bibliothèque du couvent. À part les traités sur la religion et les bonnes manières, il n'y a que des romans de Berthe Bernage et de Delly, ou bien des choses comme *Vingt Mille Lieues sous les mers* ou *Robinson Crusoé*. J'ai tout lu ça quand j'étais plus jeune. J'aimerais lire les livres dont on parle dans les cours de littérature, comme *Madame Bovary*, *Le Rouge et le Noir*, *L'Assommoir*. Ou même *Agaguk* ou *Bonheur d'occasion*. Mais tous ces livres sont interdits et le fait de les lire entraîne un vrai péché mortel. Si je pouvais mettre la main sur l'un d'eux, j'aurais enfin un vrai péché mortel à confesser.

Ma mère me manque un peu, mais je ne le lui dis pas. Je ne veux pas me plaindre parce qu'elle serait bien déçue, et je trouve qu'elle en a plein le dos avec mes quatre frères. Dans ses lettres, elle écrit toujours les mêmes choses que je lis avec le plus grand intérêt du début à la fin. Papa est parti dans le bois pour trois mois. Coco et Bernard n'étudient pas tellement, mais ils font beaucoup de musique dans le salon. Bernard surtout. Ils ont même installé une batterie près du piano. Lulu est dépaysé depuis mon départ, et maman lui apprend le piano pour l'occuper un peu. Elle dit qu'il a beaucoup de talent, qu'il joue par oreille et qu'il sait par cœur des tas de morceaux. Elle n'a même pas besoin de lui dire de pratiquer. Momo me réclame tout le temps. C'est normal, je le gardais souvent et j'en avais soin comme si c'était mon bébé. Heureusement que ma tante Alphonsine venait s'occuper de lui de temps en temps, ce qui me permettait de respirer un peu.

Tout le monde aime ma tante Alphonsine. Elle m'écrit parfois, de sa belle écriture égale et ronde. Ses phrases aussi sont rondes et égales. Je suis sûre qu'elle fait des brouillons qu'elle doit garder dans des tiroirs. Chaque fois, elle annexe quelques dollars à ses petits mots, ce qui la rend encore plus sympathique.

Je reçois une lettre d'Eddy. De belles pattes de mouches en anglais me caressent les yeux. Il ne me raconte presque rien, mais dans les choses les plus banales qu'il écrit, dans ses moindres mots, transparaît la love. À la fin, il m'embrasse avec des X, puis il signe en déformant complètement son écriture, comme s'il avait signé un chèque. Avant de lui répondre, je relis sa lettre au moins vingt fois. Je recommence ma lettre autant de fois : ou bien c'est trop romantique, et j'ai peur qu'il prenne peur, ou bien c'est trop sec, et j'ai peur qu'il pense que je ne l'aime plus. À la fin, je fais une moyenne de toutes ces versions que je transcris sur du papier fin et je dessine un arc-en-ciel dans le coin droit. Je signe avec fièvre : *I kiss you*, X X X X X X X, *Love*, Claude.

À Noël, je reprends l'autobus pour aller passer les fêtes à Noranda. Je suis sûre qu'Eddy m'attendra au terminus. Ça m'énerve, on a beaucoup de retard parce qu'une tempête de neige rend la visibilité nulle. On voit des autos prises dans les fossés. Une chance que l'autobus est lourd et que le chauffeur est habile. Finalement, on arrive, et mon père m'accueille avec un grand sourire. Eddy n'est pas là, mais je suis heureuse que mon père soit venu à ma rencontre. Quand je suis loin de lui, j'oublie qu'il a un sale caractère et je pense plutôt à ses blagues et à ses histoires. Son mackinaw sent le bois, et ça me réchauffe le cœur, quand je lui saute dans les bras pour l'embrasser.

À la maison, tout le monde est content de me voir. Il y a plein de mokas et de tourtières sur le garde-manger et ma mère me demande si j'ai faim avant de m'embrasser. Coco ne bronche pas et continue de regarder sa partie de hockey à la télévision sans se préoccuper du tintamarre que mon arrivée entraîne. Il finit par relever la tête à un moment donné et il me dit qu'il a vu Eddy cet après-midi.

— Ton chum, y a pus de dents, j'y ai pété la yeule en sang sus'a bande en jouant au hockey.

— T'es pas drôle, Jacques Éthier, tu pourrais en inventer une plus comique.

— Tiens, tiens, la Suffragette fait sa suffragette.

Mon frère Coco me fait tellement enrager que je n'ai plus le goût de défaire mes valises. Je suis prête à repartir par l'autobus de nuit. Mais ma mère me calme :

— Occupe-toi pas de lui, y dit ça rien que pour te taquiner. C'est parce qu'y aime sa p'tite sœur qu'y fait ça. Veux-tu de la tourtière ? 'Est encore chaude.

— Ma p'tite sœur mon œil, dit Coco en se replongeant dans sa partie de hockey.

Je suis contente de retrouver mon lit, même si ma chambre est encombrée par les affaires de Coco. Quand je suis partie, il prend ma chambre. Ce soir, il va dormir dans le salon parce qu'il ne veut plus dormir dans la chambre des garçons avec les trois autres. Je pense qu'il est jaloux de moi, non pas parce que je suis une fille, mais parce que j'ai des privilèges de fille étant donné que je suis la seule fille. Et puis, après tout, je suis de la visite.

Tout le monde est parti ce matin. Je suis seule dans la maison et j'en profite pour fouiller dans les tiroirs de ma mère, comme quand j'étais petite. Au cas où je découvrirais un fait étrange, un secret, je ne sais trop quoi. J'essaie tous ses bijoux. Je palpe ses vêtements. Elle a un vieux carnet jauni dans lequel elle a transcrit des poèmes d'amour. J'essaie de l'imaginer à mon âge. C'est un exercice impossible. Elle a toujours été une femme de son âge. Mais pour qui a-t-elle transcrit ces poèmes d'amour avec son écriture parfaite ? Je fouille dans sa grosse collection de cartes postales. J'essaie de regarder ce qu'il y a d'écrit derrière les cartes couleur sépia qui viennent surtout de Bretagne. Il y a la mer, il y a des femmes en sabots avec des bonnets de dentelle. Ça me semble loin et ancien. C'est sa façon à elle de voyager. Elle ne va nulle part, elle dit qu'elle est bien chez elle, avec ses enfants, qu'elle ne demande rien d'autre à la vie. J'essaie de percer le mystère de son cœur, mais il y a toujours une petite barrière dans ses yeux. Un voile dans son regard pourtant franc. Je sais qu'elle m'aime. Elle le dit. Mais je ne la crois pas quand elle le dit. Je ne crois pas ses mots. Je ne crois que son sourire, parfois. Elle est très raisonnable comme mère. Elle peut s'occuper de nous toute seule pendant des mois quand mon père est parti dans le bois. Elle répète souvent la même phrase pour nous faire peur : « Attends que j'le dise à ton père. » Mais quand il revient, elle est si contente qu'elle ne lui dit presque rien. Elle ne veut pas mettre d'huile sur le feu.

En cachette, j'appelle Eddy. Il se fait tirer un peu l'oreille. Il accepte quand même finalement de venir au cinéma avec moi. Il me donne rendez-vous devant le Capitole. Nous allons voir *The Man with the Golden Arm* avec Frank Sinatra. C'est un film très dur dans lequel Frank Sinatra passe son temps à jouer aux cartes et à se piquer à l'héroïne. C'est la première fois que je vois un vrai cas de drogue et je ne suis pas certaine de comprendre. Eddy a l'air de tout saisir et il me prend la main au moment où je m'y attends le moins. Mes tempes battent très fort. Heureusement qu'il fait noir parce que je me sens rougir jusqu'à la racine des cheveux. Le reste du film se déroule dans la brume et je suis partie bien plus loin que Frank Sinatra, dans un ciel où plus rien ne m'atteint.

En sortant du cinéma, on va prendre une patate sauce au Radio Grill. Je pense revoir les copines qui ne manqueront pas de m'inviter à des partys. Mais Eddy m'apprend qu'il n'y en a pas à l'horizon : la famille Dusseault est partie en Floride ; les parents d'Yvonne et Nicole sont allés à Montréal pour les fêtes. Il ne me parle pas de Sandra Dubreuil. D'ailleurs, je ne veux plus rien savoir d'elle. Je dois donc me rabattre sur la parenté pour fêter un peu. Eddy s'en fiche pas mal des repas des fêtes. Chez lui, personne ne fête Noël à Noël. Les juifs ont aussi des fêtes, mais pas en même temps que nous. Je n'ose pas l'inviter pour le dîner de Noël chez ma tante Alphonsine. Pourtant, elle aimerait bien Eddy. Elle parle l'anglais et elle a des amis juifs très riches.

Eddy ne me donne plus de ses nouvelles. Les fêtes se fêtent. Entre les repas de dinde et de tourtière, je fais des promenades dans le soleil dur et la neige qui craque. Les maisons sont figées, les fenêtres givrées. On dirait des rangées d'iglous. Sans contours dans la neige, elles s'alignent devant des trottoirs tout blancs. Comme si les nuages s'étaient solidifiés sous nos pieds. Dîne ici, soupe là, les cousins, les cousines. C'est les fêtes. Il faut que je répète trente-six fois les mêmes choses : «Oui, j'aime ça à Ottawa; oui, ça va bien dans mes études; non, j'ai pas grandi; oui, j'ai plus de boutons qu'avant; non, j'ai pas de chum steady.» C'est plate à mort.

Mon anniversaire coïncide avec les Rois. C'est pratique, ça fait deux fêtes dans une. Avant de me souhaiter une bonne fête, ma mère dit : «Aux Rois, un pas d'oie.» Cette année, pour une fois, le jour des Rois est moins important que ma fête et j'aurai droit à des chandelles sur le gâteau dans lequel ma mère cache une fève. Pour l'occasion, elle m'a permis d'inviter une amie. J'avais droit à deux, mais Coco a déjà dit à André de se joindre à nous, parce que Danielle est partie en Floride avec ses parents et qu'il est tout seul, le pauvre André! Si au moins il avait invité Eddy. Mais non, voyons. Et moi, je ne l'appelle pas. J'invite Yvonne qui est revenue à temps de Montréal pour l'occasion.

Ma mère a fait un gros pâté à la dinde. Elle avait mis la vaisselle ordinaire sur la table, mais j'ai tout recommencé. J'ai sorti la belle nappe brodée au richelieu, la verrerie, l'argenterie, la porcelaine. Tout. C'est ma fête, et pour une fois que j'ai un vrai gâteau, j'en profite. Et puis je pars demain matin.

Les gars se gominent les cheveux. Tout le monde est là. Ça parle fort et mon père fait des blagues devant Yvonne et André. Il leur raconte ses histoires et ma mère rit de bon cœur. Le coke pétille dans nos verres à vin. Je suis la reine des Rois, et c'est moi qui trouve la fève dans le gâteau. J'ouvre mes cadeaux. Ma mère n'a pas eu le temps d'envelopper le sien, mais ça ne fait rien. Du beau papier à lettres. Un gros dix piastres enfoui dans une enveloppe. André m'offre une boîte de chocolats Laura Secord que tous mes frères s'arrachent. Yvonne me donne un collier de perles satin enveloppé dans un écrin de velours. Ma tante Alphonsine n'a pu s'empêcher de me faire cadeau d'un roman de Delly. «Pour ta fête et les fêtes», elle se pense bien spirituelle avec sa carte de souhaits et son « *sweet sixteen never been kissed*». Mes frères disent en chœur : «Ah! Ah! Mon œil.» Pourtant, je la croyais mon alliée, ma tante Alphonsine.

Après le souper, on entoure le piano. Maman joue des airs de la Bonne Chanson. Mon père chante *Parlez-moi d'amour.* Puis il retourne à la cuisine brasser la vaisselle. Maman va le rejoindre et Lulu prend sa place. Bernard l'accompagne à la guitare. Le répertoire change et, pour la première fois, on a le droit de danser sur le tapis du salon. Ma mère dit : «Pas de rock'n'roll.» Alors on ferme les lumières et on danse des slows. Coco danse avec Yvonne et moi je danse avec André. Momo regarde tout cela avec des yeux de crapaud, calé dans le fond du divan. André me serre très fort, et j'essaie de me dégager. Si Danielle savait ça, elle déchanterait. En attendant, sa blonde est en Floride et puis André, c'est loin d'être Eddy, mais c'est mieux que rien. À onze heures, ma mère allume les lumières et elle dit délicatement : «Faut que Claude prenne son autobus de bonne heure demain matin.» Tout le monde a compris. André me donne un gros baiser chaud, me chuchote à l'oreille qu'on se verra cet été. Avant que je puisse lui répondre, il s'est déjà engouffré dans une buée de froid noir. Coco va reconduire Yvonne. La fête est finie.

Je reprends l'autobus pour Ottawa. Même route longue, mêmes sapins rabougris, mêmes pins blancs égarés dans le ciel des lacs gelés. Je retrouve les filles à Maniwaki. Cette fois-ci, je fais partie de la gang et on se raconte tous nos partys en même temps. Évidemment, je suis obligée d'en inventer pas mal pour être à la hauteur. J'ajoute des fêtes aux fêtes, des cadeaux aux cadeaux, de l'amour à la love. À force d'inventer, je finis par me croire. Heureusement que ma fête a tout racheté.

J'écris à Eddy, me disant que la petite flamme renaîtra dans les lettres, dans les petits mots d'amour et les X X X X X, *Love*, Claude. Peine perdue. Il ne répond pas. Puis il écrit une lettre ordinaire, sans aucun X, sans aucun *Love*. Rien du tout. Des nouvelles plates concernant ses études qu'il commence à prendre au sérieux. Le désir s'est affadi, je ne sais trop comment ni pourquoi. J'ai perdu Eddy, ma mère a gagné la première manche. Je me jette dans les livres et heureusement que j'ai mes petits calepins noirs pour écrire ma peine.

Je retourne dans le Nord pour les vacances d'été. Je pense à Eddy tout le long du voyage en autobus vers Rouyn. Je pense qu'il va surgir de mon désir, que le vieil Indien qui boit sur le siège à côté de moi va se transformer en Eddy comme dans les contes de fées. Quand finalement l'autobus tourne sur la rue McQuaig en direction du terminus, c'est lui que je vois en premier. Il est avec Sandra Dubreuil, et tous les deux se promènent main dans la main. Mon chien est mort.

Mon père est au terminus, qui m'attend avec le sourire, comme d'habitude, quand il y a longtemps qu'on s'est vus. Il m'avertit que Coco s'est approprié ma chambre parce qu'il travaille tôt le matin et qu'il ne peut pas se coucher trop tard, ce qui priverait tout le monde du salon. Je lui dis que je comprends, mais au fond, ça m'enrage. Je pense que je n'ai plus de place, qu'il faudra que je m'installe ailleurs à mes frais le plus vite possible. Ma mère a fait un bon souper, et j'oublie tout ça. Je suis heureuse de les revoir tous, même Coco.

Je prends le salon et je fais exprès pour fermer la porte à dix heures, prétextant que je me couche. Mais, comme on a enfin une télévision, une grosse combinée comme chez Danielle Dusseault, je regarde *Ciné Club* jusque très tard dans la nuit : *Les Quatre Cents Coups*, *Hiroshima mon amour* et tous ces films qu'on ne voit jamais dans les salles de Rouyn parce qu'ils ne sont pas américains. J'éteins les lumières et je baisse le son au plus bas pour que tout le monde pense que je dors. La belle Emmanuelle Riva se tourne dans son lit en parlant doucement de la bombe d'Hiroshima. Je ne perds pas un mot de ce qu'elle chuchote dans son insomnie et je me sens solidaire de tous les bombardés du monde. Je ne dors pas, mais c'est tout comme, à cause du silence, de la solitude et de la grande noirceur. Coco veut entrer, mais je refuse en lui disant que je dors pour vrai. Ça le fait enrager, d'autant plus que parfois je laisse entrer Bernard et Lulu. C'est mon privilège. Coco se venge en me parlant tout le temps d'Eddy et de Sandra. Je n'ai aucun répit.

Ma mère, qui est une vraie mère qui s'occupe de tout, m'a trouvé du travail à l'hôtel Noranda comme serveuse. Je suis bien contente qu'elle ait fait ça pour moi, ça va me changer les idées. Elle a un peu hésité, à cause de ce lieu toujours louche qu'est un hôtel, mais l'appât du gain a eu raison de ses scrupules. On parle, ma mère et moi. On est toutes seules dans la maison. Elle m'offre une cigarette et un pepsi. Je me sens très importante, une vraie femme. C'est la première fois qu'elle me traite d'égale à égale. Elle s'est peut-être ennuyée de moi. Il faut dire qu'elle ne pouvait plus compter sur moi pour garder, faire la vaisselle, faire les repas. Quand elle est comme ça, devant moi, avec sa petite robe fleurie, sa cigarette et son pepsi, je la trouve belle un instant. Mais ça ne dure pas longtemps.

— Tu sors pus avec ton juif? Y t'a pas rappelée, hein?

— Non. On sort pus ensemble.

— C'est mieux comme ça, tu vas voir. C'est compliqué, les religions différentes, les langues différentes, les mentalités différentes. R'garde sur la 2e avenue, c'est plein de Polonais qui ont marié des Canadiennes, pis c'est pas drôle. Trouve-toi donc un bon Canadien.

59

— Facile à dire.

— Ben voyons donc, la mère des gars est pas morte. Tu vas t'en trouver un autre.

C'est le mois de juin. Ça fait déjà un an que j'ai appelé Eddy la première fois. Il vient de pleuvoir et les haies de saules embaument la rue Murdoch. Comme l'été dernier, quand je me promenais avec Eddy et qu'il me prenait la main des fois. Je la gardais toujours prête, dégagée, au cas où. Et quand il la ramassait distraitement, mes tempes valsaient.

Je me présente à l'hôtel, croyant pouvoir commencer mon entraînement. Le gérant a un geste de recul en m'apercevant. C'est un gros gérant gras qui porte de grosses lunettes de corne. Ses yeux tourbillonnent au fond d'une spirale tant ses lunettes sont fortes. Je me dis qu'il doit être plus myope que moi. Et aussitôt, par réflexe, je pense à mes lunettes qui ne conviennent pas au style de la maison, c'est évident. Pas à une waitress, en tout cas.

— Examinons ton dossier.

— Je n'ai pas de dossier, c'est ma mère qui m'a dit que j'étais engagée.

— Il y a un petit malentendu, ma belle. Remplis ce formulaire-là, pis j'te rappellerai quand on aura besoin de toi.

Sans grand enthousiasme, je laisse en blanc les espaces concernant l'expérience acquise. Je n'ajoute presque rien finalement sur le formulaire, puisqu'il n'y a aucune question concernant les études. Évidemment, le gérant ne me rappelle pas.

Je dis à ma mère que je n'aurai pas cet emploi. Elle a l'air un peu soulagée.

— Ça fait rien, tu t'occuperas de Momo pis tu m'aideras dans la maison. L'an prochain, on te trouvera quelque chose dans un bureau, ça conviendra mieux. J'vas dire à ton père d'en parler au député; avec lui, ça traînera pas, tu vas voir.

J'attends malgré tout un appel d'Eddy. Quelque chose me dit que je vais le revoir. Yvonne Théroux et Danielle Dusseault m'ont appris que Sandra a étudié toute l'année à Ottawa et qu'Eddy est allé la voir quelques fois. « Le salaud, y m'a même pas appelée », voilà ce que j'ai envie de leur dire, mais je reste calme et digne. Il ne faut pas montrer que ça m'atteint, sinon de quoi aurais-je l'air? Quand une fille se fait laisser par un gars, il ne faut pas que ça paraisse. Il faut faire comme si ça ne me dérangeait pas même si en dedans j'aurais le goût de me tuer.

Mais pendant tous ces jours de grande chaleur où je m'occupe de Momo, je ne peux m'empêcher de penser à lui.

Puis un événement vient tout chambarder : au mois de mars, j'ai participé à un concours pour aller au festival de Shakespeare à Stratford, en Ontario. Il a fallu écrire une composition sur les délices littéraires de Shakespeare, que je ne connais pas. J'avais complètement oublié ça. Une lettre m'informe que j'ai gagné avec « ci-inclus des billets de train, des billets de théâtre, l'adresse où vous devez loger, l'horaire, l'itinéraire, etc. ». Tout est bilingue, mais surtout en anglais.

Coco arrive en trombe et me dit qu'il me livrerait un secret intéressant pour une piastre. À propos d'Eddy. J'hésite et je finis par flancher. Eddy ira aussi à Stratford, il a gagné lui aussi le concours, et il prendra le même train. Je cours dans ma chambre et je ferme la porte. Mon cœur bat très fort. J'ouvre la fenêtre très grand et j'allume une cigarette. Est-ce possible, est-ce possible? Je pense que Coco m'a fait marcher et je deviens triste tout à coup. Qui vivra verra. *Que sera sera,* dirait Doris Day.

Mais non, Coco était sérieux. À la gare de Noranda, la première personne que je vois, c'est Eddy, de dos, qui embrasse tendrement Sandra.

Eddy finit par monter dans le train de l'Ontario Northland. Dans le même wagon que le mien. Le voyage va durer toute la nuit, c'est écrit dans le dépliant. Eddy fait semblant de ne pas me remarquer et il se tient à la fenêtre, soufflant des baisers gras à Sandra dans le creux de sa main.

Le train s'ébranle, et je vois Eddy se diriger au bout du wagon. Je fais semblant de ne pas le remarquer. Puis, mine de rien, il s'approche et s'assoit à côté de moi sur la banquette de velours. Il me parle de tout et de rien. Les mots courent dans le vide. Je ne le regarde pas, ne sachant pas si je dois être furieuse contre lui. Après tout, il m'a laissé tomber, il m'a abandonnée, trahie. Je reste plongée dans *Othello,* même si je ne comprends presque rien à ce vieil anglais, sauf une atmosphère, l'atmosphère de la passion toute noire avec du sang entre les lignes. Les mots de Shakespeare ressemblent à des prières qu'on fait au ciel dans les moments de grand désespoir même si on ne croit pas en Dieu. « *Thou hast...* », un impératif majestueux.

Puis je lui fais un grand sourire parce que j'en ai envie depuis un moment, et on se met à parler avec chaleur, de très près, comme si on s'était vus la veille. Ça dure très longtemps et un boy noir vient nous demander de nous déplacer, car il veut aménager les banquettes en couchettes, ce qu'il fait en un tourne-main. On se retrouve tout naturellement dans la partie du bas d'un lit superposé. Le lit du haut restera sûrement inoccupé. Tout ce que ma mère a craint m'est offert sur un plateau pendant que le train file vers Toronto dans la nuit la plus chaude de l'été.

Je vais enfin savoir ce que cachent les définitions du dictionnaire, les entre-lignes des livres sur les origines de la vie, les sous-entendus de Sandra. On parle de nos études, de nos professeurs, de la musique et de la politique et de la religion. Eddy réussit à parler de tout sans que je sache ce qu'il pense vraiment. Son visage m'arrive dans le halo de ma myopie : cheveux noirs gominés, yeux bleus profonds derrière des petites lunettes de métal, nez judaïque, bouche sensuelle, sourire d'acteur. Tous les mots qu'il dit sonnent comme des mots d'amour. Ses grandes mains effilées virevoltent, dessinant le contour de ses phrases. Il me fait penser à James Dean quand il est amoureux de Nathalie Wood et qu'il n'en laisse rien paraître sur son visage.

C'est le petit jour. Rien ne s'est passé. On relève le store et je m'aperçois que le paysage a changé. On longe une masse d'eau grande comme la mer : le lac

Ontario. J'essaie d'imaginer ce que serait la mer, la vraie, et non pas une mer de neige comme en Abitibi l'hiver quand on ne voit que du blanc, de l'infiniment blanc, quand le ciel se confond avec la terre, quand on ne voit ni ciel ni terre, dirait ma mère. Je me sens très loin de l'Abitibi avec ses grandes épinettes efflanquées, décimées par les coupes de bois de la C.I.P.

En arrivant à Stratford, on se quitte. Moi, je vais avec les filles dans des maisons pour filles seulement; Eddy, avec les garçons dans des maisons pour garçons seulement. Je trouve bien belle cette ville romantique à l'anglaise avec ses petits ponts jetés ici et là sur la rivière. Je n'arrive pas à dormir, je suis la princesse sur un pois.

Eddy n'a pas beaucoup dormi non plus, les gars ayant fait la fête jusqu'aux petites heures, et c'est un peu fripés qu'on assiste à *Othello*. Desdémone est vêtue de rouge et Othello est tout noir. Je ne comprends pas bien leur accent, mais je sens que l'amour souffle à l'oreille de la mort. Je suis prise au piège du drame. Tout finit-il toujours ainsi? Eddy dort par moments et sa tête tombe un peu sur mon épaule. Je lui en veux d'être aussi léger devant la beauté grave qui s'étale sur la scène, devant les costumes de velours et les décors de la passion sans borne. Il se réveille en sursaut quand on se lève pour applaudir. Il me fait un sourire et on décide de se promener le long de la rivière. Je garde toujours sa main dans la mienne, et quand on traverse les petits ponts, je me prends pour Grace Kelly dans *The Swan*.

On ne parle pas de Shakespeare, ni de Sandra, ni de nos parents. On est des personnages dans un film : on ne dit que des choses qui n'ont rien à voir avec la vie de tous les jours, on parle du sens de la vie, de la différence entre l'amitié et l'amour, de la couleur de l'après-midi. Tout le monde autour de nous croit qu'on sort steady. C'est à s'y méprendre et on s'y méprend nous-mêmes, la tête la première dans la love.

Hier, on est rentrés tard. Trop tard, même. Quand on est revenus à la maison des filles, la porte était fermée à clé, et tout était éteint. Eddy était joyeux, il avait son petit sourire taquin, puis il a dit comme ça :

— Viens, on va dormir dans la parc, ça sera drôle. *Let's go*, on va chercher des *blankets* chez où je reste.

Chez lui, tout était ouvert et illuminé. J'ai attendu sur la galerie pendant qu'il allait chercher les couvertes. Comme dans un moulin à scie, les garçons rentraient et sortaient. Certains me zieutaient, se demandant bien ce que pouvait faire une fille à lunettes devant la maison des gars. Puis Eddy est sorti avec une couverte grise camouflée dans son sac à dos. On s'est dirigés vers le parc, tranquillement. Quand il a mis son bras autour de ma taille, mon ventre a sursauté.

Sur le bord de la rivière Avon, on a vite repéré un endroit bien abrité. L'eau était noire et argent. Des cygnes glissaient et les saules pleureurs faisaient comme un arc de triomphe autour d'eux. Eddy m'a enroulée dans la couverte rugueuse qui sentait le fond d'armoire. J'étais un peu craintive. C'était plus fort que moi, j'avais peur que Sandra surgisse d'un talus. Eddy a deviné et m'a dit «Mon 'tite Claude», puis il a commencé à m'embrasser sur le bord des lèvres. Ce fut comme une explosion de dynamite dans ma bouche. Il a relevé ma robe, puis il a ouvert son pantalon. Je sentais son sexe dur appuyé sur mon jupon de dentelle. Puis les doigts d'Eddy, ses grands doigts effilés, ont lentement poussé l'élastique de ma petite culotte détrempée par les caresses et les baisers. Cela a duré longtemps, très longtemps, et soudain j'ai crié dans le ciel de l'Ontario. Eddy a fait «Chut» en retirant son doigt.

On n'a plus dit un mot. Eddy est resté bandé, les yeux tendus, grand ouverts, me suppliant de le caresser à son tour. J'ai regardé la protubérance qui se mouvait dans son sous-vêtement et je n'ai pas osé la toucher. Une sorte de peur s'est emparée de moi, la peur de ne pas être à la hauteur. Il aurait pu me pénétrer avec son sexe, et je me serais laissé faire sans même penser à Sandra, sans même penser à ma mère. Mais je ne pouvais plus bouger. On a passé le reste de la nuit ainsi, collés l'un contre l'autre. Le jour s'est levé, rose et pâle, derrière les ponts de la rivière Avon, puis on a replié la couverte. Les cygnes paraissaient beaucoup moins blancs dans la lumière du petit matin. Eddy m'a embrassée, mais il l'a fait par convenance, sans entrain. Je l'ai senti dans sa façon de terminer son baiser. Une hâte soudaine d'en finir, difficile à cerner, inexplicable, mais bien présente. Il est déçu.

Moi aussi, je suis bien déçue. Toute la journée je me sens lourde et les yeux d'Eddy ne cessent de me reprocher quelque chose. Pourquoi ne suis-je pas allée plus loin? Pourquoi suis-je restée pantoise devant son sexe, pourquoi ai-je eu peur de le toucher, de l'effleurer? Mon esprit s'emmêle et je reste ballottée entre le regret et le désir. Quoi faire avec un sexe d'homme sinon le convoiter? Je n'arrive pas à dire un mot de tout cela à Eddy, mais j'ai l'impression d'avoir cassé une corde de sa guitare.

On se rend à la gare pour prendre le train avec les autres. Je vais faire ma toilette pour me rafraîchir et je m'aperçois que j'ai saigné un peu. Pourtant, je ne suis pas menstruée. Ça doit être ça, la cerise, comme les gars disent en riant d'une fille. «Elle a perdu sa cerise», la phrase me rebondit dans la tête. Pourtant, on n'a pas fait l'amour, pas complètement en tout cas. Tout ça m'inquiète. Un doigt peut-il remplacer un sexe?

On arrête un peu à Toronto pour visiter la ville. Faire un tour de métro. J'ai peur dans les tunnels tout noirs et je cherche Eddy qui s'arrange pour ne pas être à côté de moi. Je le suis des yeux et je vois qu'il profite de la foule pour se coller à d'autres filles. Il parle avec enthousiasme, un peu trop fort, pour que j'entende sa bonne humeur. Puis on revient prendre le train comme des moutons. C'est ici que l'Est embrasse l'Ouest, que Moncton promet d'écrire à Vancouver, qu'on s'embrasse d'un océan à l'autre et que Dieu sauve la reine.

Après North Bay, le train prend la direction de Cochrane et Timmins. On est moins nombreux et on a le temps de tous se connaître. C'est la direction nord. Eddy sort sa guitare et entraîne les autres à chanter *Alouette* et *Oh! He's a Jolly Good Fellow*. Puis il s'assoit près d'une autre fille et se met à rire aux éclats. J'ai l'impression que le vent tourne. Sherry, une *gorgeous* blonde qui a deviné mon angoisse, me dit en aparté:

— Eddy sortira jamais steady avec toi. Les juifs, ça se mêle pas aux autres en amour. Ils gardent ça pour eux, entre eux, comme les catholiques.

Il me semble que j'ai déjà entendu ça quelque part. C'est rare qu'une fille de mon âge pense ainsi. L'idée que ma mère pourrait avoir raison me bouleverse un instant. Mais je me ravise, le temps de me convaincre que tout cela n'a pas de sens. Le train s'arrête à North Bay. Les esprits se sont un peu calmés et Eddy s'est finalement assis près de moi, sur la banquette du restaurant de la gare, et m'offre gentiment de partager son coke et sa patate sauce. Je lui demande :

— T'es pas un vrai juif, toi, hein ?

— Qui ça ? Moi ?

— Oui, toi.

— Dans un sens, non, mais dans un sens, oui.

— Est-ce que c'est vrai qu' les juifs peuvent pas se marier avec les catholiques ?

— Pourquoi tu me demandes ça ?

— Pour rien, comme ça.

— C'est pas vrai, voyons, où tu vas chercher ça ?

Je le crois sur parole parce que ça fait bien mon affaire. On remonte dans le train et le reste du voyage se passe à peu près dans le silence. On fait semblant de nous assoupir chacun sur nos banquettes et, sans qu'on ait eu le temps de nous en rendre compte, on arrive à la gare de Noranda. Le boy noir nous crie de sortir avec les autres.

Ma mère attend sur le quai. Elle est toujours là, elle ou mon père, quand je reviens de quelque part, pour me faire plaisir, mais quelquefois, j'aimerais bien être seule. Comme en ce moment. Sandra est là, toute là, bien mise dans une jupe *flare* à petits pois rouges. Je regarde Eddy qui me glisse imperturbable :

— O. K., là. On fait comme si on s' connaissait pas. *All right?*

— Appelle-moi avant que je reparte pour Ottawa...

C'est tout ce que je trouve à lui dire. Il ne répond pas et descend en vitesse embrasser Sandra. J'attends qu'ils se soient engouffrés dans la Studebaker du frère d'Eddy, puis je sors du train. Ma mère me demande si j'ai fait un beau voyage, et je ne lui réponds pas. Dans l'auto, elle me dit que je dois être bien fatiguée. Je marmonne : «C'est ça, c'est ça», pour m'en débarrasser. En entrant à la maison, je m'affale sur mon lit. Lulu me réveille au bout de vingt-quatre heures en disant que tout le monde croyait que j'étais morte. Bernard et Momo sont avec lui, inquiets. J'entends Coco rire de moi dans la cuisine en chantant : «Claude love Eddy, Eddy love Sandra, ah! ah! ah!» Puis il faut bien que je me lève et que je continue à vivre.

L'été s'achève comme il a commencé. Plate à mort.

Ottawa de nouveau. L'autobus de nouveau, la route des épinettes, la route au bout de la route. Pas de nouvelles d'Eddy. Ma mère m'écrit en post-scriptum que Sandra est enceinte de quatre mois. Elle aimerait garder son bébé, mais sa mère veut qu'elle le fasse adopter. Elle est partie à Montréal pour cacher son bébé, pour que personne ne le sache à Noranda. Tout le monde fait semblant de ne pas savoir, sa mère la première. Ça fait une petite explosion souterraine. Je me demande ce qu'en pense Eddy, il me semble plus lié encore à Sandra. Ma mère me dit au téléphone :

— Tu vois, ton beau juif, j'avais raison de m'en méfier. Y ont pas la même morale que nous autres, ce monde-là.

— Mais, 'man, y a ben des Canadiens à qui ça arrive, pis y était pas tout seul. Sandra était là, elle aussi.

— C'est pas pareil. On discutera de t'ça un peu plus tard, c't un longue distance, on va pas gaspiller du temps pour ça. Pis, as-tu eu des bonnes notes, manges-tu comme il faut ?

Eddy, c'est fini. Le bébé de Sandra, c'est son bébé aussi. Il faudra bien que je me trouve un autre amoureux. C'est une entreprise loin d'être facile dans mon couvent clôturé de pierres grises. La moindre sortie ici est clandestine et soupesée avec minu-tie. Trouver un amoureux dans les parages, c'est comme trouver de la petite monnaie dans une poche trouée.

Tout est fermé le dimanche à Ottawa, comme partout ailleurs en Ontario, et c'est pourquoi on a des heures de sortie beaucoup plus longues ce jour-là. Pour se distraire, on a mis sur pied un ciné-club. Dimanche dernier, les filles ont reçu les garçons du collège Saint-Alexis pour la projection de *Douze Hommes en colère*. C'est moi qui animais la discussion après le film. Dans tout ciné-club digne de ce nom, le film est suivi d'une discussion. Les sœurs avaient préparé des sandwiches roses et verts roulés au fromage Philadelphia dans le but de montrer aux filles comment se comporter dans le grand monde. Un blond frisé dur a surmonté sa timidité pour me féliciter d'avoir animé la discussion avec autant d'aplomb. « Mon nom, c'est Pierre-Paul. » Entre deux sandwiches, il m'a jeté un regard insistant et j'ai vite compris que si je lui demandais de me rappeler, il me rappellerait. Je lui ai donc demandé de me fournir de la documentation pour le film de dimanche prochain, *Marty*.

Je me mets à rêver tout haut dans ma chambre toute blanche et tout animée de désordre, car cette année je ne suis plus au dortoir des cent lits. J'ai droit à une petite chambre avec toilettes. Je la partage avec Annie et on trouve que c'est du grand luxe. La nuit, Doris vient et on fume en parlant tout bas de nos chums. Annie parle de son beau Marc, Doris ne jure que par Louis, son militaire et moi, je parle d'Eddy. Il est cependant impossible de vérifier tous nos dires puisqu'on n'a jamais l'occasion de voir les amis de nos amies. Ce soir, un peu avant l'étude, alors que je dansais une polka avec Annie dans la salle de récréation, Doris m'a crié qu'un garçon voulait me parler au téléphone. Le silence s'est dressé autour de moi pendant que je me dirigeais vers la cabine qui sentait la sueur et le rouge à lèvres. Les filles se sont arrêtées net de jouer au canasta. Je suis sortie radieuse de la cabine téléphonique : je suis invitée en chair et en os au cinéma, avec le grand blond frisé, samedi prochain.

Même s'il a l'air d'un ange, Pierre-Paul m'a proposé d'aller voir *La Dolce Vita* de Fellini, un film controversé et décrié autant dans *Le Droit* qu'en chaire par l'aumônier. Je n'ai même pas averti la surveillante que j'allais voir un film. J'ai plutôt dit que je devais accompagner un cousin de Noranda qui était de passage à Ottawa. Tranquillement, j'apprends à mieux mentir, à moins rougir. C'est la seule façon de survivre ici. Si on dit la vérité, on se fait avoir à l'os. C'est ce qu'on se dit entre nous. Dans le fond, le pire qui pourrait nous arriver serait de nous faire expulser. Toutes les filles ont peur de se faire renvoyer, moi la première.

Je me suis préparée sérieusement à ma sortie, empruntant en cachette ici et là une jupe, des souliers à talons hauts, un soutien-gorge pigeonnant et du rouge à lèvres rose malade pâle à la Brigitte Bardot. J'attends samedi et le soir, je rêve qu'on m'appelle au parloir quand je m'endors sur le sourire du grand Pierre-Paul au milieu des fougères croulantes. La porte s'ouvre devant un nuage de confettis et je suis prête à le suivre.

C'est samedi enfin, et tout se passe exactement comme dans mon rêve, sauf pour les confettis et la porte que la surveillante vient ouvrir avec son trousseau de clés. On décide de marcher rue Rideau. Il me prend la main d'une manière brusque et excessive. Il ne dit pas un mot. Je dis n'importe quoi. Son haleine a une odeur de tabac à pipe et de Certs. J'ai un peu peur. Il insiste pour payer mon entrée au cinéma, et la confiance revient tout à fait quand Anita Ekberg et Marcello Mastroiani se baignent dans la fontaine de Trevi au petit matin. Pierre-Paul suce nerveusement ses Certs et, tout en restant de glace, il serre ma main avec compulsion. Il me fait même un peu mal au moment où les gros seins d'Anita Ekberg se baladent sur l'écran.

Après le film, on décide d'aller voir les tulipes de la reine Juliana, sur le bord du canal Rideau. Il me prend d'abord par la taille, puis il met méthodiquement sa main sur mon épaule. On passe en face du Parlement, près de la gare, et il s'anime un peu en parlant de Marcel Chaput et de l'indépendance du Québec. Je suis agacée. C'est la première fois que j'en entends parler ailleurs que dans les journaux. Je n'ai jamais pensé à l'exploitation des Français par les Anglais. Je ne me suis même jamais demandé quelle langue je parlais au juste. Quand mon père déblatère contre ses patrons, il n'insiste jamais sur le fait qu'ils sont des Anglais. Quant à moi, les Anglais, je les aime assez, surtout les beaux juifs de six pieds, genre Eddy ; j'aurais aimé naître anglaise et juive pour devenir riche et belle. Dans mon enfance d'Abitibi, sous le ciel méditerranéen de l'hiver, j'ai souvent patiné avec des amies anglaises. Comment ces filles-là peuvent-elles devenir subitement si méchantes ? Pierre-Paul prononce « les Anglais » comme un chien gruge son os. C'est la première fois que la politique m'atteint et je vois tout à coup un fossé se creuser entre mes amies et mon peuple. J'ai une langue et un peuple, je viens de m'en rendre compte pour vrai. Ça me tombe dessus comme un fardeau. Ma mère trouve que ce serait plus facile si tout le monde était catholique et parlait français par-dessus le marché.

Je pense encore à Eddy, à ses mains, à son sourire et à sa voix. Je le compare à Pierre-Paul et je trouve que celui-ci ne fait pas le poids. Il parle de politique, mais il le fait de façon mesquine et autoritaire. Eddy ne parle jamais de politique, mais il est ratoureux comme un politicien.

On marche sur le bord du canal, et le grand blond frisé délaisse ses arguments nationalistes. On s'assoit dans l'herbe saturée de vapeur d'eau froide chauffée par le soleil de mai. Près d'un pâté de tulipes flamboyantes, Pierre-Paul parle de son avenir en physique nucléaire. J'essaie de placer un mot ou deux, non pas pour le contredire, mais pour émettre des doutes, et je n'y arrive pas. Je me contente de hocher la tête et de sourire en me demandant s'il va se décider à m'embrasser. Puis je bâille, et il commence à me caresser les genoux tout en remontant ma jupe d'un cran toutes les trois minutes.

À la fin il m'applique un gros French kiss. C'est tout ce que je désirais, l'embrasser. Ce qu'il pense de la politique et des sciences m'importe peu au fond. Après cinq minutes, il extrait sa langue de ma bouche et l'odeur du tabac à pipe mêlée au goût de Certs me donne un peu mal au cœur. Tout à coup, sans prévenir, il me propose de me reconduire au pensionnat. On revient en silence, et je fais déjà l'hypothèse qu'au prochain rendez-vous, les étapes seront franchies plus vite. Dans l'escalier, ses yeux de poisson s'animent tout à coup. Il parle comme s'il s'adressait à une foule. Il dit très fort que le Québec devrait se séparer du Canada, que le Québec devrait être indépendant. Il ajoute : «Un jour, quand les Anglais s'ront pus là, on sera tous riches.» Je trouve qu'il est fou, mais je n'ose rien dire parce que je n'ai pas encore assez réfléchi à la question. C'est vrai que les patrons de la mine Noranda sont des Anglais et qu'ils ont les plus grosses maisons de la rue Trémoy. Je n'avais pas fait le rapprochement. C'est loin d'être clair, tout ça. Il faudra que j'y repense sérieusement.

Quand il finit de parler, il m'embrasse avec véhémence, et sans même me laisser le temps de lui poser une seule question, il repart en vitesse. Je me sens bouleversée. C'est comme si la guerre était ici, pour vrai, pas seulement en Europe ou dans les livres d'histoire.

Je suis seule dans ma chambre le reste de la soirée. Annie est partie chez ses parents à Maniwaki. Je me suis acheté un gros sac de chips et six bouteilles de coke. Je raconte mon aventure avec Pierre-Paul dans mon petit calepin noir. Puis je continue de lire *La Peste* jusque très tard dans la nuit. Je sais que je ne dois pas manger ni boire après minuit si je veux communier demain matin, dimanche, mais je continue de manger mes chips et de boire mon coke. Un péché véniel de plus ou de moins, ça ne changera pas grand-chose. J'irai à confesse juste avant la messe et je raconterai tout à l'aumônier : *La Dolce Vita*, les gros seins d'Anita Ekberg, le French kiss près des tulipes, le coke et les chips après minuit, *La Peste*, et il sera tenu au secret. C'est bien pratique, la confesse : on peut tout faire et tout effacer à mesure. N'empêche que le remords me ronge quand même de temps en temps.

L'aumônier est un spécialiste des péchés de volupté. En chaire, ce matin, il commence à distinguer de façon très raffinée les péchés mortels des péchés véniels, et même si je suis de plus en plus incrédule, je me surprends à mesurer les peines encourues soit par un French kiss, soit par un effleurement des lèvres. C'est une vraie comptabilité. Une fois que l'aumônier m'a mise sur la piste, je peux, pendant le reste de la messe, calculer le prix de toutes ces offenses luxurieuses en les passant en revue les unes après les autres.

De nouveau les examens, de nouveau le mois de juin. Je dois retourner à Noranda pour l'été. Chaque fois que je prends l'autobus pour revenir chez moi, je suis partagée entre la joie de retrouver les miens et la tristesse de perdre une certaine indépendance. Comme si je les aimais de loin seulement. J'ai besoin de voir mes frères quelques heures ou quelques jours, c'est tout. Mais où aller le reste de l'été, sans argent, sans travail? Au couvent, je suis un peu en prison, mais dans une prison de silence. Je peux y être seule et tranquille. Pas de mère à mes trousses pour me demander de faire le ménage, pas de père qui fronce les sourcils, pas de frères qui passent leur temps à se moquer de moi. Peu à peu, je perds l'habitude de la vie de famille et j'en arrive même à aimer ma petite vie plate de pensionnaire.

En arrivant, Coco m'annonce la grande nouvelle: André et Danielle ont cassé. Ça me donne un coup. Je les pensais agglutinés pour la vie, ces deux-là. Il paraît qu'André en avait assez de Danielle. Mais Danielle me dit au téléphone que c'est elle qui en avait assez d'André, qu'il la trichait. Entre-temps, Coco se tient avec André, ce qui réjouit ma mère.

— Peut-être qu'André va lui montrer les bonnes manières, me dit-elle en l'absence de Coco. C'est tellement un bon garçon, cet André-là. Y m'a dit qu'y viendrait nous voir au chalet cet été.

— Ah bon!

Ma mère veut passer l'été au chalet avec les deux plus jeunes, Lulu et Momo. Elle a décidé qu'il fallait que je l'aide encore cette année. Notre chalet est au bout d'un long chemin de gravier qui donne mal au cœur et qui arrache les silencieux des voitures. Tout est bien organisé. L'eau, le chauffage, les canots. Je n'aurai qu'à m'occuper de Momo au fond, qu'à le surveiller pour ne pas qu'il se noie ou se perde dans le bois. Lulu m'aidera. Je m'entends vraiment bien avec lui, c'est presque mon seul ami à Noranda maintenant que je suis partie dix mois sur douze.

Ça fait drôle. Je ne suis plus d'ici ni d'ailleurs. Je ne rencontre plus grand monde que je connais quand je me promène sur la rue Principale après souper. Danielle Dusseault se cherche un nouveau chum et, comme elle sait qu'André se tient chez nous, elle ne me parle pas très longtemps. Yvonne Théroux me salue à peine et le collège Bellevue a comme effet de lui retrousser davantage son nez retroussé. Elle s'agrippe à Élie Buckovetsky comme la misère sur le pauvre monde. Coco me dit qu'Élie lui joue dans le dos en masse quand elle est partie le reste de l'année. Nicole Gauthier a disparu de la carte. On chuchote qu'elle a eu un bébé elle aussi, tout comme Sandra.

Je passe parfois au Radio Grill, mais ce n'est plus du tout ce que c'était. La gang s'est déplacée, paraît-il, dans d'autres sous-sols d'hôtels, au Moulin rouge et au Maroon lounge. On dit : « Au Moulin p'au Maroon » comme s'il s'agissait des jumeaux. Mais je n'aime pas les vrais bars et surtout, je n'entrerais jamais toute seule là-dedans. J'irais bien avec Lulu, mais il est encore trop jeune et il est hors de question que j'y aille avec les deux plus vieux.

D'ailleurs, Coco et Bernard sont partis travailler dans le bois avec mon père. Ainsi, il ne reste personne à la maison pendant tout l'été, personne qui ne laisse les portes ouvertes et les lumières allumées, personne qui ne couche dans tous les lits en même temps, surtout à deux, en mêlant les garçons et les filles. Ma mère rappelle toujours le cas Sandra, qui a fait boule de neige :

— J'ai l'impression que cette histoire-là s'est passée pendant que monsieur et madame Dubreuil étaient à leur chalet. J'voudrais pas que ça t'arrive ; te vois-tu avec un p'tit ? Tu pourrais même pas finir tes études, pis qu'est-ce que mes sœurs diraient ? Y paraît que son juif s'occupe pas du p'tit, même si c'est lui, l'père. Tout le monde sait ça.

Je me résigne donc à passer un triste été sur le bord du plus beau lac de la terre, comme dit mon père, à rager contre les mouches à chevreuil, la rosée du matin et le manque d'électricité. Je suis là avec ma mère et mes deux jeunes frères. En vacances, elle en profite pour sortir son répertoire de phrases célèbres : « Chaque jour suffit sa peine », « On vous aime tous pareil », « La mère des gars est pas morte ». Elle dit ça pour me consoler parce qu'elle sent que je ne suis pas dans mon assiette. J'aimerais bien lui parler d'Eddy, du Eddy que je connais, pas celui des racontars. J'aimerais lui parler de Pierre-Paul aussi, mais j'ai la certitude absolue que ma mère ne connaît rien à l'amour. Je veux dire à l'amour qui brûle le cœur et qui nous coupe en deux. La love. Les péchés de l'amour. Je suis incapable d'associer cette sorte d'amour aux tartes aux pommes qu'elle nous fait, aux vêtements qu'elle coud ou qu'elle raccommode, aux discussions qu'elle a avec mon père au sujet de mes frères. J'ai du mal à m'imaginer qu'elle a eu ses enfants autrement que par l'opération du Saint-Esprit. Quand je la regarde, je crois toujours à l'opération du Saint-Esprit, comme avec Ronnie Turner derrière les traques. J'en suis restée là avec elle. Je ne la vois même pas donnant un baiser un peu long, surtout pas faisant du necking. Enfin, ce n'est pas grave. Je l'aime bien, même quand elle sort ses quatre vérités de La Palice.

Après souper, je lave la vaisselle. Ensuite, j'assois Momo sur l'évier de la cuisine et je le lave en lui racontant des histoires. C'est la seule chose qui fait rire Momo, les histoires. Le reste du temps, il est sérieux. Bien plus que Coco. Trop pour son âge, mais ma mère dit que ça la repose des plus vieux. Quand Momo est bien propre, en pyjama, on sort sur la galerie regarder le soleil qui n'en finit plus de se coucher. Rose, vert, mauve. La seule chose vraiment belle sur ce lac, c'est le soleil qui flambe au-dessus d'une bande d'épinettes bien noires et bien tassées. Le chalet dans l'ensemble, c'est plate à mort, mais à bien y penser, rien ne vaut la douceur de l'eau quand on se baigne l'après-midi. Une petite écume se forme à la surface quand on nage. Je plonge et je plonge comme un canard huppé, je vois jusqu'au fond et je cueille des huîtres d'eau douce. L'eau est jaune et claire comme la lumière du soleil qui nous chauffe la peau. Je pense que la seule place où je voudrais passer mon éternité, c'est dans les joncs de ce lac moelleux, à flâner avec les brochets, à deviner les couleurs du coucher de soleil, à entendre les huarts la nuit, à me faire bercer par les moutons de la vague. L'hiver, je serais bien à l'abri sous des tonnes de glace et les dorés viendraient me rendre visite. Ah oui, ce serait le meilleur paradis de la terre. Ah oui! C'est quand même moins plate que tout le reste, il faut bien l'avouer.

Au moment où ma mère dit : «Claude, va donc coucher Momo, y est assez tard», un bruit de moteur attire notre attention. On hésite quelques instants entre un moteur d'auto, un moteur de bateau et un moteur d'hydravion. Finalement, une auto surgit, une grosse Chrylser de l'année qui déploie ses ailes entre les sapins. On finit par distinguer André au volant de l'auto de sa mère, accompagné de nul autre que mon frère Coco. Lucien court les accueillir : «C'est Coco, c'est Coco.»

J'aurais pu me passer de ces moineaux-là, mais je suis quand même contente d'avoir de la visite. André extrait du coffre à bagages tout ce qu'il a apporté : une tente, un tourne-disque et un radio à batterie, du coke, des chips. Il offre une boîte de Laura Secord à ma mère, qui n'arrête pas de glousser en me regardant de travers.

— T'es ben fin, mon André. Une chance que vous avez apporté une tente parce qu'il y aurait pas eu assez de place dans le chalet. C'est ben fin d'être

80

venu. Dis-moi donc, Coco, où est-ce qu'y est passé, Bernard?

— Y est resté avec papa dans le bois.

— Une chance, j'aurais pas voulu qu'y reste tout seul en ville.

Les deux gars ont faim et ma mère s'empresse de leur faire réchauffer des spaghettis. Elle leur donne ensuite un morceau de tarte au sucre qu'ils dévorent et, quand ils sont gavés, ils sortent pour monter leur tente. Je ne peux les accompagner parce que c'est l'heure de coucher Momo, de lui conter une dernière histoire et de l'endormir. Ma mère me demande de faire leur vaisselle. Lucien reste avec moi pour m'aider parce que Coco l'a reviré en disant :

— Va-t'en, p'tite femelle. On n'a pas besoin de toi.

Lucien rage et, s'il était plus gros, je crois bien qu'il le battrait. On dirait que Coco s'arrange toujours pour faire de la peine à quelqu'un. C'est plus fort que lui. Ma mère ne s'en rend pas compte, elle répète qu'elle nous aime tous de la même façon. Lulu et moi, on pense qu'elle préfère Coco parce que c'est le plus vieux et le plus tannant. Elle lui pardonne toutes ses frasques.

C'est vrai que ma mère ne se plaint jamais et que, pour elle, tout va toujours bien. Elle ne supporte pas qu'on dise que ça va mal. Par exemple, s'il se met à pleuvoir, elle dit tout de suite qu'il va faire beau. Elle ne parle jamais de la mort et personne n'a le droit d'en parler. Seule la maladie scande sa vie, la vraie maladie, les opérations, la polio, les césariennes. C'est sa façon à elle de combattre la mort.

Coco et André rentrent finalement après s'être baignés longtemps. Ils sont tout grelottants, et ma mère allume le poêle à bois pour les réchauffer. C'est un grand poêle blanc avec un réservoir d'eau chaude. Ma mère a une grande expérience des feux de bois. Dès qu'elle jette l'allumette après avoir disposé les journaux, les éclats et les morceaux de bouleau, le poêle se met à chauffer, à gronder, à craquer et son odeur nous atteint jusqu'à la moelle des os. Jusque très tard dans la nuit, on joue au cribbage en buvant du coke dans la lumière jaune et vacillante du fanal à gaz, qu'André appelle une lanterne.

Vient le moment de se coucher, et André me regarde droit dans les yeux en disant :

— Claude, tu devrais m'appeler un de ces jours pour qu'on aille ensemble au cinéma.

— J'sais pas.

Je m'en sors ainsi, mais je sais que je ne l'appellerai jamais. Parce que premièrement je ne le trouve pas trop trop de mon goût et que deuxièmement j'ai décidé de ne plus jamais appeler les garçons.

André me demande d'aller faire une promenade avec lui dans le bois cet après-midi. J'hésite avant d'accepter. Il arrive mal à faire comprendre à mon frère qu'il veut être seul avec moi, et je finis par céder pour faire enrager Coco. Entre nous, c'est toujours le pied de guerre et toutes les occasions sont bonnes pour faire des étincelles. Avec Coco, on ne peut jamais être calme et de bonne foi. On doit choisir ses mots et se demander ce qu'il a derrière la tête quand il dit les choses les plus banales. Être sur le qui-vive m'énerve. J'aimerais pouvoir lui parler comme à tout le monde et non pas comme à mon frère-qui-cherche-la-bagarre-pour-se-montrer-le-plus-fort-et-le-plus-fin.

On ne sait pas trop quoi se dire, André et moi. Le soleil chauffe le gravier et ravive l'odeur des framboises qui bordent le sentier. Des gros taons se gavent de sucre et on les voit vriller dans l'air sec. On ramasse un peu de framboises qui s'écrasent entre nos doigts tant elles sont mûres. Soudain, à brûle-pourpoint, je lui demande : «Veux-tu venir avec moi voir la dam de castors?»

— Le *barrage*, tu veux dire, répond-il avec un aplomb qui me fait rougir.

— Mais nous autres, on appelle ça une *dam*, même que ça fait bien rire Momo. Y est jamais allé pis y pense que c'est une vraie dame castor, avec un chapeau et des souliers à talons hauts, qui élève ses bébés castors et tout et tout.

En riant, André me prend doucement par la taille pour me faire passer devant lui dans la petite trail qui longe le ruisseau écumant et noir. Il n'y a plus de framboises, à cause de l'ombre. On écrase des fougères en marchant. Arrivés près du barrage, nous nous assoyons dans l'humus fumant et il se met à me frencher. Je ne veux pas qu'il fasse de bruit pour que personne ne se rende compte de quoi que ce soit, surtout pas Coco, qui pourrait être caché derrière un bouleau, on ne sait jamais. André me renverse dans les fougères et quand j'entrouvre les yeux, je vois le cristal bleu du ciel, avec des nuages de coton qui passent à grande vitesse. C'est la première fois qu'un garçon m'embrasse sans que je ressente autre chose que de l'ennui. Pourtant, la terre est odorante et humide.

Je réussis à me défaire de son étreinte et il me demande :

— Mais, Claude, qu'est-ce qui te prend?

— Ce qui me prend, c'est que je trouve que t'es vite en affaire, mon André.

Les baisers gras d'André me font lever le cœur, tout comme son empressement et sa politesse à tout casser. Quand il me serre contre lui, je vois ses pores dilatés dans son visage huileux. Des points noirs ici et là. Des taches de rousseur. Finalement, je retourne au chalet. On entend les taons qui butinent dans les framboises. On n'a plus le goût d'en cueillir. André a le caquet bas. Je ne dis rien. Ah, et puis, qu'il aille au diable! Après tout, je ne vais tout de même pas me contenter des restes de Danielle Dusseault.

Coco veut repartir à Noranda, mais ma mère ne veut pas qu'il soit seul à la maison. Devant son insistance, ma mère exige qu'André nous ramène tous. Je m'assois de mauvaise grâce sur la banquette avant, juste à côté de lui, et je prends Momo sur moi, pour être sûre qu'en changeant de vitesse André ne soit pas tenté de me frôler les genoux.

Ma mère est très contente de revenir en ville parce qu'au fond elle déteste la vie de chalet. Pas d'eau chaude, pas de télévision, et surtout pas de téléphone pour appeler ses sœurs pendant des heures. Aussi, elle a peur des orages du mois d'août. Et moi, je ne suis pas fâchée d'aller faire un tour au Radio Grill, question de couper l'été en deux. Il fait très chaud et Momo vomit deux fois dans l'auto. Je m'excuse chaque fois, comme si c'était ma faute, et j'essuie tout pendant que les autres font semblant de dormir. André me regarde avec des yeux d'épagneul. Moi, je fixe le coucher de soleil qui occupe tout le ciel devant nous, chargé d'oranges, de roses et d'ors.

Quand on arrive à Noranda, la maison est tout ouverte, tout allumée : mon père est là, avec mon oncle Edmond, le frère de ma mère. C'est étrange, ils picotent tous les deux dans une assiette de binnes en canne. Tout traîne dans la maison. Ils ont l'air abattu et ils nous dévisagent. Mon père a les sourcils froncés et ne dit pas un mot. On dirait qu'il a envie de pleurer, tout comme mon oncle Edmond.

— Comment ça se fait que t'es déjà revenu ? dit ma mère.

— On s'en allait vous voir au chalet. Y est arrivé quelque chose, Honey, quelque chose...

— Où c'est qui est Bernard ?

— Bernard s'est blessé tout à l'heure.

— C'est-tu grave ?

— Pas mal grave.

— Ben parle, dis quelque chose, que c'est qu'y est arrivé, oùsqu'il est ?

— C'est correct astheure, le docteur a dit qu'y était pus en danger. Y a un arbre qui est tombé sur lui... Fracture du crâne.

Ma mère se met à crier. Son cri nous perce les tympans et entre dans tous nos pores. On reste debout, mon père pleure, je suis atterrée. Ma mère

85

ne pleure pas, elle crie. Puis elle arrête de crier et elle commence à ramasser la vaisselle. Un silence gros comme un bulldozer passe dans la cuisine. André casse la glace et dit une niaiserie comme : « Bernard a peut-être pas été assez prudent. » Mon père devient tout rouge et lui fait une face de beu. André dit bonjour en promettant de me rappeler. C'est ça, André, fais de l'air.

Une fois André parti, ma mère s'affaisse sur une chaise du salon et se met à pleurer en silence. Je n'ai jamais vu ma mère pleurer. Mon père pleure parfois, surtout de joie, quand il est ému par un cadeau, un mot tendre, un poème. Il a pleuré quand son père est mort. Il était inconsolable. Je pleure de voir ma mère pleurer en silence. On l'entend à peine se moucher. Ça dure une éternité. Puis elle arrête net :

— Où est-ce qu'y est ?

— À l'hôpital Youville.

— À quelle heure que c'est arrivé, ou que c'est arrivé, comment c'est arrivé ? Y était-tu avec toi ? Qu'est-ce qu'y est arrivé ?

— C'est arrivé au bout du lac Opasatika, t'sais, le lac Long, la baie d'Orignal. L'autre bord, complètement. Y revenait du bois, y voulait se baigner, y était ben pressé. Edmond pis moi on a vu l'arbre tomber sur lui avant qu'on ait eu le temps d'y crier d'arrêter. On pensait qu'y était mort. On a couru vers lui, pis le bûcheron aussi. Y était sans connaissance, mais y respirait. Ça fait qu'Edmond est allé téléphoner à l'ambulance pendant que le bûcheron pis moi on dégageait Bernard. Une demi-heure plus tard, l'ambulance est arrivée pis y l'ont transporté tout de suite à l'hôpital. Y a été chanceux dans sa malchance, m'as te dire ben franchement, Honey. Y aurait pu mourir dret là.

— Pourquoi t'es pas venu nous chercher? dit ma mère en dévisageant mon père.

— Ça fait pas longtemps que c'est arrivé. Hein, Edmond? J'm'en allais vous le dire au chalet. Une chance que vous êtes arrivés.

— Pourquoi t'es pas venu directement?

— J'voulais reprendre mes esprits avant. J'voulais pas t'annoncer ça. J'aurais dû l'empêcher d'aller se braquer juste en dessous de l'arbre, j'aurais dû l'empêcher... J'comprends pas, le gars a pourtant crié «Timber!», ben fort. J'comprends pas.

Ma mère est partie avec mon père à l'hôpital. Je reste avec Lulu et Momo qui ne comprennent pas tout à fait ce qui se passe. Coco, pour une fois, ne dit rien. Il s'enferme dans sa chambre.

Les heures passent. La nuit. Le téléphone sonne sans arrêt. La nouvelle s'est répandue dans la parenté qui appelle de Montréal, de Notre-Dame-du-Nord. On reste là, assis, sans bouger. On répond au téléphone à tour de rôle et, chaque fois, on dit qu'on ne sait rien et on raccroche. On n'a rien à dire, on n'ose pas appeler à l'hôpital pour avoir des nouvelles. On dirait que nos parents nous ont oubliés.

Finalement, ils reviennent. Bernard a repris connaissance, mais on ne sait pas s'il sera paralysé. On ira le voir demain.

Des tonnes de gens inconnus essaient de nous encourager : des oncles, des tantes, des cousins venus de loin pour nous consoler. Mon père n'arrive pas à dire un mot. Je me couche et je pense à Bernard au moment où l'arbre est tombé sur lui. Je me rends compte que je l'ai à peine connu. Je l'entends encore jouer de la guitare dans le salon avec sa gang. Il est comme un étranger pour moi. C'est mon frère, mais ce pourrait être un pensionnaire. Il ne me dit jamais ce qu'il fait, mais il discute de tout et de rien. Il a plein de blondes, c'est tout ce je sais de lui, parce qu'elles appellent tout le temps. J'avais même reçu ordre de ne pas répondre parce que Bernard avait trop peur que je me trompe dans les noms. C'est vrai, je ne le connais pas, Bernard, il est toujours dans l'ombre de Coco.

On dirait que l'accident de Bernard a changé un peu notre vie. On ne pense qu'à Bernard, on ne parle que de lui. Il est devenu important tout à coup, comme s'il avait fallu que la mort le frôle de très près pour qu'on se rende compte de son existence. Mon père va le voir tous les jours à l'hôpital et ne se fâche presque plus, ne récite plus de poèmes. Coco ne me taquine plus. Lulu ne joue presque plus de piano et Momo reste dans son coin. Ma mère ne fredonne plus *Un Canadien errant* en faisant des gâteaux.

Petit à petit, la vie reprend son cours, à mesure que Bernard revient à la vie. Toutes nos peurs ont été vaines : il n'y aura pas de séquelles, sauf quelques cicatrices. Mais pas de paralysie. Ma mère dit que c'est l'essentiel, qu'il n'y a rien de plus précieux que la santé, etc. Je me demande si elle ne regrette pas un peu de sortir de la zone du grand malheur. Ses sœurs l'appellent de moins en moins, et le jour où Bernard sort enfin de l'hôpital, tout le monde revient à ses occupations. Mon père repart travailler dans le bois avec Coco. Ma mère reste à la maison pour soigner

Bernard qui est en convalescence un bon mois, et je continue de m'occuper de Momo.

Je pense toujours à Eddy. Je ne sais pas s'il est au courant de l'accident de Bernard. C'était son ami, Bernard. Peut-être que je le verrai au Radio Grill à un moment donné. Il n'est pas venu à l'hôpital, c'est André qui était là, à côté de moi, comme une tache. Il se prenait pour mon chum steady et j'étais vraiment trop préoccupée pour réagir. Je n'arrive vraiment pas à le trouver de mon goût même si tout le monde dit qu'il est correct, à commencer par mon frère Coco. Il m'appelle souvent, et je ne peux m'empêcher de le trouver petit, baveux, pincé. Je le compare à Eddy, c'est plus fort que moi. Ma mère adore André parce qu'il est poli et qu'il lui apporte toujours un petit cadeau quand il vient chez nous. Une fleur, des chocolats, du fudge que sa mère a fait. Il s'offre pour aider à la vaisselle. Son père est un grand comptable de Noranda que ma mère a connu avant de se marier. Il a épousé une femme de Montréal, très instruite, qui reste à la maison et qui fait du bénévolat. Ils ont tout pour être heureux, sans compter leur grosse maison sur les bords du lac Osisko.

À force d'insister, André finit par me convaincre d'aller au cinéma avec lui. Il sonne à la porte, et c'est ma mère qui lui ouvre. Elle y tient. Elle l'invite à s'asseoir sur le divan usé. J'ai honte. Le salon est une jungle. Pour arriver à s'asseoir, André doit enjamber les guitares de mes frères, contourner le kiddy car de

Momo, dégager les journaux. André fait semblant de ne rien voir et place délicatement les journaux sur ses genoux. Ma mère lui fait la conversation et le vouvoie gravement en lui offrant du sucre à la crème.

André n'aime que la musique classique et la musique militaire. Il ne manque pas de demander à ma mère de jouer du piano, ce qu'elle fait de bonne grâce. Elle sort ses feuilles du banc de piano et se met à jouer avec frénésie. Elle joue *Polichinelle* de Rachmaninov. André, en mélomane averti, se concentre pendant que ma mère s'envole en Russie sur ses touches d'ivoire véritable. Après les derniers trilles, André applaudit. Personne n'a jamais pensé d'applaudir ma mère auparavant.

Il me demande de jouer à mon tour, mais je refuse. Oh! je pourrais me débrouiller pour jouer sans me tromper la petite *Gertrude's Dream Waltz* de Beethoven, mais on va être en retard au cinéma. André devine que c'est un prétexte et il n'insiste pas. J'ai quand même mis ma belle robe blanche avec une encolure bateau bordée de guipure.

On va voir *Exodus* au Paramount. André paie mon entrée, et ça lui donne le droit de mettre son bras autour de mon cou pendant tout le film. Je suis fascinée par le beau Paul Newman : il a les mêmes yeux qu'Eddy. Je me prends pour Eva Marie Saint, en moins platine. J'imagine que, comme elle, j'ose embrasser mon beau juif à l'orée de la terre promise. Je décortique son nom à saveur angélique : Ève, Marie, sainte. Ils s'aiment, mais ils doivent se séparer à cause de leurs différences. Puis ils se retrouvent dans la mort qui rôde, mais c'est Eva Marie Saint qui embrasse sa cause. Faut-il embrasser la cause de l'autre pour arriver à s'entendre ? Plus le film avance, plus André promène sa main un peu partout. Je suis trop absorbée dans ma réflexion pour réagir. Je pense à Eddy, comme je l'aime, tel qu'il est! M'aime-t-il telle que je suis? Lequel de nous deux se serait converti? Lui au catholicisme? Moi au judaïsme? Pourtant, on ne croit pas à la religion ni l'un ni l'autre. Il m'a raconté un jour que sa mère s'était convertie au judaïsme pour épouser son père. Qu'autrement ils n'auraient pas pu se marier. À la fin, je fais un mouvement de recul quand André me frôle un sein. Je sors pour aller aux toilettes et en revenant je regarde la fin du film derrière la salle. Les Palestiniens ont l'air des méchants, ils portent des robes sombres. Ils martyrisent les juifs. On ne voit pas les juifs torturer les Palestiniens. André me fait signe de regagner ma place. Je reviens près de lui à la fin, quand Paul Newman exhorte les Arabes à vivre en harmonie avec les Juifs sur la terre qu'ils viennent de leur prendre. Je ne comprends pas. Je trouve qu'André sent la transpiration et j'ai hâte de sortir du cinéma.

En revenant, André parle de l'interprétation de Paul Newman et des paysages de l'histoire sainte. Lui, ce qui l'a étonné, c'est de voir des juifs habillés à la moderne en shorts de gymnastique se promener dans Jérusalem. Habituellement, on voit plutôt des personnages comme Moïse ou Ben Hur se promener dans les ruines de l'Ancien Testament. Je n'ai rien dit, j'étais encore dans mon personnage d'Eva Marie Saint et je me demandais comment elle pouvait faire pour se promener toujours bien coiffée en page boy avec sa jupe, son chemisier bien repassé et ses talons hauts dans les champs d'oliviers. André voulait que je discute avec lui de la position des Nations unies dans le conflit entre les Juifs et les Arabes, mais j'ai dit que je ne comprenais rien à la politique. Il m'a regardée avec son air supérieur et j'ai senti que tout était trop complexe pour commencer à parler de cette histoire. Tant pis si je passe pour une ignorante.

André est fier de ses connaissances, et il tient ma main avec assurance en marchant. Sa main est tellement moite que je dois la retenir pour ne pas qu'elle glisse. Il pense que je lui fais des avances et il m'embrasse si fort qu'on dirait qu'il veut m'aspirer l'âme. En arrivant à la maison, on se colle près de la maison dans un coin noir pour se mettre à l'abri de mes frères. Il insiste pour m'embrasser et je recule. En me débattant, je m'égratigne le coude sur le papier-brique. Ça saigne un peu.

— Ayoye, tu m' fais mal!

Il reste là, figé, les bras ballants, et je rentre en vitesse dans la maison.

— J'veux plus le revoir, celui-là, vraiment plus.

— Ben voyons donc, Claude, qu'est-ce qui te prend? dit ma mère.

— J'sais pas pourquoi, mais y m' tombe sus'es nerfs.

— Pourtant c't'un chic type. C'est vraiment un chic type.

— Regarde c'qui m'a fait au coude, ton chic type.

— C'est pas vrai..., dit ma mère, consternée, viens que j'te désinfecte ça avec du peroxyde. Dis pas ça à ton père.

Aujourd'hui, le directeur du personnel de l'hôtel Noranda m'a appelée pour me demander si je voulais toujours travailler comme waitress. Je voulais accepter l'emploi, mais après des heures de discussion avec ma mère, j'ai dû changer d'avis. De son côté, elle a décidé qu'elle allait passer la fin de l'été au chalet avec Lulu, Momo et ma tante Alphonsine. Elle dit de sa voix autoritaire :

— Tu vas rester ici, toi Claude, pour t'occuper de Bernard. T'auras rien qu'à lui faire ses repas pis son lavage. Y commence à marcher, y a presque plus besoin qu'on l'aide.

Je reste seule avec Bernard. Depuis qu'il a eu son accident, il parle davantage. Je le trouve même gentil par moments. Quand il n'est pas avec Coco, il ne fait pas de mauvaises blagues pour me faire enrager. Ce que j'aime de Bernard, c'est qu'il me laisse la paix pour lire, écrire dans mes petits calepins noirs. Je ne sors pas beaucoup, mais parfois je vais prendre une bière au Moulin rouge avec Bernard. Je découvre qu'il a tout un réseau d'amis qui rigolent beaucoup avec lui. Bernard change de personnalité quand il prend quelques bières. Ses petits yeux noirs se plissent et il se met à raconter des histoires, un peu comme mon père. Il est drôle et menteur et, à mesure qu'il boit et se réchauffe, tout double et quadruple même. Ça fait des sacrées soirées. Finalement, ce n'est pas si mal d'avoir un frère.

Mon coude est guéri. André n'appelle presque plus. Je vais parfois au Radio Grill avec Danielle Dusseault. On déblatère toutes les deux contre André. Le pauvre, les oreilles doivent lui ciller. Eddy est souvent là avec des anciens du High School. On se salue de loin. J'aimerais lui parler, mais j'ai peur qu'il rie de moi, ou quelque chose du genre. Danielle dit :

— Tu devrais y parler, y voit pus Sandra pantoute. Y l'a laissée pour de bon.

À la maison, je prépare les repas, je lave la vaisselle, je fais le ménage. Puis le soir, je sors très tard quand Bernard m'invite, ce qui est rare. Je m'endors parfois devant des reprises de *Un Homme et son péché* à la télévision. Donalda, c'est moi, mais avec des lunettes et des cheveux courts. Je nourris le désir insensé de retourner au pensionnat où je n'aurai que ma petite vaisselle à laver. André ne me rappelle plus du tout. Ma mère a perdu, j'ai gagné la deuxième manche.

Septembre arrive comme une délivrance, et je pars de nouveau à Ottawa pour y faire ma dernière année d'études. Mais je me rends compte de plus en plus que je n'ai pas le goût de faire une maîtresse d'école. Ce que je préfère, c'est lire et écrire. Je collabore au *Manuscrit*, le journal du couvent. Je lis tout le temps, surtout la nuit, dans les toilettes, avec une lampe de poche. J'ai une correspondante en France, qui s'appelle Claude elle aussi et qui m'envoie des beaux livres reliés, dorés sur tranche. C'est ainsi que j'ai pu passer au travers de *Notre-Dame de Paris*, du *Père Goriot* et de *Madame Bovary*. En toute clandestinité.

Je cache mes livres sous le matelas parce que je sais qu'ils sont strictement interdits. Ces œuvres écrites par des libre-penseurs contiennent des scènes impures, c'est ce que dit la sœur de français, sœur Jean-du-Tabernacle. On ne peut lire que des extraits dans des «petits classiques» épurés. J'aime mieux les œuvres complètes, je peux me laisser emporter par l'histoire sans me demander toujours ce qui s'est passé entre les extraits.

L'autre jour, je n'ai plus retrouvé *Madame Bovary*. Annie n'y avait pas touché, j'en étais certaine, parce qu'elle ne lit que les livres obligatoires. C'est un vrai mystère.

L'aumônier m'a convoquée. J'ai failli m'évanouir quand j'ai vu, sur son bureau, ma belle édition de *Madame Bovary*.

— Vous savez que ce livre est à l'index, n'est-ce pas Claude?

— Oui.

— Vous savez que c'est un grave péché que de lire un tel livre.

— Oui.

— L'avez-vous lu?

— Non.

— Qui vous l'a donné?

— Je l'ai trouvé.

— Où?

— Dans une librairie.

— Vous l'avez acheté?

— Oui.

— Pourquoi ne l'avez-vous pas lu?

— J'en ai pas eu le temps.

— Alors vous aviez l'intention de le lire?

— Oui.

— Donc, il faut vous confesser, parce que vous aviez l'intention de faire un péché.

— ...

— Et il va sans dire que je confisque votre livre. Pour cette fois, je n'avertirai pas vos parents, mais vous savez qu'il y a là matière à renvoi.

De retour dans ma chambre, je m'écroule en larmes. Annie m'avoue que la sœur surveillante est venue pendant mon absence et qu'elle a trouvé le livre dans les toilettes. Heureusement que la sœur s'est arrêtée là, car si elle avait cherché un peu plus, elle en aurait trouvé une dizaine d'autres cachés un peu partout.

Je caresse le désir de poursuivre des études en lettres à l'université pour avoir le droit de tout lire enfin! Comment mes parents, qui ont quatre fils à faire instruire, pourraient-ils se payer le luxe d'envoyer leur fille à l'université? Après tout, une fille peut se faire vivre par son mari! C'est peut-être ce qu'ils pensent en secret quand ils offrent à mes frères, devant moi, de payer toutes leurs études s'ils veulent bien en faire.

Ma tante Alphonsine trouve la solution. Elle a lu dans le journal que le gouvernement donne des bourses aux étudiants qui promettent de «servir» sept ans dans l'enseignement. Ma mère se rend chez le député qui m'aide à faire les démarches pour obtenir la bourse et je signe allègrement ce contrat, comme une fille signe n'importe quel contrat de mariage quand elle tient mordicus à se marier. J'ai peine à le croire, mais je suis inscrite pour vrai en lettres à l'Université de Montréal. Je partirai toute seule pour la grande ville. Youpi, je ne serai plus pensionnaire! Je suis sortie du bois.

Ma mère pense que je vais me trouver un mari à l'université et que je passerai le reste de ma vie à Montréal. Je ne suis pas sûre de vouloir me trouver un mari. Un chum, oui, mais pas un mari. Elle répète une autre de ses phrases célèbres: «Qui prend mari prend pays.»

Je suis chanceuse cet été, j'ai déniché un emploi de commis dans une compagnie d'assurances. Il faut dire que j'ai fait des pieds et des mains et du crayon et du téléphone pour y arriver, d'autant plus que je savais par mon frère Bernard qu'Eddy y travaillait l'été depuis deux ans. D'ailleurs, quelle ne fut pas sa surprise au bel Eddy de me voir arriver le premier jour. Il a un poste important. Il remplace le patron et l'assistante du patron pendant leurs vacances qu'ils prennent à tour de rôle.

Il fait semblant de ne pas me reconnaître et me traite exactement comme les autres filles du bureau, gentiment, sans plus. La cicatrice s'ouvre un peu et je me demande si je pourrai supporter son indifférence très longtemps. Sharon, la directrice du personnel, une grande blonde mariée d'au moins trente ans, a l'air d'avoir l'œil sur Eddy. Monsieur Goldstein par-ci, monsieur Goldstein par-là. Pendant la pause-café, elle me questionne tout le temps. Elle me demande si j'ai un chum, si j'en ai encore pour longtemps à étudier. Elle me dit : « C'est comme Eddy Goldstein, il a décidé de s'inscrire en médecine à McGill en septembre. »

Eddy a beaucoup changé. Il arrive au travail en complet et cravate, frais et dispos, saluant toutes les employées, avec l'aménité d'un assureur chevronné. Il est tellement sérieux qu'il prend à peine ses pauses-café, alignant ses colonnes de chiffres avec la plus grande minutie. On dirait un ange comptable.

Je voudrais lui parler. Savoir ce qui lui arrive. Il sait que je sais. Sandra est partie vivre à Montréal avec son bébé. Je voudrais lui demander comment va son bébé. Pour faire le pont, pour raviver le passé. Mais je sens qu'il ne faut pas. Chaque chose en son temps.

Puis un jour que Sharon et les autres sont parties, il me regarde enfin pour vrai, comme s'il me reconnaissait. Un désir dans ses yeux bleus. Exactement comme avant. Je le regarde aussi. Je me sens ramollir et je pense que si je m'approchais de lui, il m'embrasserait. Il se retient, le petit salaud. Il me dit seulement : « Viendrais-tu avec moi ce soir ? Il y a une course de stocks-cars à McWatters. » Il roule toujours ses *r* à l'anglaise et je fonds. Je dis oui tout de suite.

Il vient me chercher dans une vieille minoune toute bariolée un peu après souper. Il a troqué son complet veston pour une veste de cuir et des jeans moulants. Une mèche de cheveux se rabat sur son front, laquée noire, comme celle d'Elvis Presley. Ma mère lui ouvre la porte et avec toute la froideur dont elle est capable, elle revient me dire que mon «type» demande à me voir. Elle glisse entre ses dents :

— Dis-moi pas que ça recommence, cette histoire-là. Toi pis tes nations étrangères...

J'agrippe ma veste de daim et je pars sans dire un mot. *Alea jacta est.*

Dans l'auto, Eddy se met à rigoler comme avant. Il se montre vite familier, me passant la main sur le genou de temps en temps. Il y a cependant un élément nouveau dans sa façon de parler : il entrelarde ses phrases de nombreux *stie.* Je ne l'avais jamais entendu sacrer auparavant. Il a l'air d'un vrai colon. J'ai encore du mal à imaginer que ce garçon est celui que j'ai cru aimer l'an dernier, que j'aime encore.

En rentrant sur la piste de stock-cars, il met un casque de motard et me demande de monter seule dans les estrades. J'ai donc affaire à un coureur et non à un spectateur.

Peu à peu l'enthousiasme m'atteint, à cause des gens tout autour qui crient. Des gens que je ne connais pas. Qui boivent de la bière et qui sacrent à faire rougir les gars de bois, y compris mon père. Les autos se percutent dans une corrida de ferraille bigarrée. Plus rien n'est pris au sérieux, ni les autos, ni la vie, ni le soleil qui se couche derrière les nuages de la mine, violet et rose bonbon. Eddy est favori et, après plusieurs carambolages qui me font frémir, il n'a aucune peine à gagner la course.

Triomphant, il revient me chercher pour me ramener à la maison. Il conduit comme un fou, ivre de sa victoire, content d'avoir étonné la petite oie blanche que je suis. Sans que j'aie le temps de m'en apercevoir, on traverse les deux villes, on passe sur les voies ferrées, on se dirige vers Noranda-Nord, puis on bifurque dans le chemin du cimetière.

— Oùsqu'on va? dis-je en essayant de me montrer brave.

— Tu vois bien, on vient icitte, au cimetière, stie.

— Pourquoi au cimetière?

— Parce que c'est plus tranquille, stie.

— Tranquille?

— As-tu besoin d'un dessin, stie?

Après avoir franchi la porte du cimetière, il stationne son auto au beau milieu des monuments de granit. Dans le temps de le dire, il ouvre sa braguette et sort son dard. Je n'ai jamais vu d'aussi près un sexe d'homme en érection. Ceux de mes frères, quand j'ouvre la porte de la salle de bains par mégarde sans frapper, me semblent ratatinés. Je regarde la chose avec curiosité, un vrai bat de base-ball au bout renflé. Il saisit ma main et l'insère avec force entre ses deux jambes en me disant: «Fais-moi jouir, stie.» Je retire ma main aussitôt et il m'empoigne le cou par-derrière pour que j'enfouisse ma tête sur son sexe qui dégage une odeur à me faire lever le cœur. Je me débats du mieux que je peux. Je ne trouve plus la partie très drôle et je me mets à pleurer. Puis il finit par me projeter sur la portière en criant:

— Maudite agace-pissette, stie.

Il démarre en trombe et fait valser sa minoune à travers les pierres tombales pendant plusieurs minutes. Je suis paralysée, sans réaction. Je pense que mon grand-père est là quelque part sous la terre. Je l'appelle à l'aide dans ma tête en fermant les yeux. Eddy finit par se calmer, sort du cimetière et il me ramène en quatrième vitesse à la porte de la maison.

Ma mère m'attend dans la cuisine. Pour une fois, je me sens réconfortée en la voyant. Elle fait semblant de lire son *Woman's Day* au bout de la table.

— Ç'a ben été, ta petite sortie?

— Oui, m'man, ç'a ben été.

Elle ne me croit pas, c'est sûr. Elle reste encore un peu dans la cuisine, au cas où je lui raconterais quelque chose. Je vais me coucher. Toute la nuit, je revois les yeux d'Eddy, menaçants. J'ai mal au cou et je tremble pour rien. Je n'ai pas fermé l'œil et je me dis qu'Eddy était bien plus raffiné l'année dernière. Je suis en confiture. Je vais travailler à reculons, comme si j'étais en proie à une fièvre de cheval. J'ai peur d'affronter Eddy. J'ai peur qu'il raconte tout au bureau aujourd'hui. Mais non, il arrive à l'heure au travail, en cravate comme tous les matins, et il salue tout le monde avec délicatesse. Petit sourire en coin. Que penser de tout ça? Est-ce que je suis vraiment une agace-pissette? Je me sens quand même humiliée. Comment peut-il continuer à vivre comme si rien ne s'était passé? Je ne comprends pas. Je suis une zone sinistrée.

— Eddy, pourquoi as-tu fait ça? Me détestes-tu tant que ça?

Mais les mots restent au gosier. Je devrais le haïr. Je devrais le tuer. Mais je l'aime, c'est plus fort que moi, et je joue son jeu.

— Bonjour, Eddy, comment ça va?

— Oh! un 'tit peu poqué. J'pense que j'ai un peu trop bu hier soir, j'me rappelle pus trop trop ce que j'ai fait.

Je l'haïs, l'hostie.

Puis septembre arrive de nouveau. Je n'arrive pas à croire que je pars pour de bon à Montréal, qu'Eddy y sera lui aussi. Dans son appartement, près de son université. Le dernier jour, il me dit:

— Je vas t'appeler.

— Comment tu peux m'appeler, j'ai pas encore le téléphone.

— C'est pas grave, j'm'arrangerai, *you're gonna see.*

Et il me frôle la joue d'un petit bec. Un petit baiser copain copain, et je rougis. Je suis déçue, j'en voudrais davantage, un gros French kiss comme dans le bon vieux temps.

André vient me reconduire au terminus, il a insisté. J'ai dit oui, en pensant qu'Eddy nous verrait ensemble, juste pour qu'il soit jaloux. Évidemment, personne ne nous a vus à sept heures et demie du matin. André a essayé de me coller un gros baiser sur les lèvres pour payer son déplacement, mais je suis montée vite dans l'autobus, me contentant de lui faire bye bye à travers la vitre. Bye, bye, Noranda. Je ne reviendrai plus. En tout cas, pas pour un bon bout de temps. C'est trop plate.

J'espère qu'Eddy m'appellera à Montréal, qu'il ne m'oubliera pas. Je lui en veux de m'avoir coincée dans l'auto au cimetière, mais c'est plus fort que moi, je l'aime encore. Je me dis sans conviction que je l'oublierai, que je me ferai un nouveau chum à l'université. Un vrai sérieux chum qui m'aimera tout le temps, qui me téléphonera tous les jours. Mais Eddy s'améliore à mesure que le voyage avance. Cadillac, Malartic, Val-d'Or, Louvicourt, Grand-Remous, Mont-Laurier, Saint-Jovite, Sainte-Agathe. Je ramollis et, rendue à Montréal, Eddy a atteint la perfection.

Ma tante Laura m'a déniché une chambre pendant l'été. Sûrement que c'est la chambre la plus miteuse des alentours de l'université, avec une tapisserie de couleur indéfinissable, des tentures fleuries rouge et vert, un tapis de Turquie fleuri rouge et noir, un couvre-lit fleuri rouge et bleu, un lit de noyer foncé, un miroir terni et craqué, des abat-jour jaunis et sales, une commode grasse. Ça sent les vieilles toasts et le linge moisi.

Ma tante Laura me prête une table de jardin sur laquelle j'installe ma Smith-Corona verte et blanche, flambant neuve. Je veux être à la hauteur et je tape méticuleusement toutes mes notes de cours pendant les trois premières semaines. Ensuite, je me vautre dans la lecture de tous les romans que je n'avais pas pu lire. Je commence la *Comédie humaine* et je délaisse les notes de cours. Ce n'est vraiment pas comme au cinéma : les personnages vivent dans ma tête, je me promène en voiture sur les pavés de Paris, je manque d'argent, j'assiste au bal. Je suis la voisine de la cousine Bette. Je découvre la France, je découvre l'Europe.

Je vais à tous mes cours. Je suis un peu perdue et j'ai l'impression de venir d'un pays étranger, de n'avoir jamais rien appris. Je ne pose pas de questions, même si je ne comprends pas grand-chose à ce que les professeurs racontent. Les filles qui viennent de Marie-de-France posent de longues questions que je ne comprends pas non plus. Elles ont un petit accent français, portent les Chanel de leur mère et conduisent la décapotable de leur père. Je n'ose même pas leur adresser la parole. Par contre, j'ai vite trouvé deux copines, une fille de la Nouvelle-Écosse et une autre de Chicoutimi. Puis je rencontre des garçons, aussi timides que moi, qui viennent de Sudbury et de Moncton. On rigole ensemble. Ils jouent de la guitare, et je les considère un peu comme mes frères. Au fond, on se sent tous comme des réfugiés.

Chez madame Beauséjour, où je reste, il y a aussi un gars qui loue une chambre. Tony d'Ottawa. Il étudie en art dentaire et il a de beaux cheveux blonds tout frisés. Il est fiancé, et c'est la première chose qu'il me dit ou presque. Mais il vient souvent frapper à ma porte pour m'inviter à prendre un café avec lui dans la cuisine quand madame Beauséjour est partie. On discute pendant des heures. Heureusement que madame Beauséjour est très pieuse. Elle va à l'église trois fois par jour, le matin, l'après-midi et le soir. Tony et moi, on parle contre elle et on dit qu'elle doit avoir un kick sur le curé. Elle nous regarde de travers quand elle nous surprend dans la cuisine en train de rigoler. Elle fait «Tut! Tut! Tut!» et rentre dans son salon double en claquant la porte vitrée.

Sur les murs des couloirs pendent des natures mortes. Son mari était peintre et il a fait une production importante de tableaux sans jamais les vendre. Il était contre le marché de l'art, semble-t-il, et il a interdit à sa veuve, dans son testament, de vendre un seul tableau. Elle insiste sur ce détail. Je les trouve tellement laids et insignifiants, ces tableaux, que même si elle voulait les vendre, elle ne trouverait pas d'acheteurs.

Ce soir, je sors avec Tony. Il m'invite au ciné-club voir *Jules et Jim*. Jeanne Moreau chante une chanson de bracelets tout à fait anodine avec sa voix frêle, et ça m'empêche de deviner qu'elle va se suicider. J'aurais tant aimé qu'elle puisse aimer ses deux amants et qu'ils vivent à trois, sans problèmes, dans leur chalet suisse. Ils étaient pourtant bien partis, mais ça n'a pas marché. Pourquoi cela doit-il toujours finir mal dès que les sentiments sont complexes? J'aime Eddy, je vais toujours l'aimer. Je ne le dirai pas, ça ne se fait pas, c'est pourquoi je n'aurai pas à me suicider. Ce qui n'est pas dit dans les paroles de nos mères mène à la mort, c'est sûr. Il faut se taire pour vivre.

Madame Beauséjour devine que Tony et moi, on pourrait devenir de grands grands amis. Elle ne peut pas le supporter et sa patience est à bout. Elle dit en revenant de la messe :

— Mademoiselle Éthier, je vous donne une notice d'une semaine. Samedi prochain, vous devez partir d'ici. Je vais communier tous les matins et je ne veux rien avoir sur la conscience. Qu'est-ce qui m'a pris de louer mes chambres à des sexes différents ?

— Mais pourquoi moi et pas lui ? lui ai-je répondu, un peu baveuse.

— Parce que les filles, c'est plus risqué. J'ai pas envie que vous tombiez enceinte dans ma maison.

— Mais madame, j'ai pas l'intention de tomber enceinte.

— Mais vous pouvez faire des... choses quand chus partie à la messe pis j'veux rien avoir sur la conscience. Et pis, j'trouve que les filles, vous autres, vous restez trop longtemps dans la toilette à vous pomponner. J'ai fait une grave erreur, là, j'veux plutôt louer à un autre garçon, c'est plus pratique... j'vas pouvoir aller communier en paix.

Je fais mes bagages et je cherche une autre chambre. Près de l'université en plein mois d'octobre, ce n'est pas évident. Heureusement, les petites annonces me mettent en relation avec Gracia, une grande blonde pulpeuse, mère de jumeaux de quinze ans, divorcée et accotée.

Gracia est la première femme divorcée que je vois de près, en chair et en os. Je trouve plutôt scandaleux de l'entendre chanter et rire tout en cuisinant des ailes de poulet à la moutarde, son mets préféré. Il me semble que cette désinvolture ne va pas du tout avec son statut de femme divorcée.

Gracia est d'ailleurs loin d'être malheureuse, surtout lorsqu'elle passe l'après-midi avec son petit ami chauve, un Écossais qui cherche indirectement à m'inclure dans leurs ébats. Mais la morale de l'«œuvre de chair en mariage seulement» est encore ancrée solidement dans mon cerveau. Je suis restée presque vierge. Enfin, Eddy a ouvert la voie avec un doigt seulement, et je compte n'y rien changer, même si, par ailleurs, toutes les autres possibilités de contacts amoureux sont les bienvenues.

Gracia gagne sa vie à vendre de la lingerie fine importée de France. Elle fait sa propre réclame en s'affichant dans la maison avec d'élégants dessous Simone Pérèle, à peine camouflés par des déshabillés vaporeux. On voit ses taches de rousseur sur sa poitrine. On voit aussi quelques bourrelets sur son ventre.

Elle part souvent pour quelques jours offrir sa marchandise à des clients de l'extérieur. Elle vend beaucoup parce qu'elle se fait elle-même mannequin. Elle ne part jamais sans son diaphragme. Quand je vais à la toilette, je l'examine et je me demande comment elle fait pour utiliser cet objet caoutchouté au moment propice. J'aurais peur de mal l'ajuster dans l'énervement. D'ailleurs, Gracia se plaint que son diaphragme est mal ajusté. Elle en discute avec son ami écossais au sortir de la chambre certains après-midi.

Dans cette atmosphère de haute luxure, j'ai beaucoup de distractions. Il y a des chicanes, de la baise et toutes ces choses qui rendent difficile la concentration dans les études. Gracia est un personnage de roman, comme Manon Lescaut ou Emma

Bovary. De la voir ainsi manœuvrer, ça me donne le goût de passer de la théorie à la pratique. L'amant écossais devient de plus en plus pressant pendant les absences de Gracia. Chaque fois que je le rencontre, il me demande si je suis vierge, si je consentirais à coucher avec un homme que je connais à peine. Il tourne autour du pot, il voudrait bien qu'on aille faire un tour dans sa chambre. Mais il est chauve et vieux, et je décide de prendre un appartement. J'ai besoin de plus de calme pour étudier.

Je commence une vie nouvelle dans mon petit appartement d'une pièce, au 2269 Maplewood. C'est mon amie Marie-Claire, une fille débrouillarde, qui me l'a refilé. Ses parents habitent à Montréal, mais elle vit quand même en appartement. Elle connaît plein de gars et se tient avec la gang de la revue *Mots et cris*. Elle m'a demandé d'en faire la mise en pages. Ce que j'aimerais le plus au monde, ce serait d'écrire, mais je pense que l'écriture c'est pour les autres, comme la maladie, comme la mort. J'écris des textes quand j'ai le cœur gros, mais je n'oserais jamais en montrer une seule ligne à qui que ce soit de peur de faire rire de moi. Je sens d'ailleurs que mes poèmes n'ajouteraient pas une seule goutte d'eau au verre déjà rempli des Miron, Chamberland, Perreault et compagnie.

En faisant la mise en pages de la revue, je me sens plus près de l'écriture. Chez Marie-Claire, c'est ni plus ni moins le local de la revue. On y va souvent parce que c'est chouette chez elle et qu'elle n'est pas trop exigeante en matière de propreté. Il y a de la bière, de la fumée, beaucoup de discussions, un peu de pelotage et parfois quelques conversations litté-raires. Je suis fascinée par les gars de la revue qui sont tous très nationalistes. Pour eux, tout a l'air clair, précis, évident. Je suis d'accord avec leurs arguments, mais en les écoutant, j'ai toujours l'impression qu'ils sont trop sûrs d'eux pour que ce soit si simple. L'indépendance me laisse perplexe. Les gars sont pompés à l'os contre les Anglais. Ils défilent tout bas des tas de statistiques qu'ils prennent dans les numéros de *Révolution québécoise*. On dirait qu'ils ne font que penser et boire de la bière, qu'ils ne font rien d'ordinaire comme se laver, manger, acheter des choses, embrasser une fille. Pourtant, ils ont des blondes. Je me demande s'ils se déshabillent pour se coucher.

J'ai bien arrangé mon une-pièce. Avant de partir, Marie-Claire a décroché les innombrables affiches de Chagall et de Miró qui tapissaient ses murs. Ça laisse des grands carrés jaunes, et je décide de tout repeindre avant de coller mes propres affiches de Chagall et de Miró. C'est comme un vrai petit nid. Pour la première fois de ma vie, je me sens chez moi, et ça me rend euphorique. Dans mon une-pièce, j'irai jusqu'au bout, j'en suis sûre. Avant l'août, foi d'animal, intérêts et principal.

Gracia est devenue un vraie mère pour moi. Elle m'aide à coudre des petits rideaux vert canot et une housse assortie pour mon divan-lit. D'un côté, il y a un lavabo, un mini-frigidaire, une armoire de métal blanche et un petit poêle à deux ronds, et de l'autre côté, il y a une bibliothèque, un divan, une table à tout faire. Entre tout cela, des philodendrons courent dans un filet de pêche de Gaspésie, comme à la crêperie bretonne de la rue Rachel.

Je suis au ciel vingt-quatre heures sur vingt-quatre, sauf quand il faut que j'aille aux toilettes. Je partage la salle de bains avec deux autres locataires et je dois mettre beaucoup de Ajax dans la baignoire pour la nettoyer avant et après chaque bain. Comme chez moi, à Noranda, avec mes frères, je suis la seule à voir que la toilette, la baignoire et le lavabo sont sales. Des capotes usagées traînent parfois sur le bord du lavabo. La nuit, j'entends clairement les borborygmes et les râles d'orgasme chez mes voisins.

Je suis à la recherche de pilules contraceptives. Marie-Claire, une habituée de l'alcôve, m'avertit qu'il est difficile de s'en faire prescrire sans certificat de mariage. Gracia, ma bonne étoile, connaît un juif de Westmount qui ne pose pas de questions indiscrètes. J'ai son numéro et, si ça marche, je le refilerai aux copines.

Le docteur juif de Westmount ne m'a rien demandé. Seulement si j'étais allergique et si j'avais plus de dix-huit ans. J'ai une petite roulette que je camoufle dans mon sac et je fais sonner le réveille-matin à huit heures du soir pour ne pas oublier de prendre ma pilule. C'est très facile et je n'ai presque pas mal au ventre quand je suis menstruée. Mes seins sont gonflés, sensibles au toucher.

Aujourd'hui, c'est le printemps. La mince couche de glace sur les flaques d'eau est prête à céder au moindre pas hasardeux. La rue Maplewood ruisselle sous le soleil. André m'appelle de temps en temps. On jase au téléphone longtemps, mais je refuse toutes ses invitations. C'est plus fort que moi, je pense à mon bel Eddy qui ne m'a pas donné signe de vie de l'année. Je pourrais l'appeler, mon frère Coco a son numéro à Montréal. Mais je ne veux rien demander à Coco et puis je n'appelle pas les gars. Jamais. C'est ma fierté. N'empêche que j'aimerais bien qu'Eddy m'appelle. J'ai envie de lui parler, qu'il me regarde avec ses yeux de juif errant. J'ai envie d'avoir un chum. Quand je vois des amoureux qui se promènent main dans la main, j'en bave. Est-ce que ça va m'arriver un jour? Des fois je suis découragée et je pense que je passerai le reste de ma vie toute seule, indépendante et fière, mais triste au fond. «Allons, Claude, la mère des gars est pas morte.» La petite voix de ma mère me fait sortir de ma torpeur et je décide de commencer ma chasse à l'homme.

Je choisis d'abord mon territoire : l'appartement du sous-sol où restent deux gars de la revue, Guy et Jean-Guy. Leur frigidaire regorge de bactéries bien vivantes disposées autour d'innombrables bouteilles de bière. J'arrête chez eux par hasard pour remettre les épreuves parce qu'en plus de faire la mise en pages, je corrige les textes de tout le monde. Roger est là, c'est le nouveau trésorier. Il est venu leur montrer comment préparer le budget de la revue. Il semble tellement fort en chiffres et s'est rasé de si près que j'ai du mal à l'imaginer en lettres. Il a tout à fait l'air d'un comptable patenté. Il est bien habillé, bien peigné et dégage une odeur délicate d'after shave ou de déodorant. Cela contraste avec les gars de la revue qui sont plutôt barbus, poilus et dont les chandails sentent la sueur et le renfermé. Roger est sensible, je crois, à la coupe très au poil de mon petit tailleur pied-de-poule.

On boit beaucoup de bière pendant longtemps et, comme toujours, plus on devient soûls, plus la discussion s'anime et devient confuse. Roger a l'air d'être contre l'indépendance et il sort des arguments étoffés de statistiques qui nous laissent bouche bée. Je sens qu'il triture les chiffres, mais personne n'arrive à le discerner vraiment. C'est trop facile. La chicane est sur le point d'éclater, mais Roger est cool et il propose à tout le monde d'aller prendre un Brio chez Vito. Sur place, il m'offre de partager sa pizza all dressed. Ensuite, on marche un peu sur Lacombe et on entre au Bouvillon prendre quelques screw-drivers. Il tète sa cerise au fond du verre tout en me regardant dans les yeux. Il me caresse les genoux sous la table sans que personne ne voie son geste et je fais semblant de ne rien sentir. Sur la piste de danse, il fait plusieurs tentatives louables pour me montrer comment danser le cha-cha-cha, mais je ne connais que le slow et le rock'n'roll. Je n'arrive pas à faire autre chose que de lui marcher sur les pieds. En sortant, il me dit :

— Viens-tu, Claude ? On va aller au belvédère de la montagne contempler la ville de Montréal.

— O.K. !

Roger a une petite Simca Zephyr grise. Il me fait monter en ouvrant galamment la portière. Une fois stationnés sur le belvédère de la montagne, on se met à faire du necking. Je n'ai pas embrassé de garçon depuis longtemps et ça m'électrise tellement, ce baiser, que je ne regarde même pas la ville. Le jour se lève et je crois bien que je suis mûre comme une figue sous le soleil de Tunis.

Une fois dans l'appartement, j'ouvre le divan-lit et je commence à me déshabiller. Puis je me calme bien vite parce que Roger n'est plus très pressé. Il prend soin de vérifier les draps, de se déshabiller méthodiquement en pliant ses vêtements. Il est nu et se promène avec aisance comme un habitué des camps de nudistes. Je n'arrive pas à ôter ma jupe et ma blouse. Il prend le temps de me dévêtir morceau par morceau en me caressant longuement. Je deviens folle, je me tords. Il me lèche partout. Je comprends pour la première fois toute la complexité et toute la profondeur de l'expression «œuvre de chair». Mais pourquoi «en mariage seulement»?

Il me fait l'amour avec délicatesse. J'en redemande. Roger semble déçu: il pensait que c'était la première fois et sur les draps, il n'y a rien de rouge, aucune tache, aucune preuve. J'essaie de lui expliquer que c'est la vraie première fois, en insistant sur le mot «vraie». Je ne veux pas lui parler d'Eddy. Je trouve ça très compliqué et je décide de me taire.

Il remet ses vêtements tranquillement en commençant par ses chaussettes. L'air songeur, il me dit sèchement au revoir en me laissant pantelante, les cuisses encore toutes mouillées.

Une semaine a passé depuis ma nuit de «noces» et Roger ne me fait pas signe. J'ai bien aimé la petite intrusion qu'il a faite dans ma vie privée et je me demande comment m'y prendre pour renouveler l'expérience. J'essaie par toutes sortes de stratagèmes de le rencontrer à l'université. Il ne suit pas les mêmes cours que moi, mais en parlant aux gars de la revue, je me suis arrangée pour connaître son horaire.

Par pur hasard donc, je revois Roger à la sortie d'un cours d'histoire. Je veux lui présenter mes excuses et lui dire ce qu'il voulait entendre à propos de ma virginité ratée. Mais il me fait un de ces grands sourires, et j'oublie de m'expliquer.

— Allô! chère! Comment vas-tu? me dit-il, toujours aussi guilleret.

— Ben, c't'une chance que j'te rencontre, imagine-toi que je voulais justement t'avertir qu'y a une réunion de la revue mercredi soir prochain, chez Guy et Jean-Guy. Penses-tu de pouvoir venir?

— Sais-tu, j'sais pas trop trop ce que j'vas faire là avec c'te gang de barbus-là, j'ai décidé de pus r'mettre les pieds là. Si jamais tu les vois, fais la commission, chère.

— Compte pas sus moi.

Bon, encore un autre qui fait comme si rien ne s'était passé. Un soir, il met sa langue dans la fond de ma bouche et un peu partout sur mon corps, il me caresse les seins et le reste, il introduit son pénis gonflé dans mon sexe, et le lendemain il fait comme si rien ne s'était passé. C'est donc ça, la love?

Je ne suis pas à la hauteur de l'amour. Ma mère me l'a bien dit, c'est à cause de mes lunettes, à cause de mes cheveux raides, de mes ongles rongés. Peut-être que je ne suis pas assez riche, assez intelligente? Peut-être que mon désir géant comme un sac de pop-corn lui fait trop peur? Je ne comprends pas la coupure brutale des peaux, des âmes. Je reste engourdie dans mon désir comme si j'avais bu cinquante Labatt 50 d'affilée.

Je me remets à la lecture. J'ai au moins trente romans à lire. J'espère trouver des réponses claires dans les histoires des autres. Mais non, Claude, tu sais bien, les amours des livres sont de vraies amours qui durent et qui meurent dans la passion absolue, dans le feu de forêt, dans les mots qui ravagent. Comment font-ils pour s'aimer dans les livres, avec des rebondissements, des trahisons, des meurtres et des emprisonnements? Je voudrais être une page de roman.

Pâques arrive, tendre. Je ne m'habitue pas à la lumière tamisée, ni au muguet qui pointe sous les balcons. C'est congé et, pour une fois, je décide de ne pas aller à Noranda. Je suis bien ici.

Vendredi après-midi. Je reçois un appel d'Eddy. Je n'en crois pas mes oreilles.

— Qui t'a donné mon numéro?

— C'est ton frère Coco.

— T'es-t-allé à Noranda?

— Oui, le semaine dernier, mon mère est morte.

— Hon !... mes sympathies.

— J'aimerais ben ça te voir.

— Moi aussi.

— Je peux aller chez toi ?

— Oui, oui, ben sûr.

— O.K. Je vas être là vers sept heures. Coco m'a donné ton adresse aussi.

— O.K.

— *See you.*

Je sors ma panoplie sexy : un chandail moulant, un pantalon, un soutien-gorge noir pigeonnant, une petite culotte de dentelle, noire elle aussi. Je me suis fait teindre les cheveux noir de jais pour ressembler le plus possible à Juliette Gréco.

Je ne pense qu'à ce moment béni où je reverrai Eddy et je me prépare mentalement à faire l'amour avec lui. J'ai pris mes pilules consciencieusement tout le mois et quand Eddy arrive, je me sens tout à fait prête à redevenir sa blonde steady. Je le trouve séduisant dans son jacket de cuir. Il n'a plus du tout l'air d'un coureur de stock-car. Il ne met plus de wave set dans ses cheveux. Il m'entoure de ses grands bras et n'arrête pas de dire : « Mon 'tite Claude, mon 'tite Claude. » Je me méfie un peu. Ma cicatrice du cimetière veut s'ouvrir, mais heureusement qu'il ne sort pas un seul « stie ».

Eddy a de la peine. Il me parle de sa mère. Sa mère morte. Il est comme un petit garçon. J'ai du mal à compatir avec lui. Je lui en veux de ne pas m'avoir fait signe quand mon frère Bernard s'est blessé. Je voudrais le lui dire, mais je n'ose pas. Je l'écoute parler de sa mère et à chaque mot qu'il dit, j'imagine mon frère Bernard au moment où l'arbre tombe sur lui au bord du lac Opasatika. Je me mets à pleurer. Eddy s'excuse et je dis, non, c'est pas de ta faute. Toujours la méprise, même en parlant de tragédie.

On boit tranquillement notre bière. Vers minuit, au moment où je pense qu'on va ouvrir le divan-lit, il se ranime. Il a un plan dans ses yeux.

— Viens faire un tour d'auto.

— Où ça?

— Aux States. Es-tu déjà allée aux States?

— Non, mais j'sais pas si j'ai le goût d'y aller tout de suite, j'ai des cours demain matin pis y faut que j'prépare mes examens.

— Espèce de fille à lunettes! Apprends donc à faire des petits folies.

Fille à lunettes, c'est quand même mieux qu'agace-pissette. J'ai un petit serrement de cœur quand j'entre dans la Valiant d'Eddy. Au fond, j'ai peur qu'il m'amène dans un cimetière et qu'il recommence ses niaiseries. Mais il a de la peine et sa mère est morte. Ça me rassure. Puis il parle sans arrêt, comme avant. Il me fait penser à mon père avec ses histoires à plusieurs étages, qui prennent une éternité à aboutir. Vers deux heures du matin, je sors pour la première fois de mon pays. Dans sa Valiant, Eddy me fait découvrir les escarpements d'Ausable Chasm. J'ai perdu le sens de l'orientation. Ausable Chasm pourrait être au Colorado dans les canyons, en Norvège dans les fjords ou en Ontario près des chutes du Niagara. Je suis prête à n'importe quoi, n'importe où. On s'arrête en chemin pour commander des frites huileuses qu'on déguste avec un gros Coke dans la voiture tout en s'embrassant goulûment.

À la frontière du matin, je découvre les États-Unis dans le lit crasseux d'un motel *nowhere*. Des abîmes de sable devant le thermopane. Une enseigne de néon clignote : *Ausable Chasm Motel*. « Au sable ». Les Américains aussi déforment les mots français pour les utiliser dans leur langue. Eddy me laboure sans poser de questions, et il suce mes seins en même temps qu'il introduit quelques doigts dans mes parties sensibles et mouillées. On s'endort très tard pour se réveiller presque aussitôt dans l'odeur âcre des draps, face au soleil cru.

Au restaurant du motel, avant même d'avoir commandé, une waitress, mâchant sa gomme baloune, fait glisser sur la table deux cafés clairs. Elle dit quelques mots nasillés. Eddy comprend tout de suite : « *An order of toasts, eggs sunny side up.* » Quelques minutes plus tard, elle livre la marchandise : deux toasts bien grasses, enduites de confiture aux fraises et de beurre de peanut, avec des œufs au ketchup nageant dans du beurre fondu. Je dis à Eddy que j'ai mal au cœur.

— J'espère que t'es pas enceinte ! dit-il, pour faire une blague.

Ça me rappelle que j'ai oublié ma roulette de pilules. J'aimerais en parler à Eddy, mais j'ai peur qu'il se remette à sacrer. J'ai très hâte de retourner à Montréal.

— On part !

— Non, viens donc dans' chambre un peu, répond Eddy, en me frôlant la joue de ses doigts un peu graisseux.

On fait de nouveau l'amour. Je regarde les chromos de velours sur les murs. Eddy m'arrache quelques cris de jouissance en faisant des va-et-vient très en profondeur. J'ai une idée fixe : prendre ma pilule.

En sortant du motel, on marche un peu le long des rochers. J'écris des poèmes sur le sable, des poèmes de Rina Lasnier que j'ai étudiés dans un cours de poésie canadienne-française : « est-il nuit plus nouvelle que la naissance / est-il jour plus ancien que l'âme ? » Eddy me trouve folle, les efface à mesure en les lisant tout de travers avec son accent terrible. Les enseignes du motel clignotent toujours, et on pourrait tourner en rond le reste de notre vie dans Ausable Chasm comme à cheval sur un carrousel désaffecté.

Eddy et moi, c'est steady. Assez pour en parler à ma tante Laura et à Marie-Claire en tout cas. On se voit souvent. Il me parle enfin de son fils qui marche déjà. Sandra lui permet de le voir en cachette de temps en temps. Les parents de Sandra paient pour tout et ils ne veulent plus que Sandra revoie Eddy. Ils lui en veulent à mort d'avoir mis leur fille enceinte et de l'avoir abandonnée. Tout est de la faute d'Eddy et quand Eddy en parle, il devient grave. Il dit : «Je ne veux plus avoir d'enfant, jamais.»

Il passe parfois deux semaines sans m'appeler. Et moi, je ne l'appelle jamais, par principe. Mais je reste près du téléphone, je ne sors presque pas, de peur qu'il m'appelle pendant mon absence. Je pense à lui jour et nuit. Il me dit que ses études de médecine lui prennent tout son temps. Si ma mère savait que je sors avec Eddy, elle ne me le pardonnerait pas. Mais s'il parvient à terminer ses études de médecine, peut-être qu'elle changera d'idée à son sujet. Je me vois à Noranda dans ma maison à deux étages avec Eddy et ma petite famille. Ça ne dure pas longtemps. Il y a quelque chose qui cloche dans ce rêve, comme s'il ne m'appartenait pas.

Quand Eddy arrive comme un cheveu sur la soupe, les yeux tristes et les cheveux en broussaille, je lui saute au cou. On boit de la bière, on jase longtemps, puis on baise et on baise. Je commence à croire que je ne suis pas si moche après tout. Il faut dire que j'ôte mes lunettes au lit.

Je ne présente pas Eddy à Marie-Claire, ni à Guy, ni à Jean-Guy, ni à personne. Ils sont tellement indépendantistes qu'ils me reprocheraient de sortir avec un Anglais, un juif surtout. Nous sommes seuls au monde, comme dans les meilleurs films de love.

Arrive l'été. Je n'ai pas pu me trouver du travail à Montréal et je reviens seule à Noranda. Eddy reste à

Montréal, le chanceux. En été, la ville est grasse et chaude comme l'amour. Il m'accompagne au terminus bondé de voyageurs venant de partout et de nulle part et m'embrasse jusqu'au moment où l'autobus démarre dans une odeur forte d'huile crue.

Depuis trente et quelques jours que je suis là, je ne vois toujours rien venir et je m'en inquiète suffisamment pour prendre rendez-vous en cachette avec le docteur Cohen, le nouveau médecin de Noranda.

Avec Danielle Dusseault, j'ai trouvé un emploi comme monitrice dans un camp pour jeunes retardés. Les après-midi, quand il fait beau, j'emmène les enfants au parc. Ils sont ravis de se balancer. Quelques-uns portent des couches, même à dix ans. D'autres bavent et n'arrêtent pas de se masturber. Le soir, on rentre à moitié mortes. On n'est même plus capables d'aller au Radio Grill.

Après mon travail, cet après-midi, je vais chez le médecin. Il m'examine, puis je lui fais répéter plusieurs fois ce que j'ai parfaitement bien entendu : « *You are pregnant.* »

Le monde s'écroule.

Je lui dis tout de suite que je ne peux pas garder le bébé, que je dois me faire avorter, que je ne veux pas que ma mère le sache, que je veux le secret absolu. Rien à faire, ce n'est sûrement pas la première fois qu'il entend ces phrases. C'est clair qu'il ne veut pas m'aider. Tout ce qu'il peut faire pour moi, c'est d'écrire le mot *flu* sur ma fiche médicale. Puis il me prescrit un laxatif puissant, au cas où... Mais il m'avertit que si le bébé est accroché, ce laxatif ne me sera d'aucun secours.

Je sors du bureau du médecin en imaginant la petite âme qui flotte dans mon ventre. Je passe par la pharmacie, mais je ne veux pas rentrer chez moi tout de suite. Il me faut élaborer un plan pour aller me faire avorter à Montréal. Je ramasse les cennes que je peux trouver dans mes poches et je me rends au Radio Grill pour téléphoner à Eddy. C'est une fille qui répond. J'aimerais raccrocher, mais je me domine :

— Est-ce que je pourrais parler à Eddy, s'il vous plaît ?

— Ben là, y est parti au lac Louise pour un mois.

— Au lac Louise ?

— Ben oui, au lac Louise, en Alberta.

— Bon, O.K., laissez faire, bonjour.

Je raccroche puis je retourne m'asseoir sur une banquette du restaurant. Je commande des frites avec un Coke, mais le cœur me lève et je ne peux rien avaler. Je pense à Sandra, à son bébé, puis je sors. En tournant le coin de la *Main*, je vois André qui se promène tout seul. Je presse le pas pour qu'il ne me voie pas. Je marche vers la maison lentement. Je longe le lac Osisko, en passant devant l'hôpital, et je m'engage dans le chemin Trémoy.

C'est un soir frisquet de juin. L'air est piquant. Je regarde les salons de toutes les maisons où les rideaux n'ont pas été tirés. Une lumière jaune m'arrive de ces intérieurs de riches et me calme un peu. Ma mère a peut-être raison, je devrais me trouver un petit mari canadien-français pour vivre dans une maison blanche à deux étages et tout ce qui s'ensuit : un beau jardin, des fleurs, une bay-window, un chien, un foyer, des enfants. Un gars comme André, par exemple, ça ferait plaisir à ma mère. Quand j'arrive à la maison finalement, elle m'attend dans la cuisine :

— Veux-tu ben me dire où t'es passée?

— Ch't'allée au cinéma.

— Toute seule?

— Oui, toute seule.

— Dis-moi donc, toi, t'as pas eu ton mal de ventre ce mois-ci?

— J'ai été menstruée, mais j'ai pas eu mal au ventre.

— Tant mieux si ça peut s'arranger, c'est pas drôle d'avoir mal comme ça tous les mois.

— T'inquiète pas, ça va mieux.

— Bon, va te coucher, y est tard. Si tu veux être en forme pour travailler demain.

La double dose de laxatif fait effet. Aux petites heures du matin, une crampe me réveille et je cours aux toilettes. Impossible d'aller travailler. J'ai l'impression que tout mon intérieur se vide, les intestins compris. Le sang coule abondamment, avec d'énormes caillots brunâtres et d'innombrables flocons rouge vin. Je reste ainsi à me répandre pendant une bonne demi-heure, toute en sueur, évitant de crier même si la douleur m'agrippe par moments, me traverse de bord en bord. Puis mon père, qui se lève toujours bien avant tout le monde pour avoir le temps de se raser et de lire son journal de la veille, frappe à la porte de la salle de bains.

— Une minute, 'pa, attends un peu, j'en ai pour une minute.

— Es-tu malade?

— Oui, j'ai la diarrhée, j'pense.

— As-tu besoin d'aide? J'peux aller chercher ta mère.

— Non, laisse faire, j'vas m'arranger.

— Prends ton temps, Chouchoune.

Je déroule presque un rouleau entier de papier de toilette et je le mets entre mes deux jambes en vitesse. Je sors de la salle de bains sans regarder mon père, de peur qu'il ne voie mon visage défait par les crampes.

— Gêne-toi pas pour frapper à la porte si t'as besoin d'revenir, Chouchoune.

Je m'affale sur mon lit, me tordant chaque fois que le sang afflue dans mon bas-ventre. J'ai l'habitude de cette douleur qui m'assaille chaque mois. Mais cette fois, je ne peux pas vomir ni perdre connaissance parce que je ne veux pas que ma mère me pose de questions.

Je garde le lit, prétextant la diarrhée, mettant mes Kotex dans des boîtes de chaussures que je camoufle derrière mon divan-lit. Toute la journée, j'entends ma mère au téléphone qui raconte en détail ma maladie à toutes ses sœurs. Enfin une maladie, une vraie. Pas seulement des sales menstruations dont on ne parle jamais parce que ce n'est pas une vraie maladie. La vraie maladie, tout comme les accidents, ponctue la vie des mères, tissant la trame de leur mémoire jour après jour. La maladie bénie

124

réchauffe la conversation et attire l'affection. Seule la vraie maladie fait fléchir les mères.

Je finis par retourner au travail, et le reste de l'été s'écoule sans incident. Je suis toujours sans nouvelles d'Eddy. Un soir, pour me consoler et pour me débarrasser, je vais à l'aréna avec André faire du patin à roulettes. Personne ne nous a vus, évidemment. Encore un été de passé.

Je reviens à Montréal et j'appelle Eddy du terminus pour lui donner rendez-vous au Bouvillon. Je me montre plutôt froide et je lui demande de but en blanc pourquoi il ne m'a pas appelée.

— Ch't'allé au lac Louise, me répond-il.

— Je l'sais. Étais-tu tout seul?

— Non, j'tais avec Sandra pis le p'tit.

— Avec Sandra?

— On s'est mariés finalement, c'était trop difficile avec les familles.

— Tu t'es pas marié avec elle?

— Ben quoi, c'est le mère de mon enfant.

— Pis moi?

— Toi, y a pas de problème, j'vas te garder toute ma vie comme un maîtresse. C'est simple ça, tu vas être mon maîtresse toute ma vie et pis...

Je ne le laisse pas finir sa phrase. Je le quitte sans le regarder et je regagne en tremblant mon appartement. J'essaie de pleurer, mais ça ne vient pas. Je ne veux plus jamais revoir Eddy. Point à la ligne.

Tranquillement, je reviens à la vie.

J'ai gagné assez d'argent pendant l'été pour m'acheter un phono, ce qui me permet de ressasser ma tristesse célibataire. Juliette Gréco, Jacques Brel et Boris Vian me remplissent la tête de leurs chansons que j'apprends par cœur. Je fais tourner mille fois *Fais-moi mal Johnny* parce que j'aime bien le bout où il remet ses petites chaussettes. La poésie de Paris m'entre dans l'âme comme un onguent qui soulage le mal sans le guérir complètement. Ma tante Laura m'apprend au téléphone que le président Kennedy est mort. Elle a peur de la troisième guerre mondiale. Je ne vois pas le rapport, mais ça me fait quelque chose. Je vais voir Jackie et son tailleur taché de sang à la télévision chez ma tante Laura et j'achète le Paris-Match. Non, il n'y a vraiment rien comme le Paris-Match pour consoler, et c'est sûrement pour ça qu'on en trouve dans les salles d'attente des dentistes.

Je découvre la linguistique et les découpages maniaques de mots et de phrases. Les mots ont une histoire, tels des animaux familiers qui vivent et qui s'usent avec le temps et qui meurent. Tout cela me fascine et me repose de la littérature. J'en ai ras le bol des héroïnes romantiques. Elles finissent toujours par s'en sortir après avoir rencontré l'homme de leur vie. On ne sait rien de leur amour quotidien. Il nous reste entre les mains au dernier chapitre et il faut tout réinventer.

André m'a appelée pour qu'on aille faire une promenade dans le cimetière Côte-des-Neiges. Qu'est-ce qu'ils ont tous avec leur cimetière? J'ai accepté pour une fois. Je viens de finir les *Histoires extraordinaires* et les feuilles des arbres, à moitié tombées, sont illuminées par des rayons de soleil jaunes. Jaune sur jaune. Je suis contente de revoir André, et il me semble bien élégant parmi les glaïeuls, les chrysanthèmes et les monuments de granit. On marche l'un près de l'autre tout en parlant de nos études, de Noranda, de nos familles. Je parle d'Eddy et de Sandra, je me vide le cœur, et André reste un moment noyé dans son petit passé déjà encombré de déceptions. Il me dit qu'il a aimé Danielle Dusseault à la folie. On se tait sur ce qu'il aurait pu y avoir entre nous.

— Je me sens pas mal tout seul, mais j'étudie, et ça me passionne.

— C'est la même chose pour moi, tu vois.

J'ai répondu sans y penser et je vois qu'il a compris autre chose. Soudain, il me prend la main et m'invite solennellement à souper avec lui samedi prochain dans un grand restaurant.

— J'vas venir te chercher vers quatre heures.

— O.K.!

Puis il me serre dans ses bras. Sacré André, toujours au poste! Rendue à la maison, je veux le rappeler pour lui dire que j'ai changé d'idée, mais c'est la première fois que quelqu'un m'invite officiellement à souper. Puis j'ai envie de sortir un peu. Avec Eddy, tout se passait dans l'appartement et dans l'auto. Jamais il ne me faisait des invitations comme un vrai chum en fait à sa blonde steady. À part rouler ses *r* à l'anglaise, mesurer six pieds, avoir de beaux yeux bleus, faire l'amour comme un dieu grec, il ne fait rien pour me conquérir. Avec André, c'est autre chose. Il est un véritable chevalier servant. Après tout, André, en m'efforçant un peu, j'arriverai peut-être à l'aimer. Je fais une visite à ma tante Laura, qui me prête un petit tailleur vert très chic et un collier de cristal de roche.

André vient me chercher. Il me baise la main, comme on fait à une duchesse. J'éclate de rire. Il ouvre la portière de l'Acadian que son père lui a donnée en cadeau et qui sent le tapis neuf. C'est un beau jour d'automne, et les couleurs des arbres du mont Royal sont ramollies par un soleil faiblard.

— Je t'emmène au Berkeley. C'est là que mon père vient avec ma mère quand ils sont de passage à Montréal.

Puis il se met à me parler d'une exposition de Molinari qu'il vient de voir sur la rue Crescent.

— Molinari?

— Tu ne connais pas Moli? dit-il sur un ton de reproche qui me ramène quelques années en arrière, quand je le trouvais baveux.

— Non, je regrette.

— Voyons, c'est un grand peintre. Mon père a quelques tableaux de lui dans sa collection. Y dit que c'est un bon investissement.

— Un bon investissement?

— Ben oui, un jour, tu vas voir, ça va valoir une fortune.

— T'aimes vraiment ça c'qu'y fait?

— Non, mais c'est moderne et ça vaut cher.

André décide de parler d'autre chose. Il me trouve sûrement ignare, inculte.

La salle à manger de l'hôtel Berkeley est majestueuse. Sur les tables, il y a des nappes empesées comme des nappes d'autel, des fleurs naturelles avec des bougies. Un garçon de table avec la serviette sous le bras nous indique un coin très intime. Il m'appelle madame et me parle à la troisième personne. Un peu paralysée par tout ce décorum, assise juste en face d'André, je crois que je vais défaillir en voyant les fourchettes, les couteaux et les cuillères d'argent massif alignés de chaque côté de l'assiette de porcelaine.

— C'est du Limoges.

— Ah oui? Ma grand-mère en avait, dis-je, me rappelant les chicanes de testament qui avaient porté justement sur le fameux set de Limoges.

— Ah bon, tu connais ça?

— Ben oui.

Devant mon manque flagrant d'assurance, André dit: «T'en fais pas. T'as rien qu'à me regarder pis à faire comme moi. Tu vas voir, c'est pas difficile.»

Je jette un coup d'œil au menu en forme de parchemin sur lequel il n'y a pas de prix d'indiqués. André commande le vin avec aisance, un pommard, parce que son père a dit que c'est le meilleur vin. Je me sens étourdie rien qu'à l'écouter me suggérer des plats que je ne connais pas : des escargots bourguignonne, un tournedos au poivre et un sabayon. Je dis simplement oui, ça va.

Chaque fois que j'ouvre la bouche pour manger ou pour boire ou pour parler, j'ai la certitude de commettre une erreur. Au dessert, mon ventre se met à gargouiller et une crampe me coupe en deux. J'ai à peine le temps de me rendre à la toilette. Mon repas passe tout droit. Je suis complètement épuisée, comme après une longue séance de travail. Je voudrais rester là, assise dans ce petit compartiment privé, pour le reste de mes jours. Mais je refais mon maquillage et je rejoins André qui triomphe au-dessus d'un café irlandais. Il m'offre un digestif, mais je fais comme si je n'avais rien entendu. Il n'insiste pas, à cause sûrement de mon teint qui verdit à vue d'œil. Il règle ostensiblement l'addition avec un bill de cinquante.

Sur le chemin du retour, enflammé par le vin, André n'arrête pas de commenter le repas. Chaque fois qu'il dit le mot «escargot» ou le mot «tournedos», la tête me tourne. Il passe par le belvédère du mont Royal où il stationne son Acadian. Il se met à m'embrasser de but en blanc pendant que je me concentre sur les lumières du centre-ville. Il ne se rend pas compte que sa main sous ma petite jupe verte ne me fait aucun effet. Mais j'ai trop mal au cœur pour lui résister.

Quand il me croit bien à point, il fait démarrer sa voiture et me ramène chez moi. Je veux lui dire au revoir devant la maison, mais en deux temps trois mouvements, il fait le tour de l'auto pour m'ouvrir la portière et m'aider à descendre. Il se sent le maître de la situation, comme un client qui a toujours raison et qui réclame sa marchandise, facture en main.

La tête me tourne encore plus. Je me laisse faire. Pour me débarrasser. Je me sens trop mal pour lui expliquer. Après s'être soulagé avec des grognements de satisfaction, il s'endort en ronflant. Il m'a prise comme pousse-café, c'est mon sentiment.

Je ne dors pas jusqu'au petit matin, et avant qu'il ne se réveille, je me lève, j'enfile mes jeans et je lui écris un mot : «Merci beaucoup, André, pour le bon repas. Je te souhaite du succès dans tes études. Ne me rappelle pas, s'il te plaît.»

Je sors prendre l'air et je marche jusque chez ma tante Laura, à qui je raconte ma soirée de long en large, sans oublier les crampes et les autres malaises. Cette soirée, bien moche au fond, devient tout à fait loufoque. Je reviens chez moi le soir, et, en entrant je vois que le lit est fait. Sur la table, il y a un gros chrysanthème avec une note : «Adieu.»

C'est ça, *Farewell to Arms*. Non, maman, il n'y a rien à faire, je ne l'aimerai jamais, ce gars-là. Il a tout pour faire un bon chevalier servant, un bon mari, un bon n'importe quoi. Mais je ne peux pas m'empêcher de voir ses points noirs quand il m'embrasse. Rien à faire. Deux *tu l'auras* valent mieux qu'*un tien*.

Marie-Claire a tout un réseau d'amants de transit. Parmi eux, il y a Olivier Thiers, un Français de grande famille. Elle dit que c'est un beau jeune homme qui est venu faire des études d'architecture à Québec. Il est tout le portrait (du moins c'est l'idée que je m'en fais) d'Olivier Hauteville, le fiancé de Brigitte dans les romans de Berthe Bernage. Il vient voir Marie-Claire toutes les fins de semaine. Pendant la semaine, elle héberge plutôt de grands professeurs européens qui font une tournée de conférences au Québec. Je ne sais pas comment elle s'y prend, mais elle s'arrange toujours pour qu'ils aboutissent dans son lit. Ensuite, quand ils sont repartis chez eux, en France, en Italie ou en Allemagne, elle me donne des détails intéressants sur leur femme, sur leurs enfants, sur la couleur de leurs chaussettes et sur l'état de leurs bobettes.

Marie-Claire trouve que son ami Olivier est moins expérimenté que ses amants européens. Les parents d'Olivier habitent en France et son père enseigne l'histoire de l'art aztèque à l'université d'Aix-Marseille. Marie-Claire est davantage séduite par l'idée du père d'Olivier que par Olivier lui-même, qu'elle trouve bien cute mais qu'elle n'aime pas plus qu'il ne faut.

De mon côté, après mes mésaventures avec Roger, Eddy et André, je veux prendre une pause dans la passion et les hommes. J'étudie, faute de mieux. J'ai hâte de gagner de l'argent et de voyager. J'étouffe à Montréal dans le bruit incessant et la saleté. Je n'en peux plus de ce ciel toujours coupé par les hauts buildings. J'aimerais voir l'horizon une fois de temps en temps. Il me semble que mon cerveau rapetisse. J'ai la nostalgie du ciel du nord parsemé de nuages qui ont l'air de sortir tout droit de la terre. L'odeur du bois, de la moque et des saules après la pluie me manque. Il me faut partir vers le nord.

Mais je ne veux pas retourner chez mes parents. Ma vie n'a plus rien à voir avec la leur. Je tiens à ma petite vie privée, à pouvoir amener quelqu'un dans mon lit de temps en temps. Pour garder la forme.

Hier soir, Olivier est arrivé à l'improviste chez Marie-Claire. Il tenait un bouquet de jonquilles dans ses mains, ce qui nous a bien émues toutes les deux. J'ai voulu partir, mais il a dit : « Non, reste. » On a commandé des cigarettes, de la bière et une pizza large all dressed. Vers la fin du repas qui s'éternisait, Olivier a dit à brûle-pourpoint :

— Je m'en vais en Europe samedi prochain pour six mois.

— Chanceux! a crié Marie-Claire.

— Oh oui! chanceux, ai-je dit timidement.

— Vous n'avez qu'à venir avec moi toutes les deux!

J'ai senti que Marie-Claire hésitait. Quant à moi, je n'osais rien dire parce que j'avais peur de la vexer en acceptant l'invitation. J'ai dit :

— Moi, j'pourrais y aller, mais j'pense pas que ça ferait l'affaire de Marie-Claire.

— Moi, si tu veux y aller, ça m'dérange vraiment pas, a répondu Marie-Claire.

Au fond, je n'attendais que cette permission bien involontaire pour dire à Olivier que ça me tentait beaucoup aussi d'aller avec lui en Europe. C'est plus excitant en tout cas que de retourner passer mon été à Noranda. Marie-Claire a ajouté :

— Moi, j'peux pas y aller, parce que j'ai pas une cenne qui m'adore. Vas-y, Claude, ça m'dérange vraiment pas.

Je les regardais tous les deux, me demandant ce qu'ils pensaient. Ils me regardaient eux aussi. Puis j'ai fini par m'entendre dire que ça me tentait plus d'aller en Provence que d'aller à Noranda. En l'espace de deux minutes, j'avais perdu le nord.

Je les ai laissés seuls un peu plus tard et, en traversant la rue pour rentrer chez moi, j'avais l'impression que ma vie changeait de cap.

Mon cœur bat très fort à la perspective de fouler les pavés de Paris, à l'endroit même où mes personnages de romans se sont aimés avec passion dans la clandestinité des voitures à chevaux. Je rêve. Toute la nuit, les chapitres de la *Comédie humaine* se succèdent dans ma tête en feu. Je me lève au petit matin sans avoir fermé l'œil.

Je pense tout à coup qu'on n'a pas parlé de date ni de rien de précis. J'ai trop bu, tout est foutu. Je sirote tristement mon café, je mange mes toasts refroidies. Le téléphone sonne. C'est la voix d'Olivier Thiers. Il veut me parler seule, une minute, et il arrive.

Je m'empresse de faire un mini-ménage dans ma pièce, fourrant tout ce que je trouve dans le fond de la garde-robe. Tout revole, et en un rien de temps, la pièce devient présentable en surface.

On frappe à la porte et le cœur me bat jusqu'aux genoux. C'est bien lui, Olivier, avec son petit sourire moqueur. Il s'assoit sur mon divan et me fait des compliments sur la façon ingénieuse dont j'ai décoré mon une-pièce. Il dit que l'atmosphère a un je ne sais quoi d'européen, ce qui me flatte au plus haut point. Puis il me parle du voyage, de ses parents qui ont fait le tour du monde et qui connaissent les plus grands artistes. Ses mots semblent sortir directement d'un livre de poésie. Sa voix me séduit, mais je n'ose pas trop le montrer, à cause de Marie-Claire. Il sent mon malaise.

— Ne t'en fais pas pour Marie-Claire, dit-il. Tu sais, entre elle et moi, c'est plutôt de la camaraderie. Elle a ses aventures de son côté, puis moi, j'ai les miennes de mon côté.

— J'avoue que tout ça m' chicote un peu. Je m'demande c'que j'fais dans tout ça.

— Non, t'en fais pas. Tout va s'arranger. Mes parents vont bien te recevoir. Quand tu viendras me rejoindre, on ira en Italie tous les deux. Quand penses-tu pouvoir venir?

— Au mois de juillet, j'pense.

— On va décider de la date exacte si tu veux, parce qu'il va falloir que j'aille te chercher à Marseille.

Il déploie sur ma table encombrée une grande carte du sud de la France et de l'Italie. Avec sa voix de Claude Gauthier, il décrit le paysage, la maison de ses parents sur la route du Tholonet. Il appelle leur maison, un mas. Un mas de Provence. J'essaie d'imaginer tout cela, mais pour moi, la campagne, c'est la forêt d'Abitibi, le lac Vaudray, avec ses bouleaux, ses sapins rabougris et ses épinettes. Mon père dit parfois que la campagne près de Notre-Dame-du-Nord ressemble à la campagne française, mais il n'est jamais allé en France. À mon tour, je décris à Olivier mon pays d'enfance et j'ai dû en remettre sur la couleur du ciel et la grandeur des pins blancs parce qu'à la fin il me dit : « Sais-tu que ton patelin ressemble drôlement au mien ? » Mais lui, il n'est jamais allé en Abitibi. Quand il en parle, il confond Arvida avec Noranda. Pour lui, comme pour beaucoup de gens, le Québec est un magma de petites villes situées en dehors de Montréal.

Il me propose un itinéraire de Paris à Rome avec des arrêts à Marseille, à Aix-en-Provence, à Milan et à Venise. Je lui fais entièrement confiance, il pourrait m'amener en Espagne ou à Tombouctou, j'irais en courant. La date de mon départ est fixée, et il me donne l'adresse de ses parents sur un bout de papier : Mas des Arcanes, route du Tholonet, Aix-en-Provence. Cette adresse me semble bien imprécise. En partant, Olivier me donne quelques baisers sur les deux joues, très à la française, et je me sens rougir. Puis il m'applique un grand baiser sur les lèvres, ce qui a pour effet d'irradier instantanément mon plexus solaire.

— Sois discrète avec Marie-Claire. Je compte sur toi, je t'attends.

Même installée dans l'avion pour Paris, je n'arrive pas à croire que j'y suis en chair et en os.

Est-ce bien moi, cette petite fille à lunettes, originaire du Témiscamingue (mon père insiste toujours pour dire que Noranda est dans le comté de Témiscamingue et non dans celui d'Abitibi), qui va rejoindre le beau Olivier Thiers dans un mas de Provence? Je bois tout le champagne qu'on m'offre et je suis un peu pompette. Sous les nuages, les rues de Paris s'ouvrent au petit matin.

Ça n'a pas été facile d'annoncer la nouvelle à mes parents. J'ai procédé par lettre, comme dans les grandes occasions. Ma mère a pris sa plus belle écriture pour me donner toutes les recommandations d'usage : « Arrange-toi pour ne jamais être seule. C'est dangereux pour une fille de vingt ans de voyager toute seule en Europe. Il arrive tant de choses. Écris-moi souvent pour donner de tes nouvelles. Ta maman qui t'embrasse et qui t'aime. »

En descendant de l'avion au Bourget, une Américaine m'indique comment changer mes dollars en francs. Elle a un accent, mais comme elle a appris le français avec des professeurs français de France dans son université américaine, les Français la comprennent mieux qu'ils ne me comprennent. Elle est en transit vers la Suisse et elle me laisse partir seule, après m'avoir indiqué comment me rendre en car à Saint-Germain-des-Prés. Même si j'ai déjà pris le métro une fois à Toronto, je sens la panique me gagner. Au bout d'une demi-heure, à force de quémander des renseignements, je réussis enfin à savoir comment payer mon ticket et je prends la direction du boulevard Saint-Michel.

Avec mon énorme valise, je me promène dans Saint-Germain-des-Prés à la recherche d'un hôtel. Je dois m'arrêter à la terrasse d'un café pour manger quelque chose. Chaque fois que je dis une phrase, je me fais reprendre. Quand les mots sortent de ma bouche, ils prennent des allures de mots étrangers.

— Madame veut dire?

— Un sandwich au jambon et une bière.

— S'il vous plaît?

— S'il vous plaît.

— Madame veut dire?

— Un sandwich au jambon et une bière.

— Peut-être que madame désire un sandwich et un demi?

— Non, juste un sandwich au jambon avec une bière.

Je reçois le sandwich seulement, et ça me prend un peu de temps à comprendre que le demi, c'est la bière. Quand je m'adresse à quelqu'un, je dois préparer ma phrase longtemps d'avance, comme si je m'exprimais en allemand ou en espagnol. Par moments, épuisée, je parle carrément en anglais. Souvent je fais des gestes ou je consulte mon dictionnaire anglais-français pour trouver des équivalents en français de France.

Finalement je tombe sur un petit hôtel où il y a de la place. Rue de Tournon. La propriétaire connaît des Canadiens et, parce qu'elle ne me reprend pas à chaque mot, elle peut me louer la chambre la plus minable pour le prix le plus élevé. Ce qu'elle fait d'ailleurs. Elle m'assigne une chambre sous les combles, au sixième étage, avec un lit bosselé, un tapis luisant, un couvre-lit douteux dont le fleuri s'harmonise plus ou moins avec celui du papier peint. En entrant dans la chambre, je m'effondre en larmes sur le lit. Je finis par m'endormir là, tout habillée, ma grosse valise encore bouclée à mes côtés.

Je crois bien que j'ai dormi vingt-quatre heures d'affilée. Je veux me laver. Je sors sur le palier pour chercher les toilettes afin de prendre un bain. Je les trouve au rez-de-chaussée dans le fond d'une cour intérieure. Pas de baignoire dans ces toilettes, qui sont turques. Pourquoi « turques » ? Le dictionnaire dit des toilettes turques qu'elles sont sans siège. Hygiéniques, parfaitement hygiéniques et mons-trueuses. Il n'y a qu'une seule baignoire dans l'hôtel et, pour y avoir accès, il faut avoir la clé de la salle de bains et, pour avoir la clé de la salle de bains, il faut payer un supplément. Ce que je fais avec empresse-ment, mais quand j'aperçois la baignoire toute cernée, je rebrousse chemin et je décide de me laver par travées, comme dit ma mère, en me servant du lavabo de ma chambre.

Je descends me promener dans Paris. J'em-prunte des petites rues qui me semblent toutes pareilles. Je regarde les gens et je me sens portée par la rumeur de cette ville, par l'odeur du café et des gitanes. J'ai l'impression que je vais rencontrer Simone de Beauvoir ou Jean-Paul Sartre ou Juliette Gréco au coin d'une rue. Les Parisiens gueulent, me prennent à partie, me demandent mon avis. J'oublie tout, l'Abitibi, Ottawa, Montréal, Eddy, André, Olivier. Je suis au ciel, en chair et en os, au cœur d'une page de roman. J'aimerais être née Française. J'aimerais dire des mots, des phrases bien coordonnées, et que ça coule et que ça chante tout seul avec les bonnes conjonctions et les bonnes prépositions.

J'ai passé toute une semaine à Paris et je suis rassasiée du vert-de-gris du ciel. J'ai pris le train à la gare de Lyon à destination de Marseille. Les puces se sont régalées à même ma peau de nordique et je suis pleine de boursouflures. Pourtant, Dieu sait si je suis immunisée contre les mouches noires et les maringouins, qui s'approchent à peine de moi, même le soir dans le bois quand le vent tombe. J'essaie de me gratter le moins possible, c'est la consigne de mon père dans les cas de morsure, mais c'est plus fort que moi. J'ai des petites gales dans le visage. Je suis affreuse et j'ai peur qu'Olivier soit déçu quand il viendra me chercher à la gare de Marseille.

Le train est rapide. Sa rapidité dépasse de beaucoup, en tout cas, les vitesses additionnées du CNR, du CPR et de l'ONR. Tout ce que je vois, c'est des poteaux qui ponctuent le quadrillage des champs entre les villes. Géométrie parfaite. Pas un pouce carré n'a été laissé en friche; il n'y a plus rien à faire ici, tout est installé, organisé et hiérarchisé depuis la nuit des temps.

En face de moi sur la banquette, des Italiens parlent fort et ils rient beaucoup en me lorgnant. J'entends le mot signora et je crois qu'ils font des blagues sur moi, sur mes lunettes ou sur mes piqûres de puces. Leur panier d'osier est plein de saucissons, de vin rouge et de pain, comme dans les films de Renoir. Ils m'invitent gentiment à partager leur repas. Ils me posent des questions en anglais sur le Canada, me demandent si je connais un tel ou une telle, cousin ou cousine de Saint-Léonard. Comme à Montréal, quand les gens apprennent que je viens d'Abitibi et qu'ils me demandent si je connais Nicole Leblanc de Sainte-Rose-de-Poularies.

Je prends des lampées de gros rouge à même la bonbonne qu'ils font circuler. Je leur confie que je vais rejoindre mon «fiancé» à Marseille.

Entre Avignon et Marseille, on a si bien bu qu'ils m'invitent à aller les voir chez eux, à Rome, avec mon fiancé. Ils me donnent l'adresse d'un cousin à Venise qui y tient une auberge. Tout le monde m'embrasse chaleureusement avant que je descende du train, et c'est un peu pompette que j'arrive à Marseille.

Olivier m'attend à la gare, souriant, un petit bouquet de coquelicots dans ses mains. Il dit :

— Veux-tu voir un peu la Méditerranée ?

— Ben oui, ben oui !

Il a emprunté l'auto de son père, une deux-chevaux. Il a l'air de se demander dans quoi il s'est embarqué. Moi, je suis si heureuse que je me mets à chanter le *Petit Navire sur la mer Mé-mé-mé...*

— Mes parents ont hâte de te rencontrer, dit Olivier.

— Ah oui ?

Je trouve qu'on a l'air de vrais fiancés parce que c'est la première fois qu'un gars m'emmène chez ses parents.

On mange une bouillabaisse dans le port de Marseille. Je suis folle d'être venue comme ça à la rencontre d'un inconnu. Il me parle de ses parents, je lui parle des miens. On commence à zéro, et, au dessert, il connaît ma vie antérieure. Mon père, ma mère. Eddy, André, Roger, et même le grand Pierre-Paul. En disant tout, j'espère qu'il va me parler de Marie-Claire, de ses autres blondes. Mais non, il en reste à Jacques et Jacqueline, ses parents qu'il appelle toujours par leur petit nom.

On se promène ensuite main dans la main le long des boutiques et des entrepôts. Il s'est attardé à une vitrine. Je continue seule et, sans m'en apercevoir, je prends la main d'un autre homme qui se promène par là. La texture de sa paume est calleuse, et je retire ma main en m'excusant. Olivier court derrière moi, craignant qu'il me soit arrivé quelque chose. «Je ferais mieux de te surveiller de plus près sinon je vais te perdre», dit-il sur un ton un peu blagueur. Puis il me serre la main très fort, et je sens qu'il veut que je lui appartienne.

Olivier n'arrête pas de m'expliquer les Français et la France de A à Z. Il connaît tout. Il a un petit accent du Sud, un peu comme celui de Fernandel quand il lit *La Chèvre de monsieur Seguin*, sur le disque des *Lettres de mon moulin*. On a pris la route de Cassis afin de chercher un endroit pour passer la nuit.

On trouve assez rapidement une auberge à fleurs qui donne sur la mer, un peu plus loin en allant vers La Ciotat. La mer célèbre, celle des batailles navales de mes livres d'histoire, s'étale devant moi dans l'or du couchant. Je ne la trouve pas vraiment plus grande que le lac Ontario. La lumière si bleue dans les pins blancs me rappelle celle du lac Vaudray quand, en plein milieu du mois de juillet, ma mère dit que la journée est parfaite.

La plage est pleine de galets. Moi qui croyais qu'une plage de mer était de sable. C'est beau, mais pas du tout comme les photos de Brigitte Bardot dans le Paris-Match.

Dans la chambre, jolie et propre, il y a une vraie salle de bains avec une douche et de l'eau chaude. Je m'y précipite pour laver toute la crasse de cette semaine passée à Paris. Quand je sors de la salle de bains, Olivier a déjà déboutonné sa chemise blanche qui contraste avec sa poitrine toute bronzée. Nos peaux se rejoignent naturellement, et on part aussitôt pour l'infini sauvage de notre première nuit d'amour. On s'endort, on se réveille, on recommence à se caresser, tout va de soi, comme si on allait à la recherche de notre premier souffle.

Le matin se lève sur nos draps froissés et on prend le petit déjeuner à la française : trempette de baguette et marmelade, grand bol de café au lait. Voilà, m'sieu dame. Merci. Y pas de quoi. Tout est ancien et nouveau. Je suis un passage de roman étranger.

Sur la route en direction de la montagne Sainte-Victoire, on emprunte des chemins en lacet et des cols qui débouchent sur des paysages aériens. Les maisons sont toutes de la même couleur, saumon pâle, avec des toits de tuile rouille. Olivier m'explique la différence entre les mas, les bastidons et les bergeries. Je suis bien loin des bungalows, des cottages et des triplex.

Jacques et Jacqueline sont des gens plutôt ridés. Ils sont petits, ont le teint foncé et ils se ressemblent tellement qu'ils ont l'air d'être frère et sœur. C'est ce qui m'a frappée le plus quand je les ai vus venir à notre rencontre sur la route du Tholonet. Un bouvier des Flandres presque aussi grand qu'eux les accompagnait. Ils étaient contents de nous voir et j'ai senti tout de suite qu'ils approuvaient le choix de leur fils. La mère d'Olivier a préparé le repas et tout est comme dans une livre de recettes françaises : pissaladière, daube, clafoutis. Rosé de Provence. Nappe à carreaux. Ail, ail, ail. Les odeurs me soûlent. Le père d'Olivier parle beaucoup et très fort. D'art aztèque seulement. Parfois, Jacqueline essaie de dire une chose ordinaire comme : «Vous avez fait un bon voyage?» mais Jacques la rabroue en disant :«Voyons, Jacqueline, n'entre pas dans les détails.»

Je voudrais bien entrer dans les détails justement, parler simplement de choses et d'autres, mais comme je ne connais rien à l'art aztèque, je me contente d'écouter intelligemment.

La politique française arrive sur le tapis. Jacques critique tout, les gaullistes, les communistes, les socialistes. Je lui demande : «Mais vous, monsieur Thiers, de quel parti êtes-vous?» Il répond avec son fort accent marseillais : «Mais moi, madame, vous saurez que je suis anarchiste.» Puis en se retournant vers sa femme, il dit en riant : «Quel accent elle a, cette petite. On dirait qu'elle est du Poitou.» Il me regarde dans les yeux et il continue : «Parlez un peu, mademoiselle, que j'entende votre accent.»

Je rougis et je ne sais pas quoi dire. D'autant plus que je n'arrive pas à comprendre comment quelqu'un peut être à la fois riche et anarchiste. Je n'ai pas connu beaucoup d'anarchistes, mais il me semble qu'ils sont tous révolutionnaires et pauvres. En tout cas ils ne sont pas professeurs d'université et surtout pas propriétaires d'un mas en Provence. Même pas d'un bungalow à Noranda-Nord. Les riches que je connais sont tous associés de près ou de loin au Parti libéral ou au parti de l'Union nationale. Je continue donc à me taire. Puis Jacqueline place un timide : «Peut-être qu'ils sont fatigués, ces petits. Si nous allions nous coucher.» À ma grande surprise, Jacques ne rouspète pas; il dit simplement d'un ton las :«Tu as raison, Jacqueline, allons nous coucher.» Je veux aider Jacqueline à desservir la table, mais elle dit : «Non, laissez, ma femme de ménage viendra tout ranger demain matin.»

La maison est grande, et il y a au moins six chambres à coucher à l'étage. Je m'attendais à me séparer d'Olivier pour la nuit, mais Jacqueline a préparé un seul lit pour nous deux. Je trouve que la mère d'Olivier est bien en avance sur ma mère dans ce domaine. Jamais ma mère n'offrirait le même lit à des gens non mariés, ça ne se fait pas. Je dis à Olivier :

— Ta mère est bien *sport*.

— Tu veux dire qu'elle a l'esprit ouvert?

— Ben oui, j'aurais jamais pensé qu'a nous aurait donné la même chambre.

— Mes parents sont des libres-penseurs. Pour eux, toutes ces pudibonderies sont des détails.

— Ah bon! Je t'avertis que si tu viens chez moi en Abitibi, on a besoin d'être mariés en bonne et due forme si tu veux qu'on couche dans la même chambre.

Olivier tique quand je prononce le mot «mariés», mais il n'ajoute rien. Moi non plus. Je m'endors dans ses bras, après une séance d'amour chauffée à blanc par le soleil du Midi, entre le silence et les cris des grillons.

Je me réveille en sursaut. Il fait clair, c'est le petit matin. Jacqueline crie. Jacques crie encore plus fort. «Espèce d'imbécile, va te faire foutre!» «Ton café est infect.» «Tu peux bien partir si tu veux, j'aurai enfin la paix.» «Tu as sauté ton étudiante, j'en ai la preuve.» Je ne sais plus qui dit quoi. Les paroles me parviennent sur un fond sonore de bris de vaisselle et de jappements de chien.

Je dis à Olivier :

— Fais quelque chose, y vont se tuer, tes parents.

— T'en fais pas, c'est tous les matins comme ça. Ma mère se lève de mauvais poil.

— Mais c'est épouvantable c'qu'y se disent, y faut faire venir la police, y se battent, y vont se tuer.

— T'en fais pas, t'en fais pas, j'ai dit. Pour eux, c'est normal. Essaye de dormir encore un peu, le temps qu'ils se calment.

— J'peux pas me calmer, j'peux dormir encore moins.

J'éclate en sanglots. Olivier me prend dans ses bras.

— Il va falloir que tu t'habitues. Ils sont toujours comme ça le matin.

— J'peux pas supporter ça. Allons-nous-en.

146

— Bon, ça va, on partira cet après-midi, si tu veux. Tu vois, ils sont déjà calmés. Ils sont probablement en train de baiser. On dirait que ça les excite de s'engueuler.

On descend une demi-heure plus tard dans la cuisine, et Jacqueline est toute souriante. Jacques lit tranquillement son Monde en buvant son café au lait.

— Bonjour, mes agneaux. Vous avez passé une bonne nuit? dit Jacqueline en faisant un clin d'œil à son mari.

— Oui, maman, répond Olivier en l'embrassant.

— Quel est votre itinéraire, Claude? Olivier m'a dit que vous partiez en Italie, n'est-ce pas?

— Oui... mais je croyais que tu viendrais avec moi, Olivier.

— Ah oui? C'est vrai qu'on en avait parlé comme ça. Pour moi, c'était seulement une possibilité. Tu tiens vraiment à ce que j'aille avec toi en Italie? À vrai dire, ça ne me tente plus tellement. J'ai plutôt envie de rester ici à me reposer. D'ailleurs, je dois rentrer à Montréal plus tôt que prévu.

— ...

— Eh oui! Imagine-toi donc que je me suis trouvé du travail dans mon domaine à Montréal.

— Bon... chus ben contente pour toi.

— T'inquiète pas, j'irai te reconduire à la gare de Marseille. T'inquiète pas. Puis on se reverra à Montréal à ton retour. Dans un mois, je pense?

J'ai les yeux dans l'eau. L'Italie amoureuse que j'ai toute imaginée depuis deux mois s'évanouit, et je n'entends plus rien. Je retournerais tout droit à Noranda. Je me donne quand même une contenance pour dire : «Est-ce que je peux rester ici une journée de plus?» Je monte dans ma chambre en retenant mes larmes. Puis je m'effondre. Olivier ne vient pas me rejoindre.

Ce matin, Olivier me reconduit à Marseille, juste à temps pour le train de huit heures. Ses parents dormaient encore quand on est partis dans le rose de la route bordée de grands pins noirs. Je n'ai pas pu les saluer. Olivier me fait toutes sortes de recommandations du genre de celles de ma mère : «Ne parle pas à des inconnus. Avec les Italiens, il faut faire attention, ils sont des chanteurs de pomme professionnels. Des Casanova. Des Don Juan.» J'ai envie de lui répondre : «Mais si t'as si peur que ça, viens avec moi.» Mais je n'ose pas et je monte toute seule dans le train en direction de Venise. Ça n'a pas de sens d'aller toute seule dans cette ville d'amoureux en gondoles. Je suis comme dans un *no man's land* et je me laisse porter par les événements.

J'essaie de lire *Le Rouge et le Noir*, mais le cœur n'y est pas. Qu'est-ce qui m'a pris de partir comme ça sur un coup de tête pour aller faire un semblant de voyage de noces avec un homme que je connais à peine? Tu es vraiment folle, Claude Éthier, vraiment folle, et Coco a raison sur toute la ligne. Passé Milan, un monsieur très bien en complet-veston me demande la permission de s'asseoir près de moi. « *Prego ?* » « *Si, si, signor.* » Il parle bien l'anglais et s'appelle Roberto. Ses moustaches vont bien avec ses yeux très noirs. Sa voix est exactement comme celle de Rossano Brazzi, ornée d'un peu de velours au bout des phrases. Il me fait penser à Eddy. Il y a longtemps que je n'ai pensé à Eddy. Je me demande bien ce qui lui arrive. J'ai le goût de lui envoyer une carte postale d'Italie, juste pour le faire baver. Mais je n'ai pas son adresse.

— *But why do you travel alone?*

Cette question, c'est la seule question qui tourne en rond dans ma cervelle depuis deux jours. Je dis comme ça, sans y penser : « *Because my fiancé has to work.* » Roberto n'a pas l'air de comprendre. Et après tout, pourquoi une femme ne voyagerait-elle pas toute seule ?

Il parle. Du Canada. De l'Italie. Je l'écoute et je le trouve séduisant. Je n'ai jamais couché avec un homme marié, et ça m'intéresse de voir de plus près ce dont Marie-Claire parlait. Quelle est donc cette expérience tant décriée et tant convoitée ? Il s'assoupit à un moment donné. Je fais semblant de m'assoupir moi aussi. Il me prend par la taille dans son pseudo-sommeil, et je me laisse faire. À la fin de l'après-midi, on arrive dans l'or de Venise. Là, devant la lagune, Roberto me dit ce que je voulais entendre :

— *You have a room for tonight?*

— *No, I'll see.*

— *Well, you can have my apartment if you want. My wife...*

— *No, thank you.*

Pourquoi ai-je dit non, comme ça, alors que je voulais dire oui? En y pensant bien, je préfère être seule, réfléchir un peu à toute cette histoire. Je ne réfléchis pas assez et je me mets toujours les pieds dans les plats.

Toutes les phrases célèbres de ma mère me parviennent en même temps, sèches et lapidaires, comme des formules de carte postale. «Attention à ta santé, ne parle pas aux étrangers», et le reste et le reste.

Je salue Roberto qui se montre moins galant et je descends du train. Je monte dans un canot moteur. Ce n'est pas tout à fait l'idée que je me fais d'une gondole, mais en entrant dans Venise, je vois des gondoliers au chandail rayé, qui chantent le vrai *O sole mio* avec une voix à la Mario Lanza et non pas *Prends ma jeunesse* comme dans *La Bonne Chanson*.

Je me promène dans les dédales des rues d'eau verte. Je suis perdue, perdue. Finalement, j'arrive devant une petite auberge qui a l'air d'une vraie maison, très belle, avec des boîtes à fleurs sous les fenêtres. À l'intérieur, c'est blanc et propre, et on oublie tout de suite qu'il y a de l'eau sous nos pieds. L'aubergiste est gentille et me conduit à ma chambre. Je me couche, fourbue, dans le *letto matrimoniale*, et je m'endors sur le qui-vive, croyant à chaque instant que la clé tourne dans la porte et que je vais me faire violer. Mais non! La nuit est bonne pour moi et, au réveil, le *caffè con latte* me remet sur le piton. Il n'y a rien comme une bonne nuit de sommeil. On voit la vie différemment, je le sais par cœur, ma mère me l'a tellement répété.

150

Je consulte souvent mon dictionnaire italien-français et les commerçants sont ravis de voir que je m'efforce de parler leur langue. Je passe ma journée dans les églises, et à la fin j'en ai assez. À Venise ou ailleurs, elles ont beau être architecturales, les églises restent des églises. Je me sens crouler sous la civilisation, sous la religion et sous les doges de Venise. Chaque fois que je vois le mot «doge», je pense aux Dodgers de New York. Ou de Milwaukee... je ne sais plus, je demanderai à Coco. C'est plus fort que moi, j'ai besoin d'air, j'ai besoin de neuf. Vite le train pour Paris, l'avion pour Montréal, l'autobus pour l'Abitibi.

J'ai la tête pleine d'images vénitiennes. Pas seulement des pigeons, des doges, des Canaletto et des gondoles, mais des petits diables remplis de fruits, de légumes, de fleurs, des sourires de femmes, des jeux d'enfants et des clins d'œil du soleil qui se couche sur une eau forte.

Seule, je ne suis jamais seule. Quelqu'un, toujours, vient s'asseoir près de moi pour me raconter sa vie en anglais de niveau 1. Au fond, les histoires sont toutes des histoires d'amour.

J'ai envoyé plusieurs cartes postales à Olivier. Je ne lui ai parlé que d'architecture et de peinture. De toute façon, le reste ne l'intéresse pas. Il m'a écrit deux longues lettres, poste restante, pour me dire à quel point il avait envie de me revoir, qu'il avait du mal à se passer de moi et le reste. Les petits dessins qu'il a faits au bas de ses lettres m'ont émue plus que ses mots, que je trouve préfabriqués. Je n'arrive pas à franchir la distance entre sa peau et ses mots.

De retour à Paris, je trouve la vie plus dure. Mon accent, mon terrible accent canadien contre lequel je ne peux pas grand-chose, fait enrager ou rigoler les Parisiens. Je me sens vraiment la dernière des dernières chaque fois que je demande un renseignement ou que je commande quelque chose au restaurant. J'ose à peine ouvrir la bouche, me contentant de parler par signes comme le font les sourds-muets. Ça gâche mon plaisir, parce qu'à part les Parisiens qui me reprochent mon accent, tout m'intéresse à Paris : les Parisiens «corrects», les quais pleins de livres introuvables à Montréal, le Louvre, le Jeu de Paume, les cafés, l'odeur de la gitane, les boutiques. Il me reste un peu d'argent, et j'en profite pour acheter des livres de poésie et des romans, qui sont bien meilleur marché qu'à Montréal.

Puis je retourne au Bourget avec une valise en sus, remplie de livres pour moi et de souvenirs pour les autres. Je regrette de quitter l'Europe parce que j'ai aimé m'y sentir libre et seule, me baigner dans les décors des romans que j'ai lus depuis ma petite enfance, mais il me manque la luminosité crue du ciel d'Abitibi, les espaces inhabités. Il me manque une vie à vivre. C'est presque la fin d'août, et je dois me trouver du travail pour rembourser ma tante Laura qui m'a avancé de l'argent pour faire mon voyage. Je lui dirai que tout était parfait, et elle sera contente.

À Dorval, Olivier est là, avec un petit bouquet de pensées. Il a l'air heureux de me voir et il me propose d'aller habiter chez lui, dans son nouvel appartement de la rue Coronet. Je dis oui et je monte dans sa Volkswagen bleue toute déglinguée qu'il vient d'acheter pour une bouchée de pain.

Son appartement est sombre, car les fenêtres sont à peine plus grandes que des meurtrières. Tous les meubles sont anciens et austères, sauf le lit, qui n'est qu'un matelas à même le plancher de bois. C'est samedi, et on veut passer le reste de la fin de semaine au lit. Olivier me demande tout le temps si je l'ai trompé en Italie, mais je lui réponds en riant que je n'en ai même pas eu la chance. Puis il se décide à me poser la bonne question : « Prends-tu la pilule anticonceptionnelle ? »

— C'est le temps que tu t'en inquiètes. Qu'est-ce que tu ferais si j'te disais que j'la prends pas ?

— Je suis certain que tu es une fille responsable et que tu ne me jouerais pas de vilain tour, hein, ma petite Claude ?

— T'en fais pas, j'la prends, j'la prends.

J'oublie de la prendre parfois, mais je ne le lui dis pas. Je me le dis à peine à moi-même pour ne pas vivre dans la peur d'être enceinte. Mais ça me prend à la gorge parfois, cette peur, comme l'idée de la mort en plein cœur de la nuit.

Je dois me chercher du travail, mais avant je veux aller voir mes parents et mes frères à Noranda. Olivier me propose de m'y amener pendant le congé de la fête du travail.

— Je t'ai fait rencontrer mes parents, tu peux bien me présenter les tiens.

— Si tu veux, mais je t'avertis que c'est très loin, pis que l'Abitibi, c'est pas le Lac Saint-Jean, pis encore moins la Provence.

Vendredi soir. On part dans la Volkswagen bleue avec notre tente et nos sacs de couchage. Olivier n'est jamais monté plus haut que Val-David, qu'il trouve au bout du monde. On file sur la grand-route, puis vers neuf heures, on arrive à Grands-Remous. L'odeur du Nord arrive jusqu'au fond de mes poumons sans que j'aie besoin de respirer. C'est ça le Nord, on n'a pas à chercher l'air, il s'agit de relever la tête, et il nous atteint comme si on nous plaquait une bonbonne d'oxygène en plein sur la bouche. Ça grise. Je n'arrive pas à faire partager ma joie à Olivier, qui commence à être pris de panique en regardant la carte routière de plus près.

— Il n'y a plus de villes pendant des kilomètres et des kilomètres. Il faut qu'on installe notre tente. Il fait déjà nuit et c'est froid comme en hiver.

— T'inquiète pas, il y a un terrain de camping pas loin, de l'autre côté de la barrière, pis si tu trouves ça trop froid, on peut coucher dans une petite cabine.

On passe devant le camping du lac de la Vieille et je vois dans les yeux d'Olivier qu'on n'y installera pas notre tente. On continue un peu plus loin et on prend une cabine au Domaine. Je dis à Olivier :

— Tu sais, on a à peine la moitié du chemin de fait.

— C'est idiot de faire un tel voyage en deux jours. On sera à peine arrivés qu'il faudra repartir. Tu aurais dû me dire ça avant de partir. Avoir su, j'serais pas venu.

— Tu savais que c'était quatre cents milles, voyons, Olivier.

— Idiote, tu aurais dû me dire que ça prenait dix heures pour y arriver.

— Tu savais ben que c'était quatre cents milles, six cents kilomètres, Paris-Avignon, Montréal-New York...

— Va te faire foutre avec ton humour à la con.

— Hé! Fais pas ton petit Jacques. J'm'appelle pas Jacqueline.

Ç'a été plus fort que lui, il m'a giflée. Je me suis tue et je me suis retournée dans le lit, me disant que c'était fini entre nous. Je ne pleurais même pas. C'est fini entre nous, un point c'est tout. Je ne veux plus lui adresser la parole.

La nuit est froide, les huarts hurlent sur le lac. Je me colle une dernière fois contre Olivier, et on fait l'amour comme des sauvages. Je n'arrive pas à dormir parce que j'ai un peu peur qu'il me tue. Je me dis que je suis folle, mais je n'arrive pas à me contrôler. J'attends le matin.

Olivier essaie de faire un feu dans la truie. Il n'arrive qu'à faire de la fumée. Je lui propose d'essayer, mais il refuse. Il a son orgueil de mâle. Je sais faire du feu, c'est une chose que mon père m'a apprise très jeune. Finalement il abdique et, piteux, il me laisse la place. Ça marche et, au bout d'une demi-heure, il y a assez de braise dans la truie pour qu'on fasse griller du pain. Olivier trouve ça sauvage. Moi, l'odeur des toasts et du feu de bois me réchauffe le cœur.

On reprend la route. On ne parle pas de ce qui s'est produit hier soir. On ne parle pas du tout. Je bois les paysages qui m'arrivent comme des cadeaux. Les barrages ont noyé les épinettes qui émergent de la rivière des Outaouais comme des totems. La route est droite, droite. On dirait qu'au bout, elle entre dans le ciel. C'est ma notion à moi de l'infini.

Vers midi, la Volks réussit à gravir la côte de Joanès et au loin, les cheminées de la mine Noranda crachent un tas de gros nuages dans le ciel trop grand.

Mes parents et mes frères sont tous rassemblés pour mon arrivée. Ça fait plus d'un an que je les ai vus. Momo a grandi et s'est mis sérieusement à la guitare. Lulu est presque un homme et il fait de la musique de plus en plus. Bernard va beaucoup mieux, mais il reste avec une mélancolie dans les yeux. On dirait que son accident l'a fait vieillir de dix ans en quelques mois. Il me dit qu'il s'est inscrit en psychologie à l'université, qu'il part à Montréal dans quelques jours. Coco, quant à lui, en avait assez du collège et il travaille pour une compagnie d'électricité. Il s'est marié pendant l'été. Un vrai mariage. Il paraît que c'était bien émouvant. Ma mère a touché l'orgue pour l'occasion, mon père a chanté. Le curé a même donné une autorisation spéciale pour que Momo joue de la guitare classique pendant la communion. Tout le monde dit que j'aurais dû être là.

La maison me semble plus grande, parce que presque tout le monde est parti, sauf Maurice. Lucien est pensionnaire dans une école de musique et il ne vient presque jamais à la maison. Mais il est là ce soir avec sa guitare. Mon père a creusé la cave pour faire un vrai sous-sol comme tout le monde. La musique est descendue en bas avec les chambres des gars.

En haut, ma chambre est devenue une chambre d'invités. Ma mère l'a toute décorée, avec des tentures, un lit double en noyer massif et des commodes assorties. Je me demande comment elle a planifié la nuit prochaine, c'est-à-dire dans quelle chambre je coucherai, si je coucherai seule, si je serai invitée dans ma chambre avec Olivier ou s'il va dormir au sous-sol, dans une des chambres de gars devenue vacante à cause du mariage d'un de mes frères.

Je n'ai même pas besoin de poser la question parce que ma mère s'empresse de dire que ma tante Alphonsine a offert sa chambre d'amis à Olivier. Il y sera plus à l'aise, dit-elle.

Ma mère est heureuse de me voir et me parle sans arrêt de la femme de mon frère, de ses sœurs, de leurs maladies, de mes cousines, de mes cousins, que j'ai un peu de mal à replacer dans ma mémoire. Je regarde Olivier, qui ne comprend rien et que mon père veut intéresser. Olivier, quant à lui, se plaint de la longueur du voyage, de la fatigue et de l'aridité du paysage. Mon père, pour le consoler, lui raconte qu'il est venu de Notre-Dame-du-Nord à Noranda, avec son père, bien avant qu'il y ait une route, et qu'il a voyagé deux jours en canot, en faisant de nombreux portages. Olivier, les yeux écarquillés, cernés de fatigue, se demande sûrement s'il s'est trompé de pays, de ville, de maison ou de planète.

Le dîner est bon comme dans les grandes occasions. Ma mère a sorti sa nappe brodée, son argenterie, sa vaisselle de porcelaine et son cristal. Bernard est accompagné de sa blonde steady, Gisèle, une petite blonde décidée qu'il embrasse à pleine bouche dès que ma mère a le dos tourné. Coco s'est amené avec sa femme, Barbara. Elle est polonaise. Elle est belle et, comme elle est enceinte jusqu'aux oreilles, ses yeux sont agrandis et sa bouche gonflée. Elle parle français avec un accent anglais et souvent elle dit quelques mots ou quelques phrases en anglais. Quand elle s'adresse à mon frère, elle parle en anglais seulement.

Je le regarde attentivement. Il a à peine vingt ans et sa vie est déjà toute tracée, droite comme la route 117 entre Dorval Lodge et Louvicourt. Dans un éclair, je passe en revue sa maison, ses meubles solides, ses enfants, son chien, son chat, son sous-sol, sa télévision. Je regarde Olivier et je me vois dans ces roulières de la vie.

J'ai apporté du vin, et les yeux se mettent à pétiller. Tout le monde parle en même temps, dit n'importe quoi, dans n'importe quelle langue. Je suis heureuse de les revoir tous. Ils font les mêmes blagues qu'avant et se mettent à chanter soudain, à raconter des histoires et à dire que c'est bon d'être ensemble. Je les aime tout à coup. Un grand courant de chaleur me traverse de bord en bord et je sens mes yeux se mouiller. Tout le monde, j'en suis sûre, pense que bientôt on ne se reverra presque plus, mais personne ne dit quoi que ce soit.

Vers la fin de l'après-midi, Olivier comprend qu'il n'a rien à faire autour de cette table, qu'il ne comprendra jamais la folie du cœur. Il se lève, s'excuse à peine et je le suis dehors.

— Il faut que je parte.

— Y faut qu'tu partes? T'es fou, tu viens d'arriver.

— Viens-tu avec moi?

— Non, j'reste quelques jours.

— Viens-t'en, sinon c'est fini entre nous. J'peux pas les blairer, tes frères.

— Non, je reste.

Il descend les escaliers devant le soleil qui flambe. Il hésite un instant, puis il ouvre le coffre avant de sa coccinelle. Il en sort ma petite valise noire et la dépose sur le trottoir. Il me regarde à peine, puis il prend le volant et démarre en trombe.

Je reste seule sur le trottoir avec ma valise. Je pense à Eddy, je pense que je devrais lui parler, comme il a fait lui-même quand sa mère est morte. C'est le seul qui pourrait me consoler.

Je remplis mes poumons d'air encore une fois et je retourne dans la cuisine qui bouillonne de rires et d'affection. Je reprends ma place dans le brouhaha. Personne n'a relevé le départ d'Olivier, et je pense que c'est bien ainsi, que je suis bien toute seule parmi ces phrases à haute voix. Mon père dit à ma mère :

— Honey, joue-nous *Plaisir d'amour* avant souper, on va te chanter ça.

— Lulu, prends ta guitare, dit ma mère en faisant tourner son banc de piano. Pis toi aussi, Momo.

On se lève tous pour chanter en se distribuant les tonalités. Je pense encore à Eddy. Je pense aussi à

Olivier, parti dans le soir. Il doit être rendu à Cadillac ou à Malartic.

On soupe ensemble et on continue de fêter entre nous. Coco a beaucoup changé depuis l'accident de Bernard. Il a perdu son côté tyran. Il va même jusqu'à dire qu'il est vraiment content de me voir pour me présenter à Barbara. «Depuis le temps que j'entends parler de toi, a-t-elle ajouté, t'es comme un mystère dans la famille.»

— Ben oui! a dit ma mère, le temps passe ben vite. Claude est partie de la maison, pis on s'en est même pas aperçus. On s'est jamais aperçus qu'était là quand 'était p'tite tellement qu'a faisait pas de bruit.

Je pense à Bernard, qui n'avait presque pas d'existence avant son accident. Je pense à mes cours d'histoire, à tous ces noms de ville qu'on n'aurait jamais connus sans les catastrophes : Nagasaki, Pearl Harbour, Dachau. Faut-il un drame pour qu'on existe?

Ma mère ne comprend pas pourquoi Olivier est parti sans lui dire bonjour. Elle répète : «C'est ben les Français, ça, y sont ben mal élevés.» J'essaye de la calmer en lui disant qu'il est venu me reconduire seulement et qu'il avait prévu repartir aussitôt. Puis à brûle-pourpoint, mine de rien, je demande des nouvelles de Sandra. Après un petit silence, Barbara, la femme de Coco, dit qu'Eddy et Sandra étaient définitivement séparés. Ma mère me regarde :

— Tu vois bien, Claude, que ce gars-là valait pas grand-chose.

— Pourquoi tu dis ça, maman? On sait pas c'qui s'est passé.

— Ça marche jamais, ces mélanges-là...

Tout le monde la regarde avec de gros yeux. Coco, Barbara. Elle se rend compte qu'elle vient de faire une gaffe, puis elle va se reposer toute seule dans le salon : «Couchez-vous pas trop tard, pis fermez toutes les lumières.»

Je sors prendre l'air un peu. Il reste une pointe de soleil couchant, une larme de feu dans le ciel du Nord. Toute cette beauté violette et sauvage m'atteint. J'ai du mal à retenir mes larmes. Qu'est-ce que je fais ici, dans le désert?

Je rentre à la maison quand il fait nuit. Bernard me dit qu'il est devenu très ami avec Eddy. Ils font de la guitare ensemble et ils jouent du rock'n'roll dans des bars de Rouyn. Bernard est tout feu tout flammes. Il me parle gentiment devant Coco, sans avoir peur d'être ridicule. Eddy est à Noranda pour l'été et, en septembre, il retournera à Montréal poursuivre ses études de médecine.

— Eddy va venir pratiquer à soir.

— Où ça?

— Icitte, dans le sous-sol, comme d'habitude. Y sait que tu arrives aujourd'hui avec ton chum.

— Y sait pas que mon «chum» est déjà parti, par exemple.

Je veux revoir Eddy de toutes mes forces et tant mieux si je n'ai pas à l'appeler. Je pense à Olivier, je le vois dans le parc La Vérendrye au volant de sa Volks. C'est la nuit, il est furieux, mort de fatigue. Je suis inquiète et je me sens coupable de l'avoir laissé partir. Puis je pense à Eddy que je vais revoir. Je me demande ce que je vais lui dire. Je me répète des phrases toutes faites, comme celles qu'on lit dans les romans ou qu'on entend dans les films à grand déploiement. On se sautera dans les bras, c'est sûr. Il y aura une musique de fond genre *Liebestraum* et il dira : «Mon 'tite Claude, mon 'tite Claude.» Le temps de répondre, et il m'aura donné un majestueux baiser.

Ma mère salue à peine Eddy quand il arrive chez nous. Je le suis avec Bernard et Lulu au sous-sol. Il est un peu timide. Ce n'est pas son genre, vraiment pas son genre. Je ne lui dis même pas «Bonjour, Eddy», encore moins toutes le phrases que j'ai préparées. Il me sourit et il s'approche de moi dans les marches pour me faire une bise sur la joue : «Bonjour, Claude, c'est l'fun de te revoir.»

Il s'assoit près de Bernard sur un tabouret chromé et recouvert de cuirette. Le sous-sol est semi-fini, avec des murs de ciment peints en blanc et un plancher de ciment peint en gris souris. Ma mère a descendu ses vieux tapis de Turquie pour assourdir le son. Il y a des boîtes d'œufs fixées en rangs d'oignons au plafond pour l'acoustique. Lulu et Eddy branchent leurs guitares sur les amplis et se mettent à jouer ensemble. La maison en tremble. Je n'entends rien, je regarde Eddy en train de *djammer*. Il est absorbé par sa musique. Par moments, il me jette un coup d'œil, un sourire en coin. Je me sens comme du jello aux fraises qui fond dans la bouche.

Après la pratique, on part dans la nuit tous les trois, Bernard, Eddy et moi. On entre au Moulin rouge et on commande des bières. La band est bonne et crie à tue-tête au monde entier d'aller en enfer. On fume comme des cheminées et on boit comme des trous. On se parle à peine parce qu'on ne peut pas s'entendre. La piste de danse est vide. On a envie de danser, mais on n'y va pas. Eddy me regarde dans les yeux. Bernard comprend tout et dit : « Bon, ben, j'vous laisse, j'm'en vas rejoindre Gisèle à la Moderne. »

Une fois Bernard parti, on décide d'aller danser un slow. Ça dure longtemps. On est tout seuls sur la piste. Tout le monde nous regarde. Eddy fait voyager ses mains sous mon T-shirt et il veut les faire descendre dans mes jeans. Olivier doit être rendu à Grands-Remous. Ou peut-être qu'il s'est arrêté à Mont-Laurier prendre un café. J'ai chaud partout. Eddy voit que je suis distraite et il dit : « Allons-nous-en. »

On marche sur la *Main*. Eddy est silencieux et sa main serre la mienne très fort. Son désir m'enveloppe tout à coup et on s'embrasse comme des débiles au milieu du trottoir. Il dit : « Viens, on va prendre une chambre à l'hôtel Albert. »

— Y faudrait que j'téléphone chez nous.

— Chez vous, c'est à Montréal, dans ton appartement.

— C'est vrai, c'est ben vrai.

En montant dans la chambre de l'hôtel, j'ai quand même des petits remords. Olivier doit être rendu à Saint-Jovite ou à Sainte-Agathe. Il est presque rendu. Il doit être furieux, furieux. Peut-être qu'il est soulagé dans le fond, un peu comme moi. Ça ne nous menait nulle part, cet amour-là.

Dans la chambre, tout est brun et gris, le couvre-lit, les tentures, le tapis, qui est brûlé à plusieurs endroits. Les draps sont propres. Il y a même une chambre de bains. C'est le grand luxe.

Eddy me fait l'amour longtemps sous la douche. Il me chuchote des mots doux en me savonnant le dos et les fesses. On est couverts de mousse glissante, et je ne sais plus où j'en suis. Il me dit tout ce que je veux entendre. Vers deux heures du matin, au moment où nous allons nous mettre au lit, il me demande si je veux rentrer à la maison. Je dis que ce n'est pas de ses affaires, et il éclate de rire. Et il recommence à me faire l'amour. Et la nuit passe. Olivier est arrivé à Montréal, c'est sûr. Il va appeler chez ma mère en rentrant, et elle lui dira que je n'y suis pas, qu'elle ne sait pas où je suis. Est-ce que je sais moi-même où je suis ?

Au petit matin, on sort sur la *Main*, blêmes comme les draps qu'on a laissés tout froissés dans la chambre. La sirène de la mine part. On est comme dans un film de guerre quand les gens courent dans les abris. Mais nous autres, à Noranda, quand la sirène de la mine part, on s'arrête un instant et on pense que toutes les femmes de mineurs sont inquiètes. Qui est resté au fond, écrasé par la roche ? Eddy me serre la main plus fort, et on se promène un peu en attendant qu'il soit sept heures et demie pour aller déjeuner au Kresge. On se regarde dans les yeux et on ne dit rien. On n'a rien à se dire.

Il fait un froid gris fer. On marche sur la Lakeshore puis on descend dans le parc Trémoy. Les cheminées de la mine envoient des gros dessins de fumée dans le ciel. Les saules sentent très fort, comme après la pluie. Eddy finit par dire : « C'est qui ça, Olivier quelque chose ? »

— C'est un ami, comme ça.

— Il est venu te reconduire hier ? C'est ton nouveau chum ? Coco m'a dit que t'es allée en Europe avec lui.

— Oui, mais c'est pus mon chum. Je l'aime pus. Pus pantoute.

— Qu'est-ce qu'on va faire nous deux ?

— J'sais pas.

Tout à coup, j'éclate en sanglots. Je suis inconsolable. C'est comme si toute la tristesse du monde s'abattait sur moi. Eddy me prend dans ses bras.

— *Come on, baby, don't cry.*

La mine crache son gaz à plein ciel. Eddy me prend par la main, et on se dirige vers le Radio Grill. Prendre un coke, comme avant. Mais quelque chose s'est brisé en moi.

— Eddy, j'veux que tu m'aimes.

— Mais je t'aime bien, Claude.

— J'veux que tu m'aimes plus que ça.

— Qu'est-ce que tu veux dire ?

— J'veux qu'on se marie tous les deux.

Un instant il hésite, et je pense qu'il m'offrira de partir avec lui. Mais il ne dit rien et continue de téter sa paille.

Je me lève et je mets trente sous dans le juke-box. Je presse une touche au hasard. Ça joue *Are you lonesome tonight...* Je me dirige vers la porte et je sors du Radio Grill, toute seule. Ça sent le gaz, la gorge me pique.

Il est neuf heures du matin. Je me relève la tête, je retourne chez moi en passant devant l'hôpital, en longeant le lac Osisko. Ma mère prend son déjeuner et ne réagit pas plus que ça à mon arrivée.

— T'as passé une bonne nuit, Claude?

— Oui, oui, m'man. Je prends l'autobus pour Montréal ce soir.

— De nuit? T'es ben pressée d'aller le rejoindre, ton Français?

— Olivier a-tu appelé?

— Non, pourquoi?

— Rien. Pour rien. Je veux avoir la paix, c'est tout.

Je me mets à pleurer, et ma mère ne bouge pas. Elle ne dit pas un mot et, tranquillement, elle se lève, me met la main sur l'épaule. C'est la première fois que ma mère met sa main sur mon épaule. Elle dit: « Ma petite Claude, ma petite Claude. »

Je dis n'importe quoi. Olivier est parti. Je l'ai laissé partir. Peut-être que j'aurais dû le retenir. Pourquoi n'est-il pas resté? Il a eu peur de moi, du ciel d'Abitibi, des arbres morts, de la route trop

166

longue. Olivier Thiers est sorti de ma vie. Olivier Thiers, mon beau Français de France.

Mais qu'est-ce que j'aurais fait d'Olivier? Et qu'est-ce que je ferais d'Eddy? Les raisins sont vraiment trop verts. Et je pleure et je pleure. À la fin, ma mère met une boîte de Kleenex devant moi et elle dit sérieusement:

— La mère des gars est loin d'être morte, fais-toi-z-en pas ma Claude.

On se regarde et puis, tout à coup, comme s'il n'y avait rien d'autre à faire, on éclate de rire toutes les deux.

Je crois bien qu'après tout je ferais mieux de rester quelque temps à Noranda avant de retourner à Montréal. Le temps d'oublier Olivier. Complètement. Ce soir j'irai voir *For whom the Bell tolls* au Paramount avec Gary Cooper et Ingrid Bergman. Un bon film de guerre et de love, ça me fera le plus grand bien. Et qui sait? Je rencontrerai peut-être Eddy par hasard sur la *Main*.

Achevé d'imprimer
en septembre 1993 sur les presses
des Ateliers Graphiques Marc Veilleux Inc.
Cap-Saint-Ignace (Québec).